Other Information Security Study Guides from Sybex

CISM Certified Information Security Manager Study Guide — ISBN 978-1-119-80193-1, May 2022

IAPP CIPM Certified Information Privacy Manager Study Guide — ISBN 978-1-394-15380-0, January 2023

ISC2 CISSP Certified Information Systems Security Professional Official Study Guide, 10th Edition — ISBN 978-1-394-25469-9, June 2024

ISC2 CCSP Certified Cloud Security Professional Official Study Guide, 3rd Edition — ISBN 978-1-119-90937-8, October 2022

CISA Certified Information Systems Auditor Study Guide Covering 2024-2029 Exam Objectives — ISBN 978-1-394-28838-0, December 2024

IAPP
CIPP/US®
Certified Information
Privacy Professional
Study Guide
United States Exam
Second Edition

IAPP
CIPP/US®
Certified Information
Privacy Professional
Study Guide
United States Exam
Second Edition

Mike Chapple

with Joe Shelley

SYBEX®
A Wiley Brand

Published by John Wiley & Sons, Inc., Hoboken, New Jersey.

Published simultaneously in Canada and the United Kingdom.

ISBN: 978-1-394-28490-0
ISBN: 978-1-394-28492-4 (ebk.)
ISBN: 978-1-394-28491-7 (epub.)

For general information on our other products and services or for technical support, please contact our Customer Care Department within the United States at (800) 762-2974, outside the United States at (317) 572-3993 or fax (317) 572-4002.

Wiley also publishes its books in a variety of electronic formats. Some content that appears in print may not be available in electronic formats. For more information about Wiley products, visit our web site at www.wiley.com.

Library of Congress Control Number: 2024922075

Cover Image: © Jeremy Woodhouse/Getty Images
Cover Design: Wiley

SKY10091402_112024

To Matthew—I am so proud of everything you've become and can't wait to see the difference you make in the world!
—Mike

To Jessie—my best friend and the love of my life.
—Joe

Acknowledgments

Even though only the authors' names appear on the front cover, the production of a book is a collaborative effort involving a huge team. Wiley always brings a top-notch collection of professionals to the table, and that makes the work of authors much easier.

In particular, we'd like to thank Jim Minatel, our acquisitions editor. Jim is a consummate professional, and it is an honor and a privilege to continue to work with him on yet another project. Here's to many more!

We also greatly appreciated the editing and production team for the book. Our technical editor, Bobby Rogers, provided indispensable insight and expertise. This book would not have been the same without their valuable contributions. Rajesh Venkatraman, our production editor, guided us through layouts, formatting, and final cleanup to produce a great book. We would also like to thank the many behind-the-scenes contributors, including the graphics, production, and technical teams who make the book and companion materials into a finished product.

Our agent, Carole Jelen of Waterside Productions, continues to provide us with wonderful opportunities, advice, and assistance throughout our writing careers.

Finally, we would like to thank our families who supported us through the late evenings, busy weekends, and long hours that a book like this requires to write, edit, and get to press.

About the Authors

Mike Chapple, Ph.D., CIPP/US, is the author of the best-selling *CISSP ISC2 Certified Information Systems Security Professional Official Study Guide* (Sybex, 10th edition, 2024) and the *CISSP ISC2 Official Practice Tests* (Sybex, 4th edition, 2024). He is an information security professional with 25 years of experience in higher education, the private sector, and government.

Mike currently serves as a teaching professor in the IT, Analytics, and Operations department at the University of Notre Dame's Mendoza College of Business, where he teaches undergraduate and graduate courses on cybersecurity, data management, and business analytics.

Before returning to Notre Dame, Mike served as executive vice president and chief information officer of the Brand Institute, a Miami-based marketing consultancy. Mike also spent four years in the information security research group at the National Security Agency and served as an active duty intelligence officer in the U.S. Air Force.

Mike is technical editor for *Information Security Magazine* and has written more than 50 books. He earned both his B.S. and Ph.D. degrees from Notre Dame in computer science and engineering. Mike also holds an M.S. in computer science from the University of Idaho and an MBA from Auburn University. Mike holds the Certified Information Privacy Professional/US (CIPP/US), Certified Information Privacy Manager (CIPM), Cybersecurity Analyst+ (CySA+), Security+, Certified Information Security Manager (CISM), Certified Cloud Security Professional (CCSP), and Certified Information Systems Security Professional (CISSP) certifications.

Learn more about Mike and his other security certification materials at his website, CertMike.com.

Joe Shelley, M.A., CIPP/US, is a leader in higher education information technologies. He is currently the vice president for Libraries and Information Technology at Hamilton College in New York. In his role, Joe oversees central IT infrastructure, enterprise systems, information security and privacy programs, IT risk management, business intelligence and analytics, institutional research and assessment, data governance, and overall technology strategy. Joe also directs the Library and Institutional Research. In addition to supporting the teaching and research mission of the college, the library provides education in information sciences, digital and information literacy, and information management.

Before joining Hamilton College, Joe served as the chief information officer at the University of Washington Bothell in the Seattle area. During his 12 years at UW Bothell, Joe was responsible for learning technologies, data centers, web development, enterprise applications, help desk services, administrative and academic computing, and multimedia production. He implemented the UW Bothell information security program, cloud computing strategy, and IT governance, and he developed new initiatives for supporting teaching and learning, faculty research, and e-learning.

Joe earned his bachelor's degree in interdisciplinary arts and sciences from the University of Washington and his master's degree in educational technology from Michigan State University. Joe holds the CIPP/US, CIPM, and Security+ certifications.

About the Technical Editors

Bobby Rogers is a senior cybersecurity professional with over 30 years in the field. He serves as a cybersecurity auditor and virtual chief information security officer for a variety of clients. He works with a major engineering company in Huntsville, Alabama, helping to secure networks and manage cyber risk for its customers. In addition to numerous educational institutions, Bobby's customers have included the U.S. Army, NASA, the state of Tennessee, and private/commercial companies and organizations. Bobby's specialties are cybersecurity engineering, security compliance, and cyber risk management, but he has worked in almost every area of cybersecurity, including network defense, computer forensics and incident response, and penetration testing.

Bobby is a retired master sergeant from the U.S. Air Force, having served for over 21 years. He has built and secured networks in the United States, Chad, Uganda, South Africa, Germany, Saudi Arabia, Pakistan, Afghanistan, and several other remote locations. His decorations include two Meritorious Service medals, three Air Force Commendation medals, the National Defense Service medal, and several Air Force Achievement medals. He retired from active duty in 2006.

Bobby has a master's degree in science in information assurance and is currently writing his dissertation for a doctoral degree in cybersecurity. He also has a bachelor's of science in computer information systems (with a dual concentration in Russian language), and two associate of science degrees. His many certifications include CISSP-ISSEP, CRISC, CEH, CySA+, and MCSE: Security.

He has narrated and produced over 30 computer training videos for several training companies. He is the author of McGraw-Hill Education's *CompTIA CySA+ Cybersecurity Analyst Certification Passport (Exam CS0-002), 1st Edition* and *CISSP Certification Passport, 1st Edition*; a coauthor for the *Certified in Risk and Information Systems Control (CRISC) All-in-One Certification Guide*, first and second editions; and a contributing author and technical editor for the popular *CISSP All-in-One Exam Guide* (seventh, eighth, and ninth editions).

Contents

Introduction

If you're preparing to take the Certified Information Privacy Professional/US (CIPP/US) exam, you'll undoubtedly want to find as much information as you can about privacy. The more information you have at your disposal and the more hands-on experience you gain, the better off you'll be when attempting the exam. We wrote this study guide with that in mind. The goal was to provide enough information to prepare you for the test—but not so much that you'll be overloaded with information that's outside the scope of the exam.

We've included review questions at the end of each chapter to give you a taste of what it's like to take the exam. If you're already working in the privacy field, we recommend that you check out these questions first to gauge your level of expertise. You can then use the book mainly to fill in the gaps in your current knowledge. This study guide will help you round out your knowledge base before tackling the exam.

If you can answer 90 percent or more of the review questions correctly for a given chapter, you can feel safe moving on to the next chapter. If you're unable to answer that many correctly, reread the chapter and try the questions again. Your score should improve.

Don't just study the questions and answers! The questions on the actual exam will be different from the practice questions included in this book. The exam is designed to test your knowledge of a concept or objective, so use this book to learn the objectives behind the questions.

The CIPP/US Exam

The CIPP/US certification is designed to be the gold standard credential for privacy professionals working in the United States and those seeking to enter the field. It is offered by the International Association of Privacy Professionals (IAPP) and fits into the IAPP's suite of geographic-based privacy certifications.

The exam covers five major domains of privacy knowledge:

1. Introduction to the U.S. Privacy Environment
2. Limits on Private-Sector Collection and Use of Data
3. Government and Court Access to Private-Sector Information
4. Workplace Privacy
5. State Privacy Laws

These five areas include a range of topics, from building a privacy program to understanding U.S. privacy laws and regulations. You'll find that the exam focuses heavily on scenario-based learning. For this reason, you may find the exam easier if you have some real-world privacy experience, although many individuals pass the exam before moving into their first privacy role.

The CIPP/US exam consists of 90 multiple-choice questions administered during a 150-minute exam period. Each of the exam questions has four possible answer options. Exams are scored on a scale ranging from 100 to 500, with a minimum passing score of 300. Every exam item is weighted equally, but the passing score is determined using a secret formula, so you won't know exactly what percentage of questions you need to answer correctly to pass. IAPP does publicly state that passing scores typically range between 65 and 80 percent correct, depending upon the specific questions on your exam.

Exam Tip

There is no penalty for answering questions incorrectly. A blank answer and an incorrect answer have equal weight. Therefore, you should fill in an answer for every question, even if it is a complete guess!

IAPP charges $550 for your first attempt at the CIPP/US exam and then $375 for retake attempts if you do not pass on the first try. More details about the CIPP/US exam and how to take it can be found in the IAPP Candidate Certification Handbook at `iapp.org/certify/candidate-handbook`.

You should also know that certification exams are notorious for including vague questions. You might see a question for which two of the possible four answers are correct—but you can choose only one. Use your knowledge, logic, and intuition to choose the best answer, and then move on. Sometimes, the questions are worded in ways that would make English majors cringe—a typo here, an incorrect verb there. Don't let this frustrate you; answer the question and move on to the next one.

IAPP uses a process called *item seeding*, which is the practice of including unscored questions on exams. It does this as part of the process of developing new versions of the exam. So, if you come across a question that does not appear to map to any of the exam objectives—or for that matter, does not appear to belong in the exam—it is likely a seeded question. Of the 90 questions on your exam, only 75 are scored—15 are unscored. You never really know whether or not a question is scored, however, so always make your best effort to answer every question.

Taking the Exam

Once you are fully prepared to take the exam, you can visit the IAPP website to purchase your exam voucher:

`iapp.org/store/certifications`

IAPP partners with Pearson VUE's testing centers, so your next step will be to locate a testing center near you. In the United States, you can do this based on your address or your ZIP code, while non-U.S. test takers may find it easier to enter their city and country. You can search for a test center near you at the Pearson Vue website, where you will need to navigate to "Find a test center":

`www.pearsonvue.com/iapp`

In addition to the live testing centers, you may also choose to take the exam at your home or office through Pearson VUE's OnVUE service. More information about this program is available here:

`home.pearsonvue.com/Test-takers/OnVUE-online-proctoring.aspx`

Now that you know where you'd like to take the exam, simply set up a Pearson VUE testing account and schedule an exam. One important note: once you purchase your exam on the IAPP website, you have one year to register for and take the exam before your registration will expire. Be sure not to miss that deadline!

On the day of the test, take two forms of identification, and make sure to show up with plenty of time before the exam starts. At least one of the forms of identification must be a government-issued photo ID. Both of your forms of identification must have your first and last name, and the name must match your test registration.

Remember that you will not be able to take your notes, electronic devices (including smartphones and watches), or other materials into the exam with you.

Exam policies can change from time to time. We highly recommend that you check both the IAPP and Pearson VUE sites for the most up-to-date information when you begin your preparing, when you register, and again a few days before your scheduled exam date.

After the CIPP/US Exam

Once you have taken the exam, you will be notified of your score immediately, so you'll know if you passed the test right away. You should keep track of your score report with your exam registration records and the email address you used to register for the exam.

Maintaining Your Certification

IAPP certifications must be renewed periodically. To renew your certification, you must either maintain a paid IAPP membership or pay a $250 non-member renewal fee. You must also demonstrate that you have successfully completed 20 hours of continuing professional education (CPE).

IAPP provides information on the CPE process via its website:

`iapp.org/certify/cpe`

Study Guide Elements

This study guide uses a number of common elements to help you prepare. These include the following:

Summaries   The summary section of each chapter briefly explains the chapter, allowing you to easily understand what it covers.

Exam essentials   The exam essentials focus on major exam topics and critical knowledge that you should take into the test. The exam essentials focus on the exam objectives provided by IAPP.

Chapter review questions   A set of questions at the end of each chapter will help you assess your knowledge and if you are ready to take the exam based on your knowledge of that chapter's topics.

Additional Study Tools

This book comes with a number of additional study tools to help you prepare for the exam. They include the following.

> Go to www.wiley.com/go/sybextestprep, register your book to receive your unique PIN, and then, once you have the PIN, return to www.wiley.com/go/sybextestprep and register a new account or add this book to an existing account.

Sybex Online Learning Environment

Sybex's online learning environment lets you prepare with electronic test versions of the review questions from each chapter and the practice exams that are included in this book. You can build and take tests on specific domains, by chapter, or cover the entire set of CIPP/US exam objectives using randomized tests.

Audio Reviews

Mike Chapple, one of the authors of this book, recorded files containing the exam essentials for each chapter in a convenient audio form. Use these audio reviews in the car, on the train, when you're out for a run, or whenever you have a few minutes to review what you've learned.

Electronic Flashcards

Our electronic flashcards are designed to help you prepare for the exam. Over 100 flashcards will ensure that you know critical terms and concepts.

Glossary of Terms

Sybex provides a full glossary of terms in PDF format, allowing quick searches and easy reference to materials in this book.

Practice Exams

In addition to the practice questions for each chapter, this book includes access to two full 90-question online practice exams. We recommend that you use them both to test your preparedness for the certification exam.

CIPP/US Exam Objectives

IAPP goes to great lengths to ensure that its certification programs accurately reflect the privacy profession's best practices. It also publishes ranges for the number of questions on the exam that will come from each domain. The following table lists the five CIPP/US domains and the extent to which they are represented on the exam:

Domain	Questions
1. Introduction to the U.S. Privacy Environment	27–35
2. Limits on Private-Sector Data Collection	15–25
3. Government and Court Access to Private-Sector Information	3–7
4. Workplace Privacy	5–9
5. State Privacy Laws	9–15

CIPP/US Certification Exam Objective Map

OBJECTIVE	CHAPTER
I. Introduction to the U.S. Privacy Environment	
I.A Structure of U.S. Law	Chapters 2 and 3
I.A.a Branches of government	Chapter 2
I.A.b Sources of law	Chapter 2
I.A.c Legal definitions	Chapter 2

IAPP occasionally makes minor adjustments to the exam objectives. Please be certain to check the IAPP website for any recent changes that might affect your exam experience. Additionally, whenever changes arise, we publish a free online supplement to this book at https://www.wiley.com/go/iappcippstudyguide.

Assessment Test

1. What kind of liability may only be asserted in court by governmental authorities and not by a private citizen?
   A. Civil
   B. Negligence
   C. Criminal
   D. Invasion of privacy

2. Which of the following preemployment screening activities would turn a regular consumer report into an investigative report?
   A. The report includes information about prior bankruptcies.
   B. The CRA furnishing the report includes information about a job seeker's mortgage payments.
   C. The preemployment screening includes a criminal background check.
   D. A third-party agent interviews a job seeker's neighbors about their character.

3. Dana is frustrated because she continues to receive telemarketing calls from her current internet service provider (ISP), even though she added her number to the national do-not-call (DNC) list. Is Dana's ISP breaking the law?
   A. Yes, because it is the responsibility of the ISP to maintain an updated copy of the national do-not-call registry.
   B. No, because she is a customer of the ISP and the Telemarketing Sales Rule (TSR) provides an exemption for firms that have an existing business relationship with a consumer.
   C. No, because Dana's ISP may not know she has added her number to the do-not-call registry.
   D. Yes, because the DNC does not provide an exemption for existing customers.

4. Nick and Jenny often meet with other employees in the company cafeteria to advocate for collective bargaining. One day, Jenny notices that a security camera has suddenly been installed in the cafeteria, near where they usually sit. Why might this be a problem?
   A. Employees have not consented to video surveillance during their lunch hours when not conducting company business.
   B. Video surveillance may inadvertently reveal an employee's physical disability and lead to compliance risks under the Americans with Disabilities Act (ADA).
   C. The company did not post adequate signage to notify the employees of the new video surveillance system.
   D. The National Labor Relations Board (NLRB) may view the security camera as an attempt to intimidate employees engaging in unionizing activities.

5. Gary's firm was recently sued by an athlete who claimed that the firm used his picture in marketing materials without permission. What type of claim was brought against Gary's firm?

   A. False light

   B. Appropriation

   C. Invasion of solitude

   D. Public disclosure of private facts

6. Which one of the following statements about workforce privacy training is incorrect?

   A. Computer-based training is an acceptable training option.

   B. Training should include content on specific regulatory requirements.

   C. Training should include details on an individual's role in minimizing privacy risks.

   D. Every user should receive the same level of training.

7. Which one of the following categories would include any information that uniquely identifies an individual person?

   A. PII

   B. PHI

   C. PFI

   D. PCI

8. Carla is building an inventory of the information maintained by her organization that should be considered within the scope of its privacy program. Which one of the following types of information would not normally be included?

   A. Customer transaction records

   B. Manufacturing work order records

   C. Employee payroll records

   D. Job candidate application records

9. Which of the following laws was primarily intended to help combat money laundering?

   A. RFPA

   B. SCA

   C. BSA

   D. EPCA

10. What term is used to describe a voluntary agreement between a firm and the federal government where the firm agrees to engage or not engage in certain business practices?

    A. Conviction

    B. Retainer agreement

    C. Theory of liability

    D. Consent decree

11. What article in the U.S. Constitution defines the powers of the judicial branch?

    A. Article II

    B. Article I

    C. Article III

    D. Article IV

12. What federal privacy law contains specific requirements for how organizations must dispose of sensitive personal information when it is no longer needed?

    A. FERPA

    B. FACTA

    C. GLBA

    D. SOX

13. Which one of the following is an example of a check-and-balance held by the executive branch of government?

    A. Power of the purse

    B. Veto

    C. Confirmation

    D. Judicial review

14. Why are antidiscrimination laws relevant to workplace privacy?

    A. Pro-privacy lawmakers have used large antidiscrimination legislation as an opportunity to include unrelated privacy regulations.

    B. Antidiscrimination laws require employers to collect personal data on employees to prove they have diverse workforces.

    C. Antidiscrimination laws require large employers to conduct surveillance of employees to prevent discrimination.

    D. Personal data about workers may be used in discriminatory decision making.

15. Which of the following is not likely to appear as a state breach notification requirement?

    A. Notifications to the three major CRAs to monitor for identity theft

    B. Notification to state regulators about individuals affected in their state

    C. A notification to the families of victims to warn them of potential identity fraud

    D. Notice to local media outlets, in case all affected individuals cannot be contacted

16. What individual within an organization is likely to bear overall responsibility for a privacy program?

    A. CIO

    B. CFO

    C. CPO

    D. CEO

17. Tom recently filled out a survey about his political and religious views. The survey data is maintained by a nonprofit research organization. What term best describes Tom's role with respect to this data?

    A. Data controller

    B. Data processor

    C. Data steward

    D. Data subject

18. It is probably permissible to use a polygraph test in preemployment screening for all of the following jobs except:

    A. U.S. Treasury employee

    B. Daycare worker

    C. Armored car driver

    D. Pharmacist

19. Which one of the following firms was sanctioned by the Federal Trade Commission (FTC) after an investigation showed that it was not diligently carrying out privacy program recertifications of its clients?

    A. Snapchat

    B. Nomi

    C. TRUSTe

    D. GeoCities

20. The Washington State Biometric Privacy Law protects all of the following forms of biometric data except:

    A. Fingerprint

    B. Eye retinas

    C. Voiceprint

    D. Photographs

Answers to Assessment Test

1. **C.** The two types of liability are criminal and civil. Only governmental prosecutors may bring a court case alleging criminal liability. Anyone may bring a case alleging civil liability.

2. **D.** Under the Fair Credit Reporting Act (FCRA), a consumer report becomes an investigative report when the process includes interviews with a person's contacts to learn more about factors in the report such as "mode of living."

3. **B.** The Telemarketing Sales Rule (TSR) does provide an existing business relationship (EBR) exemption that would allow Dana's ISP to call her even though she has added her phone number to the national do-not-call registry.

4. **D.** The National Labor Relations Board (NLRB) has ruled that certain management actions, such as targeting labor union advocates for surveillance, may be seen as attempts at employee intimidation to discourage lawful union activity.

5. **B.** Appropriation is the unauthorized use of someone's name or likeness. False light is a legal term that applies when someone discloses information that causes another person to be falsely perceived by others. The public disclosure of private facts involves the disclosure of truthful information when the release of that information would offend a reasonable person. Invasion of solitude is a physical or electronic intrusion into the private affairs of a person.

6. **D.** Not every user requires the same level of training. Organizations should use role-based training to make sure that individuals receive the appropriate level of training based on their job responsibilities.

7. **A.** Personally identifiable information (PII) includes any information that uniquely identifies an individual person, including customers, employees, and third parties.

8. **B.** Privacy programs should encompass all personal information handled by the organization. This would include employee payroll records, job candidate application records, and customer transaction records. Manufacturing work orders would not normally contain personal information and, therefore, would not be included in the scope of a privacy program.

9. **C.** The Bank Secrecy Act (BSA) requires that financial institutions maintain records to make transactions traceable and to monitor transactions for signs of money laundering.

10. **D.** Federal agencies often enter into consent decrees that prohibit offending firms from engaging in offending behavior in the future and often impose substantial fines.

11. **C.** The legislative branch powers are defined in Article I of the U.S. Constitution. Executive branch powers are defined in Article II of the U.S. Constitution. Judicial branch powers are defined in Article III of the U.S. Constitution.

12. B. The Fair and Accurate Credit Transactions Act (FACTA) includes specialized guidance for organizations that use consumer reports. The basic requirement of the FACTA Disposal Rule is that covered organizations must take "reasonable measures to protect against unauthorized access or use of the information in connection with its disposal."

13. B. These are all examples of checks and balances. However, only veto power is an executive branch power. The power of the purse and confirmation of nominees are legislative branch powers. Judicial review is a judicial branch power.

14. D. Antidiscrimination laws incentivize employers to minimize the collection and use of personal information about a person's race, religion, or sex or any other information about their status as a member of a protected class in order to lower the risk of any discriminatory decision-making.

15. C. Although state breach notification laws require notifications to many different parties, none currently require notification to the families of victims.

16. C. The chief privacy officer (CPO) of an organization often bears overall responsibility for carrying out the organization's privacy program. Other executive officers, including the chief executive officer (CEO), chief information officer (CIO), and chief financial officer (CFO), may have shared responsibility, but the CPO has primary accountability.

17. D. Tom is the individual about whom the data was collected. Therefore, he can be best described as the data subject in this instance.

18. B. The Employee Polygraph Protection Act (EPPA) forbids the use of polygraph tests for employment purposes for all but a few jobs. Exceptions include government agencies, certain private security jobs, and certain pharmaceutical positions.

19. C. TRUSTe is a privacy firm that provides other companies with certifications of their privacy practices. The FTC charged TRUSTe with failing to conduct annual recertifications of clients as required.

20. D. The state of Washington excludes photographs, video, and audio recordings from its definition of protected biometric data.

Chapter

1

Privacy in the Modern Era

THE CIPP/US EXAM OBJECTIVES COVERED IN THIS CHAPTER INCLUDE:

✓ **Domain I. Introduction to the U.S. Privacy Environment**

- I.C. Information Management from a U.S. Perspective

  - I.C.b Privacy Program Development

  - I.C.c Managing User Preferences

  - I.C.f Accountability

  - I.C.h Online Privacy

  - I.C.i Privacy Notices

Privacy concerns surround us in our daily lives. We hear troubling reports of companies acquiring and misusing personal information about their customers. News stories inform us of data breaches where massive quantities of personal information wound up in unknown hands. Legislators at the federal and state levels debate these issues and often pass new laws regulating different aspects of privacy.

We are left to navigate a confusing environment full of ambiguous and overlapping ethical obligations, laws, regulations, and industry standards. Companies and consumers alike find themselves confused about the requirements they face and the appropriate course of action. Privacy professionals play a crucial role in helping their organizations navigate these confusing waters.

Introduction to Privacy

Privacy is one of the core rights inherent to every human being. The term is defined in many historic works, but they all share the basic tenet of individuals having the right to protect themselves and their information from unwanted intrusions by others or the government. Let's take a brief look at the historical underpinnings of privacy in the United States.

In 1890, a young lawyer named Louis D. Brandeis wrote an article for the *Harvard Law Review* titled "The Right to Privacy." In that article, Brandeis wrote:

> Recent inventions and business methods call attention to the next step which must be undertaking for the protection of the person, and for securing to the individual . . . the right "to be let alone." Instantaneous photographs and newspaper enterprises have invaded the sacred precincts of private and domestic life; and numerous mechanical devices threaten to make good the prediction that "what is whispered in the closet shall be proclaimed from the house-tops." For years there has been a feeling that the law must afford some remedy for the unauthorized circulation of portraits of private persons; and the evil of the invasion of privacy by the newspapers, long keenly felt, has been but recently discussed by an able writer.

Reading that excerpt over a century later, it's easy to see echoes of Brandeis's concerns about technology in today's world. We could just as easily talk about the impact of social media, data brokerages, and electronic surveillance as having the potential to cause "what is whispered in the closet to be proclaimed from the house-tops."

The words that this young attorney wrote might have slipped into obscurity were it not for the fact that 25 years later its author would ascend to the Supreme Court, where, as Justice Brandeis, he would take the concepts from this law review article and use them to argue for a constitutional right to privacy. In a dissenting opinion in the case *Olmstead v. United States*, Justice Brandeis wrote:

> The makers of our Constitution undertook to secure conditions favorable to the pursuit of happiness . . . They conferred, as against the Government, the right to be let alone—the most comprehensive of rights and the right most valued by civilized men. To protect that right, every unjustifiable intrusion by the Government upon the privacy of the individual, whatever the means employed, must be deemed a violation of the Fourth Amendment.

This text, appearing in a dissenting opinion, was not binding upon the courts, but it has surfaced many times over the years in arguments establishing a right to privacy as that right "to be let alone." Recently, the 2018 majority opinion of the court in *Carpenter v. United States* cited *Olmstead* in an opinion declaring warrantless searches of cell phone location records unconstitutional, saying:

> As Justice Brandeis explained in his famous dissent, the Court is obligated as "[s]ubtler and more far-reaching means of invading privacy have become available to the Government"—to ensure that the "progress of science" does not erode Fourth Amendment protections. Here the progress of science has afforded law enforcement a powerful new tool to carry out its important responsibilities. At the same time, this tool risks Government encroachment of the sort the Framers, "after consulting the lessons of history," drafted the Fourth Amendment to prevent.

This is just one example of many historical precedents that firmly establish a right to privacy in U.S. law and allow the continued reinterpretation of that right in the context of technologies and tools that the authors of the Constitution could not possibly have imagined.

What Is Privacy?

It would certainly be difficult to start a book on privacy without first defining the word *privacy*, but this is a term that eludes a common definition in today's environment. Legal and privacy professionals who are asked this question often harken back to the words of Justice Brandeis, describing privacy simply as the right "to be let alone."

In their Generally Accepted Privacy Principles (GAPP), the American Institute of Certified Public Accountants (AICPA) offers a more hands-on definition, describing privacy as "the rights and obligations of individuals and organizations with respect to the collection, use, retention, disclosure, and destruction of personal information."

The GAPP definition may not be quite as pithy and elegant as Justice Brandeis's right "to be let alone," but it does provide privacy professionals with a better working definition that they can use to guide their privacy programs, so it is the definition that we will adopt in this book.

What Is Personal Information?

Now that we have privacy defined, we're led to another question. If privacy is about the protection of *personal information*, what information fits into this category? Here, we turn our attention once again to GAPP, which defines personal information as "information that is or can be about or related to an identifiable individual."

More simply, if information is about a person, that information is personal information as long as you can identify the person that it is about. For example, the fairly innocuous statement "Mike Chapple and Joe Shelley wrote this book" fits the definition of personal information. That personal information might fall into the public domain (after all, it's on the cover of this book!), but it remains personal information.

 You'll often hear the term *personally identifiable information (PII)* used to describe personal information. The acronym PII is commonly used in privacy programs as a shorthand notation for all personal information.

Of course, not all personal information is in the public domain. There are many other types of information that fit into this category that most people would consider private. Our bank balances, medical records, college admissions test scores, and email communications are all personal information that we might hold sensitive. This information fits into the narrower category of *sensitive personal information (SPI)*. For example, the European Union's General Data Protection Regulation (GDPR) includes a listing of "special categories of personal data," which include

- Racial or ethnic origin
- Political opinions
- Religious or philosophical beliefs
- Trade union membership
- Genetic data
- Biometric data used for the purpose of uniquely identifying a natural person
- Health data
- Data concerning a natural person's sex life or sexual orientation

The GDPR uses this list to create special boundaries and controls around the categories of information that EU lawmakers found to be most sensitive.

What Isn't Personal Information?

With a working knowledge of personal information under our belts, it's also important to make sure that we have a clear understanding about what types of information do not fit the definition of personal information and, therefore, fall outside the scope of privacy programs.

First, clearly, if information is not about a person, it is not personal information. Information can be sensitive but not personal. For example, a business's product development plans or a military unit's equipment list might both be very sensitive, but they aren't about people, so they don't fit the definition of personal information and would not be included within the scope of a privacy program.

Second, information is not personal information if it does not provide a way to identify the person that the information is about. For example, consider the height and weight information presented in Table 1.1.

TABLE 1.1   Height and weight information

Name	Age	Gender	Height	Weight
Mary Smith	43	F	5'9"	143 lbs
Matt Jones	45	M	5'11"	224 lbs
Kevin Reynolds	32	M	5'10"	176 lbs

This information clearly fits the definition of personal information. But what if we remove the names from this table, as shown in Table 1.2?

TABLE 1.2   Anonymized height and weight information

Age	Gender	Height	Weight
43	F	5'9"	143 lbs
45	M	5'11"	224 lbs
32	M	5'10"	176 lbs

Here, we have a set of information that is about an individual, but it doesn't seem to be about an *identifiable* individual, making it fall outside the definition of personal information. However, we must be careful here. What if this table was known to be the information about individuals in a certain department? If Mary Smith is the only 43-year-old female in that department, it would be trivial to determine that the first row contains her personal information, making it once again identifiable information.

This leads us to the concept of *anonymization*, the process of taking personal information and making it impossible to identify the individual to whom the information relates. As illustrated in our height and weight example, simply removing names from a table of data does not necessarily anonymize that data. Anonymization is actually a quite challenging problem and requires the expertise of privacy professionals.

The U.S. Department of Health and Human Services (HHS) publishes a de-identification standard that may be used to render information unidentifiable using two different techniques:

 The HHS de-identification standards cover medical records, so they include fields specific to medical records. You may use them as general guidance for the de-identification of other types of record, but you must also supplement them with industry-specific fields that might identify an individual. You can read the full HHS de-identification standard at www. hhs.gov/hipaa/for-professionals/privacy/special-topics/de-identification/index.html#standard.

- *Expert determination* requires the involvement of a trained statistician who analyzes a de-identified dataset and determines that there is very little risk that the information could be used to identify an individual, even if that information is combined with other publicly available information.

- *Safe harbor* requires the removal of 18 different types of information to remove direct and indirect links to an individual. These include
  - Names
  - Geographic divisions and ZIP codes containing fewer than 20,000 people
  - The month and day of a person's birth, death, hospital admission or discharge or the age in years of a person over 89
  - Telephone numbers
  - Vehicle identifiers and serial numbers, including license plate numbers
  - Fax numbers
  - Device identifiers and serial numbers
  - Email addresses
  - Web URLs
  - Social Security numbers
  - IP addresses
  - Medical record numbers
  - Biometric identifiers, including finger and voice prints

- Health plan beneficiary numbers
- Full-face photographs and any comparable images
- Account numbers
- Any other uniquely identifying number, characteristic, or code
- Certificate/license numbers

We will cover how this standard fits into the broader requirements of the Health Insurance Portability and Accountability Act (HIPAA) in Chapter 5, "Private Sector Data Collection." We only discuss it here as an example of the difficulty of anonymizing personal information.

Closely related to anonymization is the process of *aggregation*, summarizing data about a group of individuals in a manner that makes it impossible to draw conclusions about a single person. For example, we might survey all the students at a university and ask them their height and weight. If the students include any identifying information on their survey responses, those individual responses are clearly personal information. However, if we provide the summary table shown in Table 1.3, the information has been aggregated to an extent that renders it nonpersonal information. There is no way to determine the height or weight of an individual student from this data.

TABLE 1.3   Aggregated height and weight information

Gender	Average Height	Average Weight
F	5'5"	133 lbs
M	5'10"	152 lbs

Why Should We Care About Privacy?

Protecting privacy is hard work. Privacy programs require that organizations invest time and money in an effort that does not necessarily provide a direct financial return on that investment. This creates an opportunity cost, as those resources could easily be deployed in other areas of the organization to have a direct impact on the mission. Why, then, should organizations care about privacy?

Privacy is an ethical obligation.   Organizations that are the custodians of personal information have a moral and ethical obligation to protect that information against unauthorized disclosure or use.

Laws and regulations require privacy protections.   Depending on the nature of an organization's operations and the jurisdiction(s) where it operates, it may face legal and contractual obligations to protect privacy. Much of this book is dedicated to exploring these obligations.

Poor privacy practices reflect poorly on an organization.   The failure to protect privacy presents a reputational risk to the organization, which may suddenly find its poor privacy practices covered on the front page of the *Wall Street Journal*. The reputational impact of a privacy lapse may have a lasting impact on the organization.

Generally Accepted Privacy Principles

Now that you have a basic understanding of the types of information covered by a privacy program and the reasons that organizations pay particular attention to protecting the privacy of personal information, we can start to explore the specific goals of a privacy program. These goals answer the question "What do we need to do to protect privacy?"

The *Generally Accepted Privacy Principles (GAPP)* are an attempt to establish a global framework for privacy management. GAPP includes 10 principles that were developed as a joint effort between two national accounting organizations: AICPA and the Canadian Institute of Chartered Accountants (CICA). These two organizations sought expert input to develop a set of commonly accepted privacy principles.

The 10 GAPP principles are

1. Management
2. Notice
3. Choice and consent
4. Collection
5. Use, retention, and disposal
6. Access
7. Disclosure to third parties
8. Security for privacy
9. Quality
10. Monitoring and enforcement

The remainder of this section explores each of these principles in more detail.

Exam Note

GAPP is one of many frameworks designed to help privacy professionals articulate the goals of their privacy programs and industry best practices. Other similar frameworks include the Fair Information Practice Principles (FIPPs) and the Organisation for Economic Co-operation and Development's Privacy Guidelines.

We present GAPP to you in this chapter as a framework to help you understand the basic requirements of privacy programs. The GAPP principles are not included in the CIPP/US exam objectives, so you shouldn't see exam questions specifically covering them.

You will see many of these principles come up repeatedly in federal, state, and international laws that *are* covered by the exam objectives, so expect to see questions covering these concepts, just not in the context of GAPP.

Management

Management is the first of the 10 privacy principles, and GAPP defines it as follows: "The entity defines, documents, communicates, and assigns accountability for its privacy policies and procedures." The GAPP standard then goes on to list a set of criteria that organizations should follow to establish control over the management of their privacy program.

These criteria include

- Creating written privacy policies and communicating those policies to personnel

- Assigning responsibility and accountability for those policies to a person or team

- Establishing procedures for the review and approval of privacy policies and changes to those policies

- Ensuring that privacy policies are consistent with applicable laws and regulations

- Performing privacy risk assessments on at least an annual basis

- Ensuring that contractual obligations to customers, vendors, and partners are consistent with privacy policies

- Assessing privacy risks when implementing or changing technology infrastructure

- Creating and maintaining a privacy incident management process

- Conducting privacy awareness and training and establishing qualifications for employees with privacy responsibilities

Notice

The second GAPP principle, *notice*, requires that organizations inform individuals about their privacy practices. GAPP defines notice as follows: "The entity provides notice about its privacy policies and procedures and identifies the purposes for which personal information is collected, used, retained, and disclosed."

The notice principle incorporates the following criteria:

- Including notice practices in the organization's privacy policies

- Notifying individuals about the purpose of collecting personal information and the organization's policies surrounding the other GAPP principles

- Providing notice to individuals at the time of data collection, when policies and procedures change, and when the organization intends to use information for new purposes not disclosed in earlier notices
- Writing privacy notices in plain and simple language and posting it conspicuously

Choice and Consent

Choice and consent is the third GAPP principle, allowing individuals to retain control over the use of their personal information. GAPP defines choice and consent as follows: "The entity describes the choices available to the individual and obtains implicit or explicit consent with respect to the collection, use, and disclosure of personal information."

The criteria associated with the principle of choice and consent are as follows:

- Including choice and consent practices in the organization's privacy policies
- Informing individuals about the choice and consent options available to them and the consequences of refusing to provide personal information or withdrawing consent to use personal information
- Obtaining implicit or explicit consent at or before the time that personal information is collected
- Notifying individuals of proposed new uses for previously collected information and obtaining additional consent for those new uses
- Obtaining direct explicit consent from individuals when the organization collects, uses, or discloses sensitive personal information
- Obtaining consent before transferring personal information to or from an individual's computer or device

Collection

The principle of *collection* governs the ways that organizations come into the possession of personal information. GAPP defines this principle as follows: "The entity collects personal information only for the purposes identified in the notice."

The criteria associated with the collection principle are as follows:

- Including collection practices in the organization's privacy policies
- Informing individuals that their personal information will only be collected for identified purposes
- Including details on the methods used to collect data and the types of data collected in the organization's privacy notice
- Collecting information using fair and lawful means and only for the purposes identified in the privacy notice

- Confirming that any third parties that provide the organization with personal information have collected it fairly and lawfully and that the information is reliable
- Informing individuals if the organization obtains additional information about them

Use, Retention, and Disposal

Organizations must maintain the privacy of personal information throughout its lifecycle. That's where the principle of *use, retention, and disposal* plays an important role. GAPP defines this principle as follows: "The entity limits the use of personal information to the purposes identified in the notice and for which the individual has provided implicit or explicit consent. The entity retains personal information for only as long as necessary to fulfill the stated purposes or as required by law or regulations and thereafter appropriately disposes of such information."

The criteria associated with the use, retention, and disposal principle are as follows:

- Including collection practices in the organization's privacy policies
- Informing individuals that their personal information will only be used for disclosed purposes for which the organization has obtained consent and then abiding by that statement
- Informing individuals that their data will be retained for no longer than necessary and then abiding by that statement
- Informing individuals that information that is no longer needed will be disposed of securely and then abiding by that statement

Access

One of the core elements of individual privacy is the belief that individuals should have the right to access information that an organization holds about them and, when necessary, to correct that information. The GAPP definition of the *access* principle as follows: "The entity provides individuals with access to their personal information for review and update."

The criteria associated with the access principle are as follows:

- Including practices around access to personal information in the organization's privacy policies
- Informing individuals about the procedures for reviewing, updating, and correcting their personal information
- Providing individuals with a mechanism to determine whether the organization maintains personal information about them and to review any such information
- Authenticating an individual's identity before providing them with access to personal information

- Providing access to information in an understandable format within a reasonable period of time and either for a reasonable charge that is based on the organization's actual costs or at no cost
- Informing individuals in writing why any requests to access or update personal information were denied and informing them of any appeal rights they may have
- Providing a mechanism for individuals to update or correct personal information and providing that updated information to third parties that received it from the organization

Disclosure to Third Parties

Some challenging privacy issues arise when organizations maintain personal information about an individual and then choose to share that information with third parties in the course of doing business. GAPP defines the *disclosure to third parties* principle as follows: "The entity discloses personal information to third parties only for the purposes identified in the notice and with the implicit or explicit consent of the individual."

The criteria associated with the disclosure to third parties principle are as follows:

- Including third-party disclosure practices in the organization's privacy policies
- Informing individuals of any third-party disclosures that take place and the purpose of those disclosures
- Informing third parties that receive personal information from the organization that they must comply with the organization's privacy policy and handling practices
- Disclosing personal information to third parties without notice or for purposes other than those disclosed in the notice only when required to do so by law
- Disclosing information to third parties only under the auspices of an agreement that the third party will protect the information consistent with the organization's privacy policy
- Implementing procedures designed to verify that the privacy controls of third parties receiving personal information from the organization are functioning effectively
- Taking remedial action when the organization learns that a third party has mishandled personal information shared by the organization

Security for Privacy

Protecting the security of personal information is deeply entwined with protecting the privacy of that information. Organizations can't provide individuals with assurances about the handling of personal data if they can't protect that information from unauthorized access. GAPP defines *security for privacy* as follows: "The entity protects personal information against unauthorized access (both physical and logical)." We will revisit this topic in more detail later in this chapter.

The criteria associated with the security for privacy principle are as follows:

- Including security practices in the organization's privacy policies
- Informing individuals that the organization takes precautions to protect the privacy of their personal information
- Developing, documenting, and implementing an information security program that addresses the major privacy-related areas of security listed in ISO 27002:
  - Risk assessment and treatment
  - Security policy
  - Organization of information security
  - Asset management
  - Human resources security
  - Physical and environmental security
  - Communications and operations management
  - Access control
  - Information systems acquisition, development, and maintenance
  - Information security incident management
  - Business continuity management
  - Compliance

 This list includes the ISO 27002 elements that are relevant to privacy efforts and, therefore, our discussion. ISO 27002 does include other recommended security controls that fall outside the scope of a privacy effort.

- Restricting logical access to personal information through the use of strong identification, authentication, and authorization practices
- Restricting physical access to personal information through the use of physical security controls
- Protecting personal information from accidental disclosure due to natural disasters and other environmental hazards
- Applying strong encryption to any personal information that is transmitted over public networks
- Avoiding the storage of personal information on portable media, unless absolutely necessary, and using encryption to protect any personal information that must be stored on portable media
- Conducting periodic tests of security safeguards used to protect personal information

Quality

When we think about the issues associated with protecting the privacy of personal information, we often first think about issues related to the proper collection and use of that information along with potential unauthorized disclosure of that information. However, it's also important to consider the accuracy of that information. Individuals may be damaged by incorrect information just as much, if not more, than they might be damaged by information that is improperly handled. The GAPP *quality* principle states that "The entity maintains accurate, complete, and relevant personal information for the purposes identified in the notice."

The criteria associated with the quality principle are as follows:

- Including data quality practices in the organization's privacy policies
- Informing individuals that they bear responsibility for providing the organization with accurate and complete personal information and informing the organization if corrections are required
- Maintaining personal information that is accurate, complete, and relevant for the purposes for which it will be used

Monitoring and Enforcement

Privacy programs are not a one-time project. It's true that organizations may make a substantial initial investment of time and energy to build up their privacy practices, but those practices must be monitored over time to ensure that they continue to operate effectively and meet the organization's privacy obligations as business needs and information practices evolve. The GAPP *monitoring and enforcement* principle states that "The entity monitors compliance with its privacy policies and procedures and has procedures to address privacy related inquires, complaints, and disputes."

The criteria associated with the monitoring and enforcement principle are as follows:

- Including monitoring and enforcement practices in the organization's privacy policies
- Informing individuals about how they should contact the organization if they have questions, complaints, or disputes regarding privacy practices
- Maintaining a dispute resolution process that ensures that every complaint is addressed and that the individual who raised the complaint is provided with a documented response
- Reviewing compliance with privacy policies, procedures, laws, regulations, and contractual obligations on an annual basis
- Developing and implementing remediation plans for any issues identified during privacy compliance reviews
- Documenting cases where privacy policies were violated and taking any necessary corrective action
- Performing ongoing monitoring of the privacy program based on a risk assessment

Developing a Privacy Program

At this point in the chapter, you should have a reasonable understanding of the fact that privacy issues are both complex and nuanced. There are no "quick fix" solutions to protecting the privacy of personal information. Organizations developing a privacy program for the first time will need to expend considerable effort designing that program, implementing appropriate privacy controls, and monitoring the program's ongoing effectiveness to ensure that it continues to meet the organization's legal obligations and privacy objectives.

Crafting Strategy, Goals, and Objectives

At the outset of a privacy initiative, senior leadership should outline the purpose, strategy, and goals of the privacy program. These provide the high-level direction that those implementing the program will need to guide their efforts. For example, the U.S. Department of Commerce (DOC) offers the following mission statement for their privacy program:

The DOC is committed to safeguarding personal privacy. Individual trust in the privacy and security of personally identifiable information is a foundation of trust in government and commerce in the 21st Century. As an employer, a collector of data on millions of individuals and companies, the developer of information management standards and a federal advisor on information management policy, the Department strives to be a leader in best privacy practices and privacy policy. To further this goal, the Department assigns a high priority to privacy consideration in all systems, programs, and policies.

That's a very high-level statement that clearly explains the purpose of the program. Notice that it doesn't contain any specific objectives or measures. The privacy obligations and controls used by the DOC might change over time, but it is very likely that this strategic-level mission statement will remain appropriate (at least through the end of the 21st century!). The program document also contains goals that the DOC has to guide the execution of a privacy program in support of its mission. The four goals of its plan are as follows:

1. Foster a culture of privacy and disclosure and demonstrate leadership through policy and partnerships.

2. Provide outreach, education, training, and reports in order to promote privacy and transparency.

3. Conduct robust compliance and oversight programs to ensure adherence with federal privacy and disclosure laws and policies in all DOC activities.

4. Develop and maintain the best privacy and disclosure professionals in the federal government.

These goals now start to get into the details of *how* the DOC will carry out its privacy mission. They provide four key deliverables that privacy officials can then use to align their work with the DOC's strategy.

Underneath each of these goals, the DOC then provides a series of specific objectives that will satisfy each goal. These are the activities that the DOC plans to undertake to meet its goal and, therefore, achieve the privacy program's strategic purpose. For brevity's sake, we won't cover all the objectives in this book, but let's take a look at the four objectives that align with the DOC's third privacy goal to conduct robust compliance and oversight programs:

1. Review, assess, and provide guidance to DOC programs, systems, projects, information sharing arrangements, and other initiatives to reduce the impact on privacy and ensure compliance.

2. Promote privacy best practices and guidance to the DOC's information sharing and intelligence activities.

3. Ensure that complaints and incidents at DOC are reported systematically, processed efficiently, and mitigated appropriately in accordance with federal and DOC privacy policies and procedures.

4. Evaluate DOC programs and activities for compliance with privacy and disclosure laws.

These objectives are highly specific, and you might imagine them being handed to a middle manager to execute. They also might change much more frequently than the program's high-level purpose in order to meet the changing needs of the DOC.

 Throughout this section, we draw examples from the Department of Commerce's Privacy Plan. If you'd like to review this plan in more detail, you can download it from `osec.doc.gov/opog/privacy/Memorandums/PRIVACY_PROGRAM_PLAN_2017.pdf`.

Appointing a Privacy Official

Organizations should appoint a senior leader with overall responsibility for the organization's privacy program. This establishes senior-level accountability for the program's success and provides the privacy program a seat at the executive table. This role is commonly referred to as an organization's *chief privacy officer (CPO)*, although it may also be implemented using other titles, such as director of privacy or privacy program manager.

In the DOC Privacy Plan that we have been using as an example in this section, the department identifies a position within the office of the Secretary of Commerce as the DOC's chief privacy officer. The program includes a detailed set of responsibilities for this position. Here is an abbreviated set of those responsibilities, paraphrased for brevity:

- Serve as the senior privacy policy authority
- Develop and oversee implementation of privacy policies

- Communicate the privacy vision, principles, and policy internally and externally
- Ensure the department complies with applicable privacy laws and regulations
- Advocate privacy-preserving strategies for information collection and dissemination
- Manage privacy risks
- Ensure employees and contractors receive appropriate privacy training
- Facilitate relationships with senior DOC leaders, other federal agencies, and private industry

Of course, the DOC is a very large organization, and it would be impossible for one person to be involved in all aspects of its privacy program in any type of thorough manner. For this reason, the DOC policy also specifies that each operating unit should have its own CPO and that those CPOs should meet regularly as the Department of Commerce Privacy Council.

 This type of hierarchical privacy authority is common in government agencies and other large organizations. It may not be necessary in smaller organizations, depending on the nature of the organization and the scope of its privacy program. Some organizations opt to use the role of "privacy liaisons" distributed throughout the organization. These liaisons serve as the primary point of privacy contact for their organization and work directly with the CPO office. Depending on the size of the unit they serve, the liaison role may be a full-time position or a secondary responsibility for someone in another primary role.

Privacy Roles

Depending on the nature of an individual or organization's involvement in the collection and processing of information, they may take on one or more data roles. The three primary roles are as follows:

- *Data subjects* are the individuals about whom personal information is collected. These may be the customers or employees of an organization or any other individuals about whom the organization collects personal information.
- *Data controllers* are the organizations that determine the purposes and means of collecting personal information from data subjects. If an organization collects and/or processes personal information for its own business needs, it is a data controller. It remains a data controller even if it outsources some of that collection or processing to service providers.
- *Data processors* are service providers that collect or process personal information on behalf of data controllers. For example, cloud service providers often serve in the role of data processor for their customers.

These terms take on particular importance when interpreting how laws and regulations apply to an organization. For example, some regulations allow data controllers to transfer some privacy and security responsibility to service providers, as long as the controller chooses a service provider that has gone through a certification process. Regulations, including the EU's GDPR, may also have very specific definitions of these terms, as you will discover later in this book as we explore those regulations in more detail.

Building Inventories

Once an organization has established accountable officials and privacy roles, the next step in developing a privacy program is to create a comprehensive inventory of the personal information that the organization collects, processes, and maintains and the systems, storage locations, and processes involved in those activities.

This inventory may take many different forms, depending on the nature of the organization and the level of formality desired. The end goal is for the organization to have a clear picture of the personal information that it handles and the locations where that information is stored and processed. This inventory should be maintained as a living repository of data updated when privacy practices change. It may then be used as the basis for conducting privacy assessments and implementing privacy controls.

Information security programs also depend on a similar inventory of all sensitive information maintained by the organization. The information included in a privacy-focused inventory is a subset of that sensitive information inventory. This offers an excellent opportunity for privacy and information security programs to partner and avoid redundant activity by simply including a personal information tag in the broader sensitive information inventory.

Conducting a Privacy Assessment

With a personal information inventory in hand, the organization may now turn to an assessment of the current state of its privacy program. This assessment should use a standard set of privacy practices, derived from either an industry standard framework or the regulatory requirements facing the organization. The remainder of this book will dive deeply into many of these frameworks and requirements.

For example, an organization might choose to adopt the privacy framework from the International Organization for Standardization titled "Security techniques—Extension to ISO/IEC 27001 and ISO/IEC 27002 for privacy information management—Requirements and guidelines" and documented in ISO 27701. An excerpt from this document appears in Figure 1.1.

FIGURE 1.1   Excerpt from ISO 27701

ISO 27701 is closely linked to ISO 27001 and 27002, the two ISO standards governing information security. This is another opportunity to align the interests of privacy and security programs. Annex F of ISO 27701 provides advice on applying the privacy standard in an organization that already uses the information security standards. These standards are also tightly linked to the National Institute for Standards and Technology's Cybersecurity Framework (CSF), allowing organizations to cleanly map controls between standards and frameworks that they adopt for both privacy and security.

The end result of the privacy assessment should be a *gap analysis* that identifies any places where the organization's current practices do not meet the level of control desired by the standard under which the assessment was performed. This gap analysis may then be used in remediation efforts to bring the organization up to the desired level of privacy performance.

Implementing Privacy Controls

The primary means that the organization uses to remediate privacy deficiencies is the implementation of *privacy controls* that are technical or administrative measures that improve privacy. For example, implementing mechanisms that fulfill the many GAPP criteria discussed earlier in this chapter qualify as privacy controls. Here are some examples of common privacy controls:

- Creation, review, or modification of privacy policies
- Use of encryption to protect personal information
- Purging personal information when it is no longer needed to meet the purposes disclosed when it was collected
- Configuring access controls to limit the use of personal information to authorized individuals
- Implementing and maintaining a process to manage user privacy preferences
- Developing a standard process for investigating privacy complaints and following up on potential privacy incidents
- Conducting periodic testing and assessment of the organization's privacy program

Notice that some, but not all, of these controls are technical in nature, but all the controls advance the organization's privacy efforts.

Ongoing Operation and Monitoring

Once a privacy program is well established, the organization should continue to operate the program and monitor its effectiveness. This is normally done through a combination of periodic reviews, regular updates to the privacy assessment, and dashboard-style monitoring of the program's key metrics, such as compliance with data retention and disposal standards, turnaround time for processing privacy requests, and the number and severity of privacy incidents.

Organizations may also find themselves the subject of *privacy audits* based on legal or regulatory requirements. Audits are similar to assessments in nature, because they compare the current state of the privacy program to an external standard. However, unlike assessments, audits are always performed by an independent auditor who does not have a vested interest in the outcome. Audits may be performed at the request of internal management, a board of directors, or regulatory authorities.

Online Privacy

Consumers often provide information to companies and organizations online. This may consist of *active data collection*, where the consumer directly fills out forms, or *passive data collection*, where the organization gathers information from the individual automatically when they visit a website or engage in other online activity.

An organization's privacy policy should apply to all online data collection, whether that collection is active or passive.

Privacy Notices

The *privacy notice* is the primary means that an organization uses to convey the details of its privacy policy to end users. The contents of this notice are often driven by regulatory requirements. For example, a data controller subject to the EU's GDPR might include the following:

- Contact information for the data controller and the controller's data protection officer (DPO)
- Purposes for which the organization collects personal information
- Description of the categories of data subjects from whom the organization collects information
- Description of the categories of personal information collected by the organization
- Categories of recipients to whom personal information has or will be disclosed
- Identification of any third countries or international organizations that will receive data and the safeguards put in place to protect those transfers
- Time limits for the erasure of different categories of data
- General descriptions of the technical and administrative security mechanisms used to protect personal information

Privacy notices must strike a balance between satisfying legal and ethical disclosure obligations and remaining readable to the layperson attempting to decipher the document. LinkedIn's privacy policy does an excellent job of balancing these two requirements by providing large-type summaries of each section written in plain language accompanied by the more detailed legal language of the policy. This approach, offering a brief summary of the privacy policy in plain language along with the detailed legalese, is known as a *layered privacy notice*.

Figure 1.2 shows an excerpt illustrating the layered notice approach. You can view LinkedIn's entire policy at www.linkedin.com/legal/privacy-policy.

Privacy and Cybersecurity

The fields of privacy and cybersecurity are closely related and interdependent. This occurs to such an extent that many people who do not work in either field consider them the same. However, although these fields are related to each other, they remain separate and distinct.

As you've already read, the purpose of a privacy program is to safeguard the privacy rights that individuals have to their personal information. The purpose of a cybersecurity program is to protect the confidentiality, integrity, and availability of data maintained by an

FIGURE 1.2   Excerpt from the LinkedIn privacy policy

1. Data We Collect

1.1 Data You Provide To Us

Registration
To create an account you need to provide data including your name, email address and/or mobile number, and a password. If you register for a premium Service, you will need to provide payment (e.g., credit card) and billing information.

You provide data to create an account with us.

Profile
You have **choices** about the information on your profile, such as your education, work experience, skills, photo, **city or area** and endorsements. Some Members may choose to complete a separate **ProFinder profile.** You don't have to provide additional information on your profile; however, profile information helps you to get more from our Services, including helping recruiters and business opportunities find you. It's your choice whether to include **sensitive information** on your profile and to make that sensitive information public. Please do not post or add personal data to your profile that you would not want to be publicly available.

You create your LinkedIn profile (a complete profile helps you get the most from our Services).

Posting and Uploading
We collect personal data from you when you provide, post or upload it to our Services, such as when you fill out a form, (e.g., with demographic data or **salary**), respond to a survey, or submit a resume or fill out a job application on our Services. If you opt to import your address book, we receive your contacts (including contact information your service provider(s) or app automatically added to your address book when you communicated with addresses or numbers not already in your list).

You give other data to us, such as by syncing your address book or calendar.

If you sync your contacts or calendars with our Services, we will collect your address book and calendar meeting information to keep growing your network by suggesting connections for you and others, and by providing information about events, e.g. times, places, attendees and contacts.

You don't have to post or upload personal data; though if you don't, it may limit your ability to grow and engage with your network over our Services.

organization. Before we describe the relationship between the two, let's take a deeper look at the goals of a cybersecurity program.

Cybersecurity Goals

When most people think of cybersecurity, they imagine hackers trying to break into an organization's system and steal sensitive information, ranging from Social Security numbers and credit cards to top-secret military information. Although protecting sensitive information from unauthorized disclosure is certainly one element of a cybersecurity program, it is

FIGURE 1.3   The three key objectives of cybersecurity programs are confidentiality, integrity, and availability.

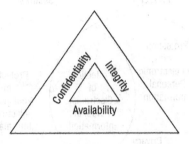

important to understand that cybersecurity actually has three complementary objectives, as shown in Figure 1.3.

Confidentiality ensures that unauthorized individuals are not able to gain access to sensitive information. Cybersecurity professionals develop and implement security controls, including firewalls, access control lists, and encryption, to prevent unauthorized access to information. Attackers may seek to undermine confidentiality controls to achieve one of their goals: the unauthorized disclosure of sensitive information.

Integrity ensures that there are no unauthorized modifications to information or systems, either intentionally or unintentionally. Integrity controls, such as hashing and integrity monitoring solutions, seek to enforce this requirement. Integrity threats may come from attackers seeking the alteration of information without authorization or nonmalicious sources, such as a power spike causing the corruption of information.

Availability ensures that information and systems are ready to meet the needs of legitimate users at the time those users request them. Availability controls, such as fault tolerance, clustering, and backups, seek to ensure that legitimate users may gain access as needed. Similar to integrity threats, availability threats may come either from attackers seeking the disruption of access or nonmalicious sources, such as a fire destroying a datacenter that contains valuable information or services.

Cybersecurity analysts often refer to these three goals, known as the CIA Triad, when performing their work. They often characterize risks, attacks, and security controls as meeting one or more of the three CIA Triad goals when describing them.

Relationship Between Privacy and Cybersecurity

Now that you have a good understanding of the nature of privacy and security programs, you may already be developing a sense of the relationship between the two. Privacy depends on cybersecurity. In fact, you've already read that security for privacy is one of the 10 GAPP principles. The bottom line is that you can't protect the privacy of information unless you can guarantee the security of that information.

FIGURE 1.4   The relationship between privacy and security

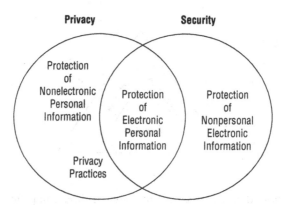

The relationship is more complex than that, however, as shown in Figure 1.4.

Cybersecurity and privacy programs share a common goal: the protection of electronic personal information. They each also have their own independent goals.

Privacy programs must also concern themselves with the protection of nonelectronic personal information, such as paper records. They also must be concerned about all 10 GAPP principles, not just security. Principles such as notice, choice and consent, and quality generally fall outside the scope of security programs.

Security programs concern themselves with the confidentiality, integrity, and availability of *all* sensitive electronic information. This includes sensitive, but nonpersonal, information, such as business plans, trade secrets, and product designs.

All differences aside, privacy and cybersecurity are close cousins in the business world. Privacy and security professionals often share a common ethos and understanding of each other's work, but it is also important that they understand the fundamental differences between their goals.

Privacy by Design

The discipline of *Privacy by Design* seeks to incorporate strong privacy practices into the design and implementation of technology systems, rather than seeking to "bolt on" privacy controls after a system is already in place. This approach leads to more effective privacy controls, more efficient design and implementation processes, and reduced rework.

Ann Cavoukian, the Information and Privacy Commissioner of Ontario, Canada, developed the concept of Privacy by Design and outlined seven foundational principles that are crucial to ensuring that individuals retain control over their personal information:

1. *Proactive, Not reactive; preventive, Not remedial.* Systems should be designed to prevent privacy risks from occurring in the first place, not to respond to privacy lapses that do occur.

2. *Privacy as the default setting.* Systems should protect the privacy of individuals even if they do not act in any way. The default approach of any system should be to protect privacy unless the user specifically chooses to take actions that reduce the level of privacy.

3. *Privacy embedded into design.* Privacy should be a primary design consideration, not a "bolted-on" afterthought. Privacy is a core requirement of the system.

4. *Full functionality—positive-sum, Not zero-sum.* Privacy should not be treated as requiring trade-offs with the business, security, or other objectives. Privacy by Design seeks "win-win" situations where privacy objectives may be achieved alongside other objectives.

5. *End-to-end security—full lifecycle protection.* Security practices should persist throughout the entire information lifecycle. Information should be securely collected, retained, and disposed of to preserve individual privacy.

6. *Visibility and transparency—Keep it open.* The component parts of systems preserving Privacy by Design should be open for inspection by users and providers alike.

7. *Respect for user privacy—Keep it user-centric.* Privacy is about protecting personal information and personal information belongs to individuals. Therefore, Privacy by Design practices maintain a focus on the individual, empowering data subjects with user-friendly privacy practices.

The principles of Privacy by Design offer an outstanding starting point for integrating privacy thinking into a systems engineering practice.

Summary

Privacy is a complex undertaking, requiring that organizations put careful thought into the nature of the personal information that they collect and process and the controls used to safeguard that information. The Generally Accepted Privacy Principles (GAPP) outline 10 principles that organizations should consider when designing their privacy programs: management; notice; choice and consent; collection; use, retention, and disposal; access; disclosure to third parties; security for privacy; quality; and monitoring and enforcement.

Organizations should consider these principles when designing privacy controls. These controls should remediate gaps discovered during privacy assessments and bring the organization up to an acceptable level of privacy practice. Ongoing audits and assessments ensure that those controls continue to operate effectively.

Exam Essentials

Know how to designate a senior individual accountable for the privacy program. Placing responsibility for the design, implementation, maintenance, and monitoring of a privacy program in the hands of a senior official provides direct accountability for the program's goals and objectives. Organizations commonly designate a chief privacy officer (CPO) to hold these responsibilities, and that CPO may also serve as the organization's point of contact for privacy regulators.

Be able to develop a privacy program designed to achieve the organization's privacy mission.   Privacy programs consist of the policies, procedures, tools, and practices used to achieve the desired level of privacy in an organization. Privacy programs should have a high-level strategic purpose/mission that is mapped to more tactical goals and even more specific objectives for achieving those goals. The purpose of a privacy program should change infrequently, whereas goals and objectives may change more frequently.

Understand that privacy programs should have strong processes for managing user preferences.   Abiding by the principle of choice and consent requires that privacy programs acknowledge user preferences for the handling of their personal information. This requires implementing procedures and mechanisms that allow users to state those preferences and for the organization to track and honor them. These activities are good privacy practices and may be required by law in some jurisdictions and industries.

Know how organizations should protect consumer privacy online and disclose their privacy practices.   Privacy notices are the primary means that an organization uses to communicate its privacy practices to data subjects. These privacy notices should be posted conspicuously on the organization's website and written in plain language accessible to the data subjects.

Review Questions

1. Which of the following types of information should be protected by a privacy program?

   A. Customer records

   B. Product plans

   C. Trade secrets

   D. All of the above

2. Barry is consulting with his organization's cybersecurity team on the development of their cybersecurity program. Which one of the following would not be a typical objective of such a program?

   A. Privacy

   B. Confidentiality

   C. Availability

   D. Integrity

3. Howard is assisting his firm in developing a new privacy program and wants to incorporate a privacy risk assessment process into the program. If Howard wishes to comply with industry best practices, how often should the firm conduct these risk assessments?

   A. Monthly

   B. Semiannually

   C. Annually

   D. Biannually

4. Of the following fields, which fits into the "special categories of personal data" under GDPR?

   A. Banking records

   B. Union membership records

   C. Educational records

   D. Employment records

5. Katie is assessing her organization's privacy practices and determines that the organization previously collected customer addresses for the purpose of shipping goods and is now using those addresses to mail promotional materials. If this possibility was not previously disclosed, what privacy principle is the organization most likely violating?

   A. Quality

   B. Management

   C. Notice

   D. Security

6. Kara is the chief privacy officer of an organization that maintains a database of customer information for marketing purposes. What term best describes the role of Kara's organization with respect to that database?

   A. Data subject

   B. Data custodian

   C. Data controller

   D. Data processor

7. Richard would like to use an industry standard reference for designing his organization's privacy controls. Which one of the following ISO standards is best suited for this purpose?

   A. ISO 27001

   B. ISO 27002

   C. ISO 27701

   D. ISO 27702

8. Which of the following organizations commonly requests a formal audit of a privacy program?

   A. Management

   B. Board of directors

   C. Regulators

   D. All of the above

9. Which element of a privacy program is likely to remain unchanged for long periods of time?

   A. Mission

   B. Goals

   C. Objectives

   D. Procedures

10. Tonya is seeking to de-identify a set of records about her organization's customers. She is following the HHS guidelines for de-identifying records and is removing ZIP codes associated with small towns. What is the smallest population size for which she may retain a ZIP code?

    A. 1,000

    B. 2,000

    C. 10,000

    D. 20,000

11. Which one of the following statements is not correct about privacy best practices?

    A. Organizations should maintain personal information that is accurate, complete, and relevant.

    B. Organizations should inform data subjects of their privacy practices.

    C. Organizations should retain a third-party dispute resolution service for handling privacy complaints.

    D. Organizations should restrict physical and logical access to personal information.

12. Which one of the following is not a common responsibility for an organization's chief privacy officer?

    A. Managing privacy risks

    B. Encrypting personal information

    C. Developing privacy policy

    D. Advocating privacy strategies

13. When designing privacy controls, an organization should be informed by the results of what type of analysis?

    A. Impact analysis

    B. Gap analysis

    C. Business analysis

    D. Authorization analysis

14. Which one of the following is an example of active online data collection?

    A. Users completing an online survey

    B. Collecting IP addresses from website visitors

    C. Tracking user activity with web cookies

    D. Analyzing the geographic locations of site visitors

15. Which one of the following would not normally appear in an organization's privacy notice?

    A. Types of information collected

    B. Contact information for the data controller

    C. Detailed descriptions of security controls

    D. Categories of recipients to whom personal information is disclosed

16. Gwen is investigating a security incident where attackers deleted important medical records from a hospital's electronic system. There are no backups and the information was irretrievably lost. What cybersecurity goal was most directly affected?

    A. Integrity

    B. Privacy

    C. Confidentiality

    D. Availability

17. When creating his organization's privacy policy, Chris wrote a simplified version of the policy and placed it at the top of the document, following it with the legal detail. What term best describes this approach?

    A. Layered policy

    B. Filtered policy

    C. Redacted policy

    D. Condensed policy

18. Under the Privacy by Design philosophy, which statement is correct?

    A. Organizations should design systems to respond to privacy lapses that occur.

    B. Privacy should be treated as requiring trade-offs with business objectives.

    C. Organizations should strictly limit the disclosure of their privacy practices.

    D. Privacy should be embedded into design.

19. In what Supreme Court case did the term "right to be let alone" first appear?

    A. *Olmstead v. United States*

    B. *Carpenter v. United States*

    C. *Roe v. Wade*

    D. *Katz v. United States*

20. Matt wants to share some information gathered from student records but is concerned about disclosing personal information. To protect privacy, he discloses only a table of summary statistics about overall student performance. What technique has he used?

    A. Anonymization

    B. Deidentification

    C. Aggregation

    D. Redaction

Chapter

2

Legal Environment

THE CIPP/US EXAM OBJECTIVES COVERED IN THIS CHAPTER INCLUDE:

A significant portion of the work performed by privacy professionals revolves around compliance with laws and regulations. In fact, the majority of the CIPP/US exam objectives, and the majority of this book, cover the specific privacy requirements imposed by various privacy laws in the United States and individual state jurisdictions. Understanding and properly applying these laws in the context of an organization requires a solid understanding of the legal environment.

In this chapter, you will learn about the structure of the U.S. legal environment, including the branches of federal government and the sources of various types of law in the United States. You will also learn common legal definitions required to help you analyze legal issues, including jurisdictional issues, private rights of action, liability, negligence, and unfair and deceptive trade practices.

Branches of Government

The U.S. federal government is divided into three coequal branches, each with responsibilities defined in the U.S. Constitution. This three-branch system is designed to provide effective governance and to include a system of *checks and balances*, where each branch has the ability to provide some degree of oversight on the other branches. The three branches of the U.S. government are as follows:

- The *legislative branch*, consisting of the two bodies of the U.S. Congress: the House of Representatives and the Senate
- The *executive branch*, led by the president of the United States and consisting of the departments, agencies, and bureaus that operate under the president's authority
- The *judicial branch*, consisting of the federal court system, with the U.S. Supreme Court as its highest body

Let's take some time to review the responsibilities of each of these branches of government and the checks and balances it holds on the other branches.

Legislative Branch

The legislative branch, also known as the U.S. Congress, is responsible for creating new laws and revising existing ones. The Congress is organized into two bodies: the House of Representatives and the Senate.

The *House of Representatives*, the larger of the two bodies, currently consists of 435 voting members, each elected by a specific congressional district. Each state has a different number of representatives determined by that state's relative population in the most recent U.S. Census. For example, California is the state with the largest population, and it has 53 members in the House. The states with the smallest populations—North Dakota, South Dakota, Montana, Wyoming, Alaska, Delaware, and Vermont—each have only a single representative. Representatives are elected to two-year terms, with every seat in the House up for election in every even-numbered year. The District of Columbia and some U.S. territories are permitted to send nonvoting delegates to the House of Representatives.

The *Senate* is the smaller body of the U.S. Congress. Each of the 50 states is represented equally in the Senate with two senators, so the Senate has a total of 100 voting members. Both of the senators from a state are elected by the entire eligible voting population of that state to serve six-year terms. The terms of senators are arranged such that approximately one-third of Senate seats are up for election every two years.

Either body of Congress can propose a new law, but any proposals must pass both the House and the Senate by a majority vote. Once a bill passes both the House and the Senate, it is sent to the president for signature. The president may sign the bill, in which case it becomes law. If the president does not sign the bill, the president is executing the president's veto authority. In that case, the bill does not become law but is sent back to Congress. Congress may override the president's veto and make the bill law by holding another vote, where the bill must receive a two-thirds majority in both the House and the Senate.

The president's veto power is an example of a check-and-balance held by the executive branch over the legislative branch. The legislative branch's ability to override that veto is a reciprocal check-and-balance. The legislative branch also holds the *power of the purse*, meaning that the executive branch may only spend money that is allocated for that purpose by legislation. This power of the purse is a check-and-balance that the legislative branch holds over the executive branch.

The powers of the legislative branch are enumerated in Article I of the United States Constitution and, therefore, are often referred to as *Article I powers*.

Executive Branch

The executive branch of the government is led by the president and is responsible for carrying out and enforcing the laws created by the legislative branch. The executive branch includes a number of departments and agencies responsible for enforcing privacy laws, such as the Federal Trade Commission, the Department of Commerce, the Department of Health and Human Services, and the Federal Communications Commission.

The departments of the executive branch often write specific rules that provide the details on how the executive branch will enforce the laws passed by Congress. These rules are also known as *administrative law*. The power of the executive branch to enforce the laws (or to decline to do so) is another example of a check-and-balance held by the executive branch over the legislative branch.

In addition to these law enforcement powers, the president has several specific powers identified in the Constitution. These include

- Serving as commander in chief of the U.S. military forces
- Granting pardons and reprieves for offenses against the United States
- Negotiating treaties with other nations on behalf of the United States
- Appointing justices to the Supreme Court, ambassadors to foreign nations, and other officers of the federal government

The powers of the executive branch are enumerated in Article II of the U.S. Constitution and, therefore, are often referred to as *Article II powers.*

The president may be removed from office by the legislative branch through the *impeachment* process defined in Article I. This process involves the House of Representatives holding a vote to impeach the president (or another federal officer) and then the Senate conducting a trial on the articles of impeachment passed by the House. If two-thirds of the senators present vote to convict the president on articles of impeachment, the president is removed from office and the vice president becomes president. The legislative branch's power of impeachment is a significant check-and-balance on the power of the executive branch.

Judicial Branch

The third branch of government is the judicial branch, which consists of the federal court system. Courts interpret the meaning of laws, resolve disputes over federal law, and determine whether laws passed by the legislative branch are consistent with the U.S. Constitution. When privacy disputes occur, the judicial branch is responsible for settling them and resolving ambiguities in the law.

The federal court system receives its power from Article III of the U.S. Constitution. However, the Constitution does not provide much structure for the judicial branch, only stating that

> The judicial Power of the United States, shall be vested in one supreme Court, and in such inferior Courts as the Congress may from time to time ordain and establish. The Judges, both of the supreme and inferior Courts, shall hold their Offices during good Behaviour, and shall, at stated Times, receive for their Services, a Compensation, which shall not be diminished during their Continuance in Office.

The *U.S. Supreme Court* is, in fact, the highest power in the judicial branch, and any opinions that it issues are binding on the entire federal judiciary system and, in many cases, on state and local courts as well. The most significant power afforded to the Supreme Court is the power to declare laws and practices unconstitutional, serving as a check-and-balance on both the legislative and executive branches. This process, known as *judicial review,* allows the Supreme Court to strike down both laws passed by the legislative branch and actions directed by the executive branch when it finds they conflict with one or more provisions of the U.S. Constitution. In cases where the Supreme Court finds a law or practice unconstitutional, this decision is final, as there is no higher avenue of appeal. The only potential recourse is to pursue a modification to the Constitution through the amendment process described later in this chapter.

Justices are appointed to the Supreme Court by the president and must be confirmed by a vote of the Senate. Once a justice is appointed to the Supreme Court, their appointment is for a life term and ends only upon the death or voluntary retirement of the justice. A justice may also be removed by the legislative branch through the impeachment process, although this has never occurred.

The Supreme Court is supported by a series of inferior federal courts, who bear responsibility for resolving the vast majority of criminal and civil cases brought under federal law. The federal courts include, in order from lesser to greater superiority, the following:

- *U.S. district courts* are the trial courts of the federal system, and most cases must first be brought in a district court before being elevated to a higher court. There are currently 670 federal district court judges assigned to 94 district courts spread across the United States. Each court serves a defined geographical area.

- *U.S. circuit courts of appeal* are the intermediate courts in the federal system and only accept cases on appeal from district courts. There are 13 circuit courts of appeal in the United States. Twelve of these cover a geographic jurisdiction illustrated in Figure 2.1. Decisions made by a circuit court are binding on all district courts within that circuit but are not binding on district courts in other jurisdictions. The thirteenth circuit court hears patent law claims and other specialized trade cases.

- The U.S. Supreme Court is the ultimate and final appeal for cases from the federal circuit court, as well as for cases from the state courts involving constitutional issues. The Supreme Court determines which cases it will accept through a process known as *certiorari*, and it accepts only a very small proportion of the cases submitted to it for review. Decisions made by the Supreme Court are final and binding on all inferior courts.

The three types of federal court described in this chapter handle the majority of cases in the federal judicial system. There are, however, some specialized federal courts with narrowly focused jurisdictions. For example, you will learn in Chapter 6, "Government and Court Access to Private Sector Information," about the significant role that the Foreign Intelligence Surveillance Court plays in adjudicating issues of government surveillance for intelligence gathering purposes.

Federal judges serving in the district and circuit courts are appointed in the same manner as Supreme Court justices. After being appointed by the president and confirmed by the Senate, federal judges serve in office until their death, resignation, or removal through the impeachment process.

FIGURE 2.1   Jurisdictional areas of U.S. Circuit Courts of Appeal

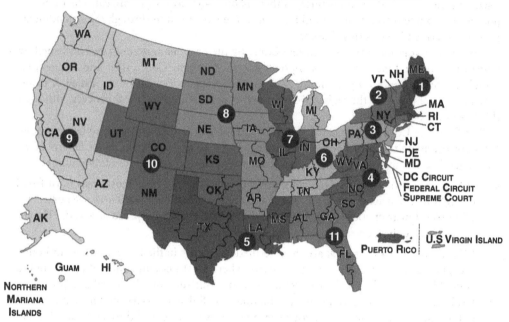

Understanding Laws

Privacy professionals often find themselves in the position of interpreting a variety of laws with different scopes and jurisdictions and, in some cases, seemingly contradictory provisions. Sorting out these issues requires a strong understanding of the sources of those laws and some foundational legal concepts.

Sources of Law

Laws in the United States come from a variety of sources. Many people are already familiar with the laws contained in the Constitution itself, as well as the laws passed through the federal and state legislative processes. Other sources of law include the administrative rules and regulations promulgated by government agencies, case law, common law, and contract law.

Constitutional Law

The U.S. Constitution is the highest possible source of law in the United States; no laws from other sources may conflict with the provisions in the Constitution and its amendments. The main text of the Constitution contains seven articles with the following purposes:

- Article I establishes the legislative branch.

- Article II establishes the executive branch.

- Article III establishes the judicial branch.

- Article IV defines the relationship between the federal government and the governments of the states.

- Article V creates a process for amending the Constitution itself.

- Article VI contains the supremacy clause, establishing that the Constitution is the supreme law of the land.

- Article VII sets forth the process for the initial establishment of the federal government.

Exam Tip

Under the U.S. legal system, the U.S. Constitution is the highest law of the land. No law may conflict with any constitutional requirements, and the only way to modify a constitutional requirement is through the amendment process.

Article V describes the process used to modify the Constitution through the use of amendments. This process is, by design, difficult, as the founders set the bar quite high for altering the terms of this important governing document. The amendment process requires that both houses of Congress pass the amendment by a two-thirds majority. After that approval by Congress, the amendment is sent to the states, who have the opportunity to ratify the amendment. Amendments are added to the Constitution only after ratification by three-quarters (38) of the 50 states.

Constitutional Conventions

The text of the U.S. Constitution was written during a Constitutional Convention held in 1787, where each state sent representatives to represent its interests and cast votes on its behalf.

Article V of the Constitution allows for the modification of the Constitution if two-thirds of the state legislatures call for a new constitutional convention. Although this has never occurred under the provisions of Article V, it remains a possibility. If the states call for such a convention, many legal scholars believe that the convened delegates would have unfettered authority to set their own rules and modify the Constitution as they wished. In the words of the late Justice Antonin Scalia, "I certainly would not want a constitutional convention. Whoa! Who knows what would come out of it?"

The U.S. Constitution currently contains 27 amendments, covering a range of topics from establishing individual rights to defining the terms of presidential succession. The first 10 of these amendments, known as the *Bill of Rights*, enumerate individual civil liberties protections, including freedom of speech, freedom of assembly, and freedom of religion.

Notably, the word *privacy* does not appear anywhere in the text of the Constitution, although there are established constitutional protections of individual privacy. These come from two sources: the Fourth Amendment and the Supreme Court precedent.

The Fourth Amendment to the Constitution reads as follows:

> The right of the people to be secure in their persons, houses, papers, and effects, against unreasonable searches and seizures, shall not be violated, and no Warrants shall issue, but upon probable cause, supported by Oath or affirmation, and particularly describing the place to be searched, and the persons or things to be seized.

This amendment establishes the right of individuals to be protected against some government interference in their private lives. Supreme Court precedent, discussed in Chapter 1, "Privacy in the Modern Era," further establishes the right of an individual "to be let alone."

Although the U.S. Constitution does not explicitly grant a right to privacy, language in several state constitutions does explicitly grant this right. For example, Article 1, Section 23 of the California Constitution reads:

> Every natural person has the right to be let alone and free from governmental intrusion into the person's private life except as otherwise provided herein. This section shall not be construed to limit the public's right of access to public records and meetings as provided by law.

The state of Florida includes the following language in Section 6 of its constitution:

> The right of the people to privacy is recognized and shall not be infringed without the showing of a compelling state interest. The legislature shall take affirmative steps to implement this right.

Similar provisions protect the right to privacy in the constitutions of Alaska, Arizona, Hawaii, Illinois, Louisiana, Montana, New Hampshire, South Carolina, and Washington.

Legislation

Most of the privacy-related laws that apply within the United States today come not from the Constitution but from the standard legislative process described earlier in this chapter. Proposed bills are passed by both houses of Congress and then signed into law by the president. These laws are, of course, only enforceable if they are compatible with the terms of the Constitution.

Laws passed by the U.S. Congress become effective and binding in all states and territories of the United States. State legislatures may also pass laws through a similar process, with the laws that they pass applying only within their own states. Most state lawmaking processes follow a process that mirrors the federal process, with a requirement that laws pass both houses of the state legislature and be signed into law by the state's governor.

 Forty-nine of the 50 states have *bicameral legislatures*, meaning that their legislatures consist of two bodies modeled after the U.S. House of Representatives and Senate. The sole exception to this is the state of Nebraska, which has a single legislative body called the Nebraska Legislature. This approach is known as a *unicameral legislature*.

Administrative Law

Agencies of the executive branch promulgate sets of rules and regulations that implement many of the laws passed by Congress. These rules make up the body of *administrative law* that is commonly documented in the *Code of Federal Regulations (CFR)*.

For example, in 1996, President Clinton signed the Health Insurance Portability and Accountability Act (HIPAA) into law. This law, in part, imposed new security and privacy obligations on healthcare providers and other covered entities. It did not, however, go into great detail on the specific privacy and security requirements that applied to those entities. Instead, it charged the Department of Health and Human Services (HHS) with creating administrative law containing those implementation details.

Responding to this mandate, HHS published the HIPAA Privacy Rule and the HIPAA Security Rule, which contained detailed requirements for organizations subject to the law's provisions. These rules were created under legislative authority, but they were not passed through the legislative process, so they qualify as examples of administrative law.

Agencies may not create administrative law on a whim. They must go through a formal rule-making process that allows for public comment and the provisions of administrative law remain subject to judicial review and may also be overridden by a legislative act.

Case Law

The main role of the judicial branch is to interpret the laws and apply them to resolve civil and criminal disputes. The interpretations made by courts over time establish a body of *case law* that other courts may refer to when making their own decisions.

In many cases, the case law decisions made by courts are binding on both that court and any subordinate courts. Courts generally follow the legal principle of *stare decisis* (Latin for "let the decision stand") that states that previous decisions on questions of law serve as precedent guiding the future decisions made by that court and its subordinates. For this reason, even the Supreme Court is reluctant to revisit decisions made by past courts, even if the justices believe that they might reach a conclusion that is different from that of their predecessors.

There is quite a bit of case law on the subject of privacy. For example, the 1996 *Smyth v. Pillsbury Corporation* decision in the U.S. District Court for the Eastern District of Pennsylvania established that employees generally do not have a right to privacy in their use of company-provided email accounts. Although this case was not appealed to higher courts, many other jurisdictions have cited it as relevant case law in their own decisions.

Common Law

The United States is among a large group of nations that observe *common law*, a set of judicial precedents passed down as case law through many generations. This subset of common law includes many long-standing legal principles that have never been codified in legislation but, nonetheless, guide many judicial decisions. The body of common law may be traced back to the English court systems and therefore is typically found in modern-day countries that were historically British colonies. Each of those nations gradually adapted common law principles to their own cultural and judicial philosophy over the years.

The body of common law in the United States includes protections of an individual's right to privacy. Later in this chapter, you will learn about the torts of negligence and invasion of privacy. Both of these concepts have their foundation in common law.

There is a delicate relationship between common law and laws with constitutional or legislative sources. Constitutional law and legislative law may override aspects of the common law. Common law also arises from other laws when those laws leave room for interpretation and common law principles guide courts in making case law that fills those gaps. For this reason, many states have codified portions of the common law in their own statutes.

Later in this chapter, we discuss the invasion of privacy tort. This is an example of a privacy-related common law.

Contract Law

Contracts are legally binding agreements between parties that they will exchange things of value with each other. When two parties have agreed to enter into a contract, they become legally liable to uphold their obligations. As long as the terms of the contract do not violate the law, they are enforceable in court. Contracts should spell out the specific liability that each party has for violations of the contract.

Several conditions must be met for a contract to be valid:

- Each party to the contract must have the capacity to agree to the contract.
- There must be an offer made by one party. This offer may be verbal or in writing, but written terms always take precedence over verbal terms and many types of transactions, such as those involving real estate, must be conducted in writing.

- The other party must accept the offer.

- Consideration must be given, meaning that both parties must exchange something of value. For example, if I enter into a contract to sell you my car, I am giving you the car, something of value, and, in return, you are paying me in cash, something of value.

- Finally, there must be mutual intent to be bound. Both parties must enter into a contract with the intention that they are agreeing to the terms.

Violations of a contract generally do not involve law enforcement agencies, so they are treated as private disputes between parties and handled in civil court. These cases are known as *breaches of contract*, and courts may take action to enforce the terms of a contract, cancel a contract, or award damages to compensate one party for harm caused by the other party's breach of contract.

From a privacy perspective, organizations often include language in contracts with vendors obligating them to protect the privacy of personally identifiable information. For example, healthcare organizations governed by HIPAA use formal Business Associate Agreements (BAAs) to document the privacy obligations of their service providers.

Analyzing a Law

Jurisdictions around the nation and the world are now frequently passing new privacy laws. These laws might cover new industries, new elements of information, or new jurisdictions. As privacy professionals, we are often called upon to read and interpret these privacy laws, determining how they apply to our organizations.

Determining Jurisdiction

When analyzing a new law, one of the first things that a privacy professional should do is determine the *jurisdiction* of the law. The jurisdiction is the geographic area over which the law applies. Determining jurisdiction is done by reading the law itself and also assessing the power of the body that created the law. Although this might seem straightforward, interpreting privacy laws is fairly complex.

For example, when the European Union first passed the General Data Protection Regulation (GDPR), the law stated that it applied to the personal information of EU residents worldwide. If a resident of the EU did business with a U.S. company and that information was physically stored in the United States, the EU claimed jurisdiction over that information. Privacy professionals at U.S. companies weren't sure that the EU actually had the jurisdiction to make this declaration.

The applicability of the GDPR is continuing to evolve, but a 2019 ruling by the European Court of Justice limited that applicability. In the ruling (*Google LLC v. Commission nationale de l'informatique et des libertés (CNIL)*), the court said that the right to be forgotten applies only within the EU. They made this decision in the context of a person requesting that their search results be removed from Google. The decision said that although Google must remove the results shown to visitors from within the EU, the law does not require Google to implement the right to be forgotten worldwide.

State data breach notification laws also create significant issues of jurisdiction, similar to those discussed in the Google case. We cover these issues in more detail in Chapter 8, "State Privacy Laws."

Just as laws have jurisdictions, courts also have jurisdictions defined by the power that a court has to render legal judgments in both their subject matter and their geographic applicability. For example, federal courts have jurisdiction only over federal law, whereas state courts have jurisdiction only over state law. Federal circuit courts have geographic authority only over specific states. For example, the Seventh Circuit Court of Appeals has authority over Indiana, Illinois, and Wisconsin. Decisions made by that court apply only within that circuit. The Supreme Court, on the other hand, has nationwide jurisdiction.

There are two elements to a court's jurisdiction:

- *Personal jurisdiction* refers to a court's authority over a person being sued or charged with a crime. Personal jurisdiction over individuals and corporations is commonly established through four mechanisms:

  - Physical presence in an area within the court's geographic jurisdiction

  - Establishing a place of residence or business in an area within the court's jurisdiction

  - The person consenting to the court's jurisdiction

  - Establishing "minimum contacts" with the region over which a court has jurisdiction, such as by conducting business within a state

- *Subject matter jurisdiction* refers to a court's authority to hear cases on a particular area of the law.

Scope and Application

Once you establish the jurisdiction of a law, you should then determine the scope and applicability of the law to your own organization's operations. In many cases, this is obvious. For example, the Family Educational Rights and Privacy Act (FERPA) regulates the ways that most educational institutions handle student records. FERPA clearly applies to the student educational records maintained by colleges and universities. HIPAA clearly applies to medical records maintained by hospitals. But you might be surprised to learn that FERPA would not apply to employee professional education records maintained by hospitals and that HIPAA might not apply to medical records maintained by student health centers.

The scope of FERPA is actually a bit more nuanced. The law applies only to educational institutions that receive federal funds under certain programs of the U.S. Department of Education. This includes virtually all institutions of higher education but excludes many private schools at the elementary and secondary level.

It's incumbent upon privacy professionals to carefully read laws, consult with attorneys, and determine what business activities fall under the scope of each law.

Legal Concepts

There are also a few important legal concepts that you will need to understand as you explore the privacy laws discussed in this book and their applications. These include the definition of a person, the concept of preemption, and the idea of a private right of action. It is important to note that although these concepts are generally true, legislation may override general definitions, making it important to always read laws very carefully.

What Is a Person?

The legal definition of a *person* is different from the common-sense definition. A person may be a human being, but under the law, a person may also be a business or other legal organization that is legally treated as a person.

The key aspects of the definition of a person under the law are that legal persons can

- Sue other legal persons
- Be sued by other legal persons
- Own property
- Sign contracts

This definition of a person holds true in most cases, but this is a particular area where many laws may contain more specific definitions that override this general approach.

Preemption

Preemption means that law that stems from a higher authority will take precedence over laws from a lower authority. For example, the U.S. Constitution contains a supremacy clause that says that federal law preempts any conflicting state laws. Similarly, decisions made by the U.S. Supreme Court preempt decisions made by any lower courts.

Private Right of Action

A *private right of action* means that individuals and corporations may bring cases to court for violations of a specific law. If a law does not contain a private right of action, it is up to state and federal authorities to prosecute violations of a law.

For example, FERPA does not contain a private right of action, so students who suffer data breaches may not sue institutions under FERPA. The U.S. Department of Education can bring enforcement actions in such a case. You will learn more about FERPA in Chapter 5, "Private Sector Data Collection." Similarly, HIPAA and the Gramm–Leach–Bliley Act (GLBA) contain privacy provisions but do not include a private right of action.

The California Consumer Privacy Act (CCPA), which protects the private information of California residents, does contain a private right of action. Under CCPA, an individual can sue an organization they believe has violated their right to privacy if that breach involved certain unredacted and unencrypted personal information. You will learn more about CCPA in Chapter 8, "State Privacy Laws."

A private right of action adds strength to a law by increasing the likelihood that an aggrieved party will bring action against the offender.

Exam Tip

As you learn about specific laws later in this book, pay particular attention to which laws do, and do not, contain a private right of action. This is an important topic to understand when preparing for the CIPP/US exam.

Legal Liability

Liability is a term of art in the law. *Black's Law Dictionary* defines liability as "responsible or answerable in law; legally obligated." Simply put, liability is what allows a party to take action against another in court.

Liability comes in two general forms:

- *Criminal liability* occurs when a person violates a criminal law. If a person is found guilty of a criminal law violation, they may be deprived of their liberty through imprisonment, fined, and/or forced to pay restitution to their victims. Charges of criminal liability are normally brought by the government, acting through a state or federal prosecutor.

- *Civil liability* occurs when one person claims that another person has failed to carry out a legal duty that they were responsible for. Cases claiming civil liability are normally brought to court by one party, the *plaintiff*, who is accusing another party, the *respondent*, of the violation. The plaintiff may be an individual, a corporation, or the government bringing a civil enforcement action.

One element required to provide a criminal violation is *mens rea*. Latin for "guilty mind," *mens rea* requires that the person had criminal intent, meaning that they either intended to commit a crime or knew that their action or lack of action would result in a crime. The standard of proof in criminal cases is that the prosecution must present evidence that demonstrates *beyond a reasonable doubt* the defendant committed the crime. This means that the prosecution must convince the jury that, after considering the evidence offered, there is no other plausible conclusion than that the defendant is guilty.

Civil penalties often use a different standard. Most commonly this is the *preponderance of the evidence* standard, which means that the prevailing party must present evidence demonstrating that there is a greater than 50 percent chance that their claim is correct. Some civil cases proceed under a different standard known as *strict liability*. The strict liability standard says that a person is responsible for the consequences of their actions even if they could not reasonably anticipate the adverse outcome.

Some laws have both criminal and civil components. For example, HIPAA contains provisions that may impose both civil and criminal penalties. On the civil side, HIPAA fines can range from as little as $100 for a first-time offense by an individual who did not know that they were violating HIPAA to $50,000 if a violation was due to willful neglect and was not corrected. On the criminal side, HIPAA-covered entities and individuals who knowingly obtain health information in violation of HIPAA may be fined $50,000 and imprisoned for up to a year. Those penalties increase to a maximum $250,000 fine and 10 years in prison if there was an intent to use the information for commercial advantage, personal gain, or malicious harm.

Theories of liability describe the conditions that must be met for someone to be found liable for a criminal or civil violation of the law. These theories differ for civil and criminal violations and also vary based on the standard written into the law, decided in case law, and appropriate for the circumstances.

Torts and Negligence

Torts are another form of civil violation. Torts do not involve a contract but, instead, involve harm to one party caused by the actions of another party. The party who caused the harm is said to have committed a *tortious act*.

Negligence is a commonly occurring tort that occurs when one party causes harm to another party by their action or lack of action. The theory of liability for negligence involves four elements:

- There must be a *duty of care*. The person accused of negligence must have an established responsibility to the accuser. This may come from the nature of the relationship between the parties. For example, physicians have a duty of care to their patients that they will exercise good medical judgment.

- There must be a breach of that duty of care. The accused person must have either taken action or failed to take an action that violated the duty of care.

- There must be *damages* involved. The accuser must have suffered some type of harm, be it financial, physical, emotional, or reputational.

- There must be *causation*. A reasonable person must be able to conclude that the injury caused to the accuser must be a result of the breach of duty by the accused.

Invasion of privacy is another tort that is established in common law. Invasion of privacy occurs when there is a violation of an individual's reasonable expectation to be left alone. There are four legal torts that may result in a successful claim of invasion of privacy:

- The *invasion of solitude* is a physical or electronic intrusion into the private affairs of a person. Breaking into someone's home or accessing their email account may both be considered invasions of solitude.

- The public disclosure of private facts involves the disclosure of truthful information when the release of that information would offend a reasonable person. This only applies when the information is not newsworthy or of public interest.

- *False light* is a legal term that applies when someone discloses information that causes another person to be falsely perceived by others.

- *Appropriation* is the unauthorized use of someone's name or likeness.

The invasion of privacy torts are a common basis for class action lawsuits against companies who have experienced data breaches.

Summary

Privacy professionals must be familiar with the legal environment in the United States because the laws and regulations governing privacy come from many different sources. Federal statutes are created by the legislative branch after passing both houses of Congress and obtaining the signature of the president. The executive branch may create administrative law to assist in the interpretation and enforcement of statutes. The judicial branch reviews, applies, and interprets both legislative and administrative law, creating a body of case law. All of these laws must remain consistent with the U.S. Constitution, which is the supreme law of the land.

When analyzing a law or regulation, privacy professionals should determine the scope and applicability of the law to the operations of their own organization. Then they must also look at the jurisdiction of the law to determine what, if any, footprint of their business is governed by the law.

Exam Essentials

Know the composition of the three branches of the U.S. federal and state governments.   The legislative branch consists of the two bodies of the U.S. Congress: the House of Representatives and the Senate. The executive branch, led by the president of the United States, consists of the departments, agencies, and bureaus that operate under the president's authority. The judicial branch consists of the federal court system, with the U.S. Supreme Court as its highest body. State governments are modeled after the same approach, with the exception of Nebraska, which has a single chamber legislature.

Explain the different sources of law in the United States.   Federal statutes are created by the legislative branch after passing both houses of Congress and obtaining the signature of the president. The executive branch may create administrative law to assist in the interpretation and enforcement of statutes. The judicial branch reviews, applies, and interprets both legislative and administrative law, creating a body of case law.

Understand the difference between personal jurisdiction and subject matter jurisdiction. Courts have two different types of jurisdiction. Personal jurisdiction refers to the court's authority over a person being sued or charged with a crime. Subject matter jurisdiction refers to the court's authority to hear cases on a particular area of the law.

Know the definition of a person under the law. A human being is certainly a person, but under the law, a person may also be a business or other legal organization that is legally treated as a person. The key aspects of the definition of a person under the law are that legal persons can sue other legal persons, can be sued by other legal persons, can own property, and can sign contracts.

Explain the concept of the private right of action. A private right of action means that individuals and corporations may bring cases to court under a specific law. If a law does not contain a private right of action, it is up to state and federal authorities to prosecute violations of a law.

Explain the difference between criminal and civil liability. Liability is what allows one party to take action against another party in court. Criminal liability occurs when a person violates a criminal law. If a person is found guilty of a criminal law violation, they may be deprived of their liberty through imprisonment. Civil liability occurs when one person claims that another person has failed to carry out a legal duty that they were responsible for fulfilling.

Describe the four elements of the tort of negligence. *Negligence* is a commonly occurring tort that occurs when one party causes harm to another party by their action or lack of action. The theory of liability for negligence involves four elements. First, there must be a duty of care. Second, there must be a breach of that duty of care. Third, there must be damages involved, and, fourth, there must be causation.

Review Questions

1. What check-and-balance does the legislative branch hold over the executive branch?
   - **A.** Power of the purse
   - **B.** Veto power
   - **C.** Prosecutorial discretion
   - **D.** Judicial review

2. What portion of the U.S. Constitution defines the powers of the legislative branch of government?
   - **A.** Article I
   - **B.** Article II
   - **C.** Article III
   - **D.** Article IV

3. Which amendment to the U.S. Constitution explicitly grants individuals the right to privacy?
   - **A.** First Amendment
   - **B.** Fourth Amendment
   - **C.** Fifth Amendment
   - **D.** None of the above

4. What source contains much of the administrative law created by the U.S. government?
   - **A.** U.S. Code
   - **B.** Bill of Rights
   - **C.** Code of Federal Regulations
   - **D.** U.S. Constitution

5. Which one of the following is the best description of the legal principle of *stare decisis*?
   - **A.** Courts should be guided by precedent.
   - **B.** Federal law overrules state law.
   - **C.** Laws must be consistent with the constitution.
   - **D.** Common law guides areas where legislation is unclear.

6. In a contract between two organizations, the parties mutually agree that disputes will be settled in the courts of the state of New York. What type of jurisdiction does this language establish?
   - **A.** Personal jurisdiction
   - **B.** Geographic jurisdiction
   - **C.** Subject matter jurisdiction
   - **D.** Consensual jurisdiction

7. Which one of the following entities would *not* normally be considered a person under the laws of the United States?

   A. A U.S. citizen

   B. A U.S. corporation

   C. A legal resident of the United States

   D. None of the above

8. Which one of the following laws contains a private right of action?

   A. CCPA

   B. FERPA

   C. GLBA

   D. HIPAA

9. During a negligence lawsuit, the court determined that the respondent was not at fault because the plaintiff did not present evidence that they suffered some form of harm. What element of negligence was missing from this case?

   A. Duty of care

   B. Breach of duty

   C. Causation

   D. Damages

10. In a lawsuit against a political opponent, the plaintiff alleged that the respondent invaded their privacy by accessing their email account without permission. What tort is involved in this case?

    A. False light

    B. Appropriation

    C. Invasion of solitude

    D. Public disclosure of private facts

11. How many voting members compose the U.S. Senate?

    A. 50

    B. 100

    C. 200

    D. 435

12. Which one of the following courts is the trial court for most matters arising under federal law?

    A. Supreme Court

    B. U.S. Circuit Court

    C. U.S. Trial Court

    D. U.S. District Court

13. What proportion of the states must ratify an amendment before it is added to the U.S. Constitution?

    A. 1/3

    B. 1/2

    C. 2/3

    D. 3/4

14. Which one of the following elements is *not* always required for the creation of a legal contract?

    A. An offer

    B. Acceptance of an offer

    C. Written agreement

    D. Consideration

15. What clause of the U.S. Constitution establishes the concept of preemption?

    A. Establishment clause

    B. Supremacy clause

    C. Commerce clause

    D. Incompatibility clause

16. What nation was the original source of the common law used in many parts of the world?

    A. Roman Empire

    B. England

    C. France

    D. Egypt

17. What category of law best describes the HIPAA Privacy Rule?

    A. Constitutional law

    B. Common law

    C. Legislative law

    D. Administrative law

18. What court has subject matter jurisdiction specifically tailored to matters of national security?

    A. U.S. District Court

    B. State Supreme Courts

    C. U.S. Supreme Court

    D. Foreign Intelligence Surveillance Court

19. Under what standard might a company located in one state become subject to the jurisdiction of the courts of another state by engaging in transactions with customers located in that other state?

    A. Physical presence

    B. Place of business

    C. Consent

    D. Minimum contacts

20. In a recent invasion of privacy lawsuit, the plaintiff claimed that the respondent disclosed information that caused them to be falsely perceived by others. What tort is involved in this case?

    A. Appropriation

    B. Disclosure of private facts

    C. Invasion of solitude

    D. False light

Chapter
3

Regulatory Enforcement

THE CIPP/US EXAM OBJECTIVES COVERED IN THIS CHAPTER INCLUDE:

✓ **Domain I. Introduction to the U.S. Privacy Environment**

- I.A. Structure of U.S. Law

  - I.A.d Regulatory Authorities

- I.B. Enforcement of U.S. Privacy and Security Laws

  - I.B.d Unfair and Deceptive Trade Practices (UDTP)

  - I.B.e Federal Enforcement Actions

  - I.B.f State Enforcement (Attorneys General (AG), California Privacy Protection Agency (CPPA))

  - I.B.h Self-Regulatory Enforcement (PCI, Trust Marks)

Many different regulators play a role in the enforcement of privacy laws and regulations. Depending on the nature of the regulation, the affected industries, and the geographic jurisdiction(s) involved, different federal, state, and industry regulators may have overlapping authority to protect the privacy of personal information.

In this chapter, you will learn about the federal agencies that play a major role in the enforcement of privacy regulations. You'll also learn about the concept of unfair and deceptive trade practices and how that concept creates privacy obligations. Finally, you will learn about the other enforcement authorities that exist in state governments and self-regulatory groups.

Federal Regulatory Authorities

As you learned in Chapter 2, "Legal Environment," the executive branch of the federal government bears responsibility for enforcing the laws enacted by the legislative branch. The executive branch carries out this authority through the U.S. Department of Justice (DOJ). The DOJ, led by the Attorney General (AG) of the United States, serves as the representative of the U.S. government in both criminal prosecutions and civil suits affecting federal interests.

There are also many regulatory agencies within the executive branch that play specific roles in the enforcement of privacy laws and the creation and enforcement of administrative law covering privacy issues. These include the Federal Trade Commission (FTC), the Federal Communications Commission (FCC), the Department of Commerce (DOC), the Department of Health and Human Services (HHS), and several financial regulatory authorities.

Federal Trade Commission

The *Federal Trade Commission (FTC)* is an independent agency that exists within the executive branch of the government but also maintains a degree of autonomy from the day-to-day workings of the executive branch. The executive authority of the commission rests with five commissioners, who are appointed by the president and serve seven-year terms upon Senate confirmation. Notably, no more than three of the five commissioners may be from the same political party, creating some bipartisan balance.

The key enabling legislation granting the FTC authority over *unfair and deceptive trade practices (UDTPs)* appears in 15 USC § 45 (a) (1), which reads as follows:

> Unfair methods of competition in or affecting commerce, and
> unfair or deceptive acts or practices in or affecting commerce,
> are hereby declared unlawful.

This law is commonly cited as giving the FTC the authority to regulate privacy and cybersecurity-related matters. There are some limits on this authority based on the scope of authority of other federal agencies to regulate certain industries, including transportation carriers, financial institutions, and nonprofit organizations.

In addition to the FTC Act, Congress passed other laws granting the FTC additional specific powers. These include the authority to regulate websites directed at children under the *Children's Online Privacy Protection Act (COPPA)*, as well as other shared authorities with the FCC, HHS, and the Consumer Financial Protection Bureau (CFPB). You'll learn more about these specific laws and the authority granted to the FTC in Chapter 5, "Private Sector Data Collection."

FTC Enforcement Actions

The FTC Act also provides the Commission with the authority to conduct investigations of possible violations of the law, including looking into unfair and deceptive trade practices. Under their formal authority, the FTC may conduct a formal investigation of a firm's practices and bring enforcement actions when they deem it appropriate. These investigations may be triggered by a consumer complaint, congressional inquiry, or other stimulus, and then may involve the collection of information from involved parties. FTC investigators work in a methodical fashion to build their case.

After conducting an investigation, the FTC may bring a formal complaint against a company they believe has violated the law. This comes in the form of a legal document that lays out the charges the agency is making and the evidence they have to support those charges. The company may then choose to negotiate a settlement with the FTC or contest the complaint.

If the company contests the complaint, an administrative trial takes place in front of an administrative law judge (ALJ). If the accused company disagrees with the ALJ's ruling, they may bring an appeal to the five FTC Commissioners. If the appeal to the commissioners is unsuccessful, companies may then pursue appeals in the federal court system.

In practice, most FTC complaints are not resolved through this formal process but use two other settlement mechanisms:

- The FTC and the accused company may decide to informally resolve minor complaints by adjusting the company's business practices.

- In more serious cases, the FTC and the company may enter into a *consent decree*. This is a formal agreement between the company and the government that dictates how the company will behave moving forward. The company does not admit guilt but enters into a formal, enforceable agreement. If the company later violates the consent decree, the FTC can bring formal legal action against the firm.

Failure to comply with FTC consent decrees can have serious consequences. In 2010, the FTC entered into a consent decree with LifeLock, requiring that the company secure personal information and refrain from deceptive advertising practices. Five years later, the FTC alleged that LifeLock failed to live up to its commitments under that consent decree. The end result this time had devastating financial consequences: LifeLock was forced to renew the consent decree and pay $100 million in damages and fines.

The enforcement process used by the FTC is a standard regulatory enforcement process for government agencies. Other regulators use similar approaches to enforce privacy and security rules.

Unfair and Deceptive Trade Practices

The FTC's ability to regulate privacy practices generally stems from the agency's authority to regulate unfair and deceptive trade practices. Therefore, privacy professionals must have a clear understanding of the terms "unfair" and "deceptive" as defined in administrative and case law.

The terms unfair and deceptive are distinct but not mutually exclusive. A given trade practice may be unfair, or it may be deceptive, or it may be both unfair and deceptive.

Unfair Practices

In 1972, the U.S. Supreme Court issued an opinion in *FTC v. Sperry & Hutchinson Trading Stamp Co.* that adopted three factors that the FTC considers when determining whether a trade practice is *unfair*:

- Whether the practice injures consumers
- Whether the practice violates established public policy
- Whether the practice is unethical or unscrupulous

The majority of FTC enforcement actions taken against unfair practices involve the first of these factors: whether the practice injures consumers. Determining whether a practice unfairly injures consumers requires the use of a three-pronged test that was documented in a 1980 FTC Policy Statement on Unfairness. The three criteria are as follows:

1. *The injury must be substantial.* Consumers must be harmed by the practice in a significant way. In the words of the FTC, "the Commission is not concerned with trivial or merely speculative harms." Typically, this means that the consumer must suffer financial

harm or an unwarranted health or safety risk. Practices are not unfair merely because a consumer suffers emotional harm or finds a practice offensive.

2. *The injury must not be outweighed by countervailing benefits to consumers and to competition.* When judging a practice, the Commission must balance whether it has a net benefit or harm to consumers overall. For example, the seller of a product may choose to not share detailed technical information about the product because it would confuse the typical consumer decision, even if some consumers might benefit from the additional information. The FTC uses its discretion to assess this balance.

3. *The injury must not be reasonably avoidable.* The law expects that consumers will take reasonable actions to protect themselves in the marketplace and will avoid making undesirable decisions.

Let's look at these criteria in the context of an example. In 2005 the FTC settled an enforcement action against Capital City Mortgage Corporation, accusing the lender of failing to release the liens it held on property after homeowners made their final mortgage payments. The FTC determined that this was an unfair practice because

- The injury was substantial. The consumer had lived up to their end of the mortgage contract, but the mortgage company did not release the claim to the property, as agreed.

- Consumers could not avoid this practice because they had no way of knowing that the mortgage company would not release the lien.

- There were no benefits to consumers or competition from this practice.

In the settlement agreement, the court ordered Capital City to pay the costs associated with the prosecution and avoid similar practices in the future.

The Capital City case was a straightforward application of the unfair practices rules, but that case did not involve any privacy issues. In a series of other cases, the courts found that a company that publishes a privacy policy may be acting unfairly if it fails to implement controls to enforce the requirements of that policy.

For example, in the case of *FTC v. Wyndham Worldwide*, the FTC alleged that the Wyndham hotel chain suffered a series of data breaches as the direct result of their failure to implement reasonable security controls. This case was the subject of extensive litigation and worked its way to the U.S. Court of Appeals for the Third Circuit, who upheld the FTC's actions, stating that

> A company does not act equitably when it publishes a privacy policy to attract customers who are concerned about data privacy, fails to make good on that promise by investing inadequate resources in cybersecurity, exposes its unsuspecting customers to substantial financial injury, and retains the profits of their business.

As you prepare for the CIPP/US exam, you should be familiar with several other unfair practices cases brought by the FTC in response to privacy issues. Along with *Wyndham Worldwide*, the IAPP cites three additional relevant examples:

LabMD   In 2016, the FTC issued a Final Order finding that LabMD suffered a data breach that impacted patient privacy as the direct result of insufficient cybersecurity practices. The agency ordered the firm to implement a cybersecurity program and subject themselves to periodic assessments.

LifeLock   LifeLock is an identity theft protection service that ran an advertising campaign claiming that it could prevent identity theft. The company settled this complaint in 2010, paying $12 million in fines to the FTC and state governments. They also agreed to avoid deceptive advertising and implement strong security controls. In 2019, the company paid an additional $100 million fine after the FTC charged them with violating the earlier court order.

DesignerWare   In 2012, the FTC accused DesignerWare, a rent-to-own company, of placing spyware on the computers it rented to customers that captured keystrokes and images of personal information. The FTC issued an order declaring this an unfair practice and prohibiting the company from engaging in similar practices in the future.

Deceptive Practices

The FTC also has the authority to regulate *deceptive* trade practices and clarified its position on the types of practices that are deceptive in their 1983 FTC Policy Statement on Deception. That policy statement set forth the following criteria to determine whether a practice is deceptive:

There must be a representation, omission, or practice that is likely to mislead the consumer.   This includes false written or oral statements, misleading price claims, sales of hazardous or defective products, the use of bait-and-switch techniques, the failure to perform promised services, and the failure to meet warranty obligations.

The practice must be examined from the perspective of a consumer acting reasonably in the circumstances.   Furthermore, if the practice is directed at a specific group of consumers, the determination of reasonableness should take place from the perspective of that group.

The representation, omission, or practice must be material.   The basic question asked is whether the practice is likely to affect the consumer's conduct or decision related to a product or service. If it is, then the practice meets the materiality test because the consumer would have behaved differently if not for the deception.

In 2019, the FTC charged the operators of the `WeTakeSection8.com` rental listing website with engaging in deceptive practices. The offenders ran a website that purported to only include rental listings where the landlords had agreed to accept Section 8 housing vouchers. In reality, the properties on the site were mostly unavailable or did not accept the vouchers. Users of the site were charged a fee to access the site. We can analyze these actions against the three criteria for a deceptive practice:

- The website claimed that consumers could access hundreds of thousands of accurate and up-to-date listings. That was not correct, so the act is misleading.

- A reasonable consumer exercising normal judgment would be misled. There's nothing in this case that would dissuade a reasonable consumer from coming to the conclusion that the site did indeed offer the listings it claimed.

- If consumers knew that the site did not have accurate information, they certainly would not have purchased access to the site, making the deception material.

The courts agreed with this analysis and ordered the website to pay a $6 million fine for their deceptive behavior.

Exam Tip

You should also familiarize yourself with the specific privacy-related deceptive practice cases that IAPP cites as examples. These are likely to come up as topics in exam questions!

GeoCities   This website hosting company collected personal information from customers, informing them that they would not resell this information. The FTC charged them with reselling information in violation of their privacy policy.

Eli Lilly   This pharmaceutical company collected patient information on their website and then inadvertently sent an email to all site users disclosing their identities to one another.

Nomi   This technology company placed sensors in retail stores that collected information about consumers' mobile devices without their knowledge or consent.

Snapchat   The social media platform informed consumers that messages and photos posted on the service lasted for a short period of time and then disappeared forever, but they were aware of methods users engaged in to preserve those messages.

TRUSTe   This privacy firm provides other companies with certifications of their privacy practices. The FTC charged them with failing to conduct annual recertifications of clients, as required.

The FTC continues to aggressively pursue deceptive practices cases against firms that it feels are not acting in the best interests of consumers. Perhaps the best example of this is the aggressive enforcement action that the FTC has taken against Facebook in recent years.

The agency first charged Facebook in 2012 with engaging in eight different deceptive privacy practices. One of those alleged that

> The company made deceptive claims about consumers' ability to control the privacy of their personal data. One specific count alleged that Facebook allowed users to choose settings that supposedly limited access to their information just to "friends" without adequate disclosures that another setting allowed that same information to be shared with the developers of apps those friends used. Put another way, suppose Consumer A restricted access to friends and designated Consumer B as a friend. If Consumer B used a particular app on Facebook—let's say a game—the game developer could access information about Consumer A, including data designated as private. That was all going on behind the scenes without a clear disclosure to Consumer A and in flagrant disregard of that person's privacy choices.

As a result of that case, Facebook agreed to an FTC order that required them to implement a privacy program and prohibited them from making misrepresentations about their security and privacy practices. In July 2019, the FTC charged Facebook with violating the terms of that order and issued them a record fine of $5 billion, the largest fine to date imposed on a firm for privacy violations.

In November 2020, the FTC entered into a consent decree with the Zoom videoconferencing serving after alleging that Zoom engaged in deceptive security practices. Specifically, the FTC charged that Zoom misled consumers into believing that their technology implemented end-to-end encryption that prevented Zoom itself from viewing the contents of videoconferences when, in reality, they used point-to-point encryption that encrypted content from each user to Zoom separately but temporarily decrypted the content on Zoom's servers. By accepting the consent decree, Zoom agreed not to make any further misleading statements about privacy and security, to put a comprehensive security program in place, and to conduct annual independent cybersecurity assessments for the next 20 years.

Federal Communications Commission

The *Federal Communications Commission* (FCC) is the regulator responsible for interstate and international communications. The agency has authority to regulate communications that originate or terminate in the United States and that occur over telephone, radio, television, wire, satellite, or cable. The FCC regulates these communications carriers and develops privacy regulations affecting their use of customer data.

For example, the Telecommunications Act of 1996 restricts the ways that communications carriers may handle customer proprietary network information (CPNI). This includes implementing safeguards to prevent the theft of CPNI, restrictions on the use and sharing of CPNI, and requirements to notify customers and law enforcement in the event of a breach of CPNI.

The FCC has enforcement authority for violations of this law. In September 2014, the agency reached a $7.4 million settlement with Verizon Communications after finding that the firm used CPNI for marketing purposes without first obtaining customer consent, as required by the Telecommunications Act.

In another significant case, the FCC entered into a consent decree in 2015 with two telecommunications firms, TerraCom, Inc. and YourTel America, assessing a $3.5 million penalty for the carriers' failure to protect sensitive personal information after posting that information on a publicly accessible website.

In December 2016, the FCC passed a set of broadband privacy rules that would have restricted the ability of Internet service providers (ISPs) to collect and share information about customer communications, location data, and browsing habits. However, in April 2017, President Trump signed a law repealing those privacy rules, removing many of the restrictions on the handling of personal information by ISPs. It is possible that future administrations may continue to adjust these rules, so privacy professionals should pay close attention to their evolution.

Department of Commerce

The *Department of Commerce* operates the U.S. portion of the Privacy Shield agreement between regulators in the European Union (EU) and the United States. Privacy Shield is a safe harbor agreement that provides a mechanism for organizations to transfer private information from Europe to the United States without running afoul of EU law. You will learn more about this safe harbor agreement later in this chapter.

Department of Health and Human Services

The *Department of Health and Human Services (HHS)* is the lead agency responsible for the implementation of the *Health Insurance Portability and Accountability Act (HIPAA)*. After Congress passed HIPAA and a series of related laws, HHS issued privacy and security rules as administrative law to implement the provisions of HIPAA. You will learn more about the scope of these requirements in Chapter 5, "Private Sector Data Collection."

HHS takes its HIPAA responsibilities seriously and is quite aggressive in issuing enforcement actions with substantial fines. Examples of recent enforcement actions taken by the agency include the following:

- Fining LifeSpan, a Rhode Island health system, over $1 million in July 2020 for suffering a data breach after the theft of an unencrypted laptop containing protected health information

- Fining Miami-based Jackson Health System over $2 million in October 2019 for a series of incidents where patient information was lost, sold without permission, and leaked to the media

- Fining an individual health care professional, Steven A. Porter, M.D., $100,000 in March 2020 for violations of the HIPAA security rule

It is striking to note the fact that these fines are quite large and were assessed against organizations ranging in size from an individual physician's practice to some of the nation's largest health systems.

> You can learn more about the fines assessed against organizations involved in HIPAA violations by reviewing the resolution agreements posted on the HHS website at www.hhs.gov/hipaa/for-professionals/compliance-enforcement/agreements/index.html.

Banking Regulators

Several federal agencies share responsibility for regulating the financial industry:

- The *Consumer Financial Protection Bureau (CFPB)*, which has overall authority for protecting consumers in the financial industry

- The *Federal Reserve*, which supervises and regulates banks operating in the United States

- The *National Credit Union Administration (NCUA)*, which performs similar supervision and regulation responsibilities for federal credit unions

- The *Federal Deposit Insurance Corporation (FDIC)*, which holds regulatory authority to examine and supervise financial institutions for safety, soundness, and consumer protection

- The *Office of the Comptroller of the Currency*, which supervises national banks and thrift institutions, as well as branches of foreign banks with federal licenses to operate in the United States

> Does all of this sound confusing and overlapping? That's because it is very confusing and overlapping! Don't worry too much about trying to distinguish between the responsibilities of these different regulators. Instead, focus your study on knowing the agencies involved in financial regulation and the fact that the CFPB is normally the lead federal agency for consumer financial protection issues.

The CFPB has taken enforcement action against firms for violations of privacy and security requirements. Here are some examples:

- A $100,000 fine against payment systems operator Dwolla for failing to implement adequate security measures after promising customers that it had strong security in place

- A $25,000 fine against GST Factoring for violations of the Telemarketing Sales Rule (TSR) after the student loan debt relief business engaged in illegal telemarketing practices
- A $575,000,000 settlement with Equifax after the firm's 2017 data breach exposed the personal information of more than 147 million individuals

Department of Education

The *U.S. Department of Education (ED)* has privacy enforcement responsibilities under the Family Educational Rights and Privacy Act (FERPA). Under FERPA, ED has the authority to regulate the handling of student educational records by institutions that receive certain types of federal funding. We'll discuss these FERPA responsibilities in greater detail in Chapter 5.

The Department of Education has not historically strongly enforced the provisions of FERPA in any meaningful way. In November 2018, the department's Inspector General issued a report citing significant failures in the department's ability to process FERPA complaints in a timely or adequate manner, stating, in part

> The Privacy Office is not meeting its statutory obligation under 20 U.S. Code Section 1232g(f) and (g) to appropriately enforce FERPA and resolve FERPA complaints. Complainants' privacy rights are also not appropriately protected as FERPA intends.

State Regulatory Authorities

State governments also have the authority to bring enforcement actions against companies accused of privacy and security violations. These actions normally take place under the authority of one or more state attorneys general bringing suit under their own state privacy laws. Each state also has a law containing provisions regulating unfair and deceptive practices, similar to those found in the FTC Act. These laws are collectively known as unfair and deceptive acts and practices (UDAP) laws, and although they do share common provisions, they also vary widely in their scope and penalties.

States also have laws regulating data breach notification, consumer privacy practices, financial institution operations, and other areas impacting privacy. We discuss these state laws in detail in Chapter 8, "State Privacy Laws."

The enforcement actions taken by states vary widely based on the nature of the offense, the regulation violated, and the authority of state regulators. Here are some examples of recent state privacy enforcement actions:

- A $10 million settlement in July 2019 between Premera Blue Cross and the attorneys general of a coalition of states. The states accused Premera of having inadequate security controls, resulting in a data breach that affected personal health information.

- A $935,000 settlement in January 2019 between Aetna and the attorney general of California after a mailing vendor used by Aetna sent letters to HIV patients that disclosed their HIV status in a manner that was visible through the window of the envelope.

- September 2020 charges brought by the New York Department of Financial Services against First American Title Insurance Company after a vulnerability on the company's website allegedly exposed the personal information of consumers.

International Regulatory Authorities

Federal and state governments aren't the only sources of regulation affecting firms in the United States. In many cases, the international affairs of U.S. firms expose them to regulation under international law. We explore this issue in more detail in Chapter 9, "International Privacy Regulation."

Established as a key part of the California Privacy Rights Act (CPRA) in 2020, the *California Privacy Protection Agency (CPPA)* is the first state-level agency in the United States specifically dedicated to privacy and data protection at the state level. CPPA has the power to enforce the CPRA and issue penalties to businesses that violate the act's provisions. The CPPA also provides guidance to businesses and individuals about their rights and responsibilities under California's comprehensive privacy laws.

Self-Regulatory Programs

Firms operating in an industry may choose to develop and participate in *self-regulation programs* where they adopt and enforce their own set of privacy and/or security standards. They then mutually commit to follow those standards and develop an enforcement program to verify to each other, and the public, that they remain compliant.

Firms participating in self-regulatory schemes may be motivated by several factors, including the following:

- Genuine desire to protect the security and privacy of sensitive personal information
- Competitive interests in preserving the integrity of their industry against unscrupulous practices
- Desire to avoid government intervention by preempting possible legislation through self-regulation

The applicability and enforceability of these requirements varies, since it is normally a matter of a contractual relationship between the regulated firms, with disputes handled under the terms of that contract.

Payment Card Industry

The *Payment Card Industry Data Security Standard (PCI DSS)* is one of the most successful self-regulatory privacy and security programs in existence. PCI DSS was created in 2004 by Visa, Mastercard, American Express, Discover, and JCB to regulate the credit card processing industry. The standard primarily focuses on security, rather than privacy, issues but does include data retention requirements that enhance consumer privacy.

Merchants become subject to the requirements of PCI DSS when they enter into contracts with banks to accept credit cards. Service providers that work with those merchants then become subject to the standard based on their contractual regulations with merchants, who are required to work only with PCI DSS–compliant service providers.

PCI DSS contains over a hundred pages of detailed specifications, but these can be summarized as 12 high-level requirements:

- Install and maintain a firewall configuration to protect cardholder data.
- Do not use vendor-supplied defaults for system passwords and other security parameters.
- Protect stored cardholder data.
- Encrypt transmission of cardholder data across open, public networks.
- Use and regularly update antivirus software or programs.
- Develop and maintain secure systems and applications.
- Restrict access to cardholder data by business need-to-know.
- Assign a unique ID to each person with computer access.
- Restrict physical access to cardholder data.
- Track and monitor all access to network resources and cardholder data.
- Regularly test security systems and processes.
- Maintain a policy that addresses information security for employees and contractors.

For more detail on PCI DSS requirements, you can download a full copy of the standard from the PCI Security Standard Council's website at pcisecuritystandards.org. The PCI DSS document available on the site includes the detailed requirements as well as testing procedures used by auditors when evaluating PCI DSS compliance.

Advertising

The *Network Advertising Initiative* (NAI) is a self-regulatory program focused on digital marketing. Businesses involved in the distribution of online advertising participate in NAI as members, and NAI claims that almost every Internet ad displayed in the United States uses the technology of one of its members.

The NAI publishes a code of conduct that contains detailed requirements describing how its members must provide notice of their privacy practices, offers consumers the ability to opt out of information processing, and describes how they must implement procedures for data security, transfer, and quality. The NAI conducts compliance reviews of its members and has the authority to sanction them and refer noncompliant companies to the Federal Trade Commission or other regulators for possible enforcement action.

The NAI is one example of an industry self-regulatory framework, but there are others that are broad in nature or that apply to specific industries. For example, the Better Business Bureau operates a self-regulatory program for organizations that advertise to children.

Trust Marks

Trust marks are another way that companies may voluntarily communicate their commitment to privacy to their stakeholders. Trust marks are symbols that appear on a company's website demonstrating that an independent third party has certified that the company meets clearly defined privacy standards.

For example, TrustArc offers the TRUSTe verified privacy seal to websites that complete a three-phase process:

Phase 1: Assessment   Organizations undergo a privacy review and receive a findings report that includes a gap analysis, a risk assessment, a summary, and remediation recommendations.

Phase 2: Remediation and certification   Organizations complete their remediation efforts and have those changes verified by TrustArc. After completing any required remediation, they receive a letter of attestation and may display the TRUSTe seal.

Phase 3: Ongoing monitoring and guidance   Organizations are subject to ongoing compliance monitoring efforts and are offered access to a dispute resolution service that manages customer privacy complaints.

For example, the Enterprise car rental company underwent this certification process and is able to display the TRUSTe seal, as shown in Figure 3.1.

In case you were wondering "Is this the same TRUSTe that I read earlier was fined by the FTC for deceptive trade practices?" the answer is yes! The FTC complaint focused on the firm's inadequate enforcement of phase 3 requirements.

Safe Harbors

Safe harbor agreements offer participating firms exemption from prosecution under certain laws if they meet certain regulatory requirements. The purpose of safe harbors is to provide legitimate firms with an opportunity to avoid prosecution when they demonstrate that they were acting in good faith and took appropriate actions to protect private information.

FIGURE 3.1 TRUSTe certification of the Enterprise car rental website

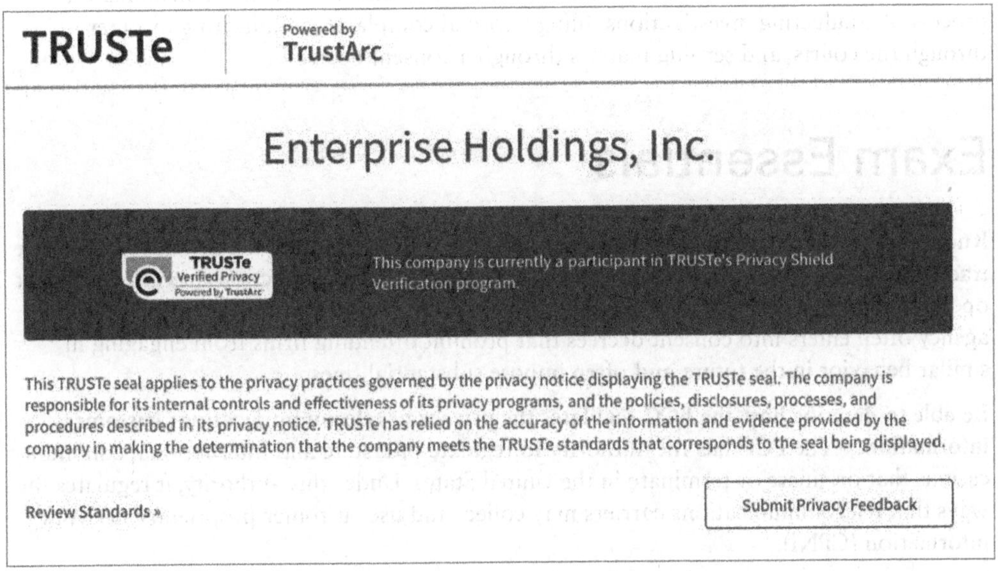

TRUSTe | Powered by **TrustArc**

Enterprise Holdings, Inc.

 TRUSTe Verified Privacy Powered by TrustArc   This company is currently a participant in TRUSTe's Privacy Shield Verification program.

This TRUSTe seal applies to the privacy practices governed by the privacy notice displaying the TRUSTe seal. The company is responsible for its internal controls and effectiveness of its privacy programs, and the policies, disclosures, processes, and procedures described in its privacy notice. TRUSTe has relied on the accuracy of the information and evidence provided by the company in making the determination that the company meets the TRUSTe standards that corresponds to the seal being displayed.

Review Standards »   Submit Privacy Feedback

The most common example of a privacy safe harbor is the Privacy Shield agreement between the EU and the United States. Organizations conducting data transfers between the EU and the United States must comply with the terms of the General Data Protection Regulation (GDPR), including transferring information only to firms that have agreed to appropriate privacy standards. Privacy Shield is one way for firms to achieve this status. Organizations may certify their compliance with privacy practices through independent assessors and, if awarded the Privacy Shield, are permitted to transfer information.

> **WARNING**
>
> The Privacy Shield safe harbor program has been the subject of extensive litigation. European Union courts have periodically ruled it invalid, leaving regulators to redesign the program's terms to bring it back into compliance. In July 2020, the EU Court of Justice issued the Schrems II ruling that declared the Privacy Shield illegal. That was followed by the implementation of a Data Privacy Framework (DPF) in 2022 that restored the ability to use safe harbor provisions. You will find more extensive coverage of this topic in Chapter 9.

Summary

Many different federal and state regulatory agencies share responsibility for protecting the privacy of personal information in the United States. This creates a confusing situation for privacy professionals, who must understand the different jurisdictions of these agencies as well as which agencies have authority to regulate their firms' operations. Privacy professionals should understand the nature of different federal enforcement actions, including the process of conducting investigations, filing a formal complaint, adjudicating disputes through the courts, and settling matters through a consent decree.

Exam Essentials

Know that the FTC has authority over privacy issues that constitute unfair and/or deceptive trade practices.   Under this authority, the FTC takes enforcement actions against firms that operate unfairly or in contradiction to their published security and privacy policies. The agency often enters into consent decrees that prohibit offending firms from engaging in similar behavior in the future and often impose substantial fines.

Be able to describe how the FCC regulates the privacy of telecommunications customer information.   The FCC has the authority to regulate interstate and international communications that originate or terminate in the United States. Under this authority, it regulates the ways that telecommunications carriers may collect and use customer proprietary network information (CPNI).

Know that the Department of Commerce maintains the EU/U.S. Privacy Shield.   This safe harbor agreement provides a mechanism for U.S. firms to exchange data with European subsidiaries and business partners without running afoul of the EU's General Data Protection Regulation (GDPR) requirements.

Know that the Department of Health and Human Services (HHS) enforces HIPAA requirements.   HHS is responsible for promulgating the administrative law that implements the provisions of HIPAA, regulating the use of protected health information. It publishes both privacy and security rules governing this information.

Know the federal agencies that regulate the financial sector.   The Consumer Financial Protection Bureau has enforcement authority for many matters of consumer interaction with the financial industry. Other agencies involved in financial regulation include the Federal Reserve, the Federal Deposit Insurance Corporation, the Comptroller of the Currency, and the National Credit Union Administration.

Know that state attorneys general have enforcement authority over the laws of their states.   Each state has an unfair and deceptive acts and practices (UDAP) law that provides the state's attorney general with enforcement authority similar to that granted to the FTC. States also have other laws governing data breaches and consumer privacy that the attorney general may enforce.

Be able to name self-regulatory schemes that provide a means for industry to regulate itself.   Examples of these schemes include the Payment Card Industry Data Security Standard (PCI DSS) and the Network Advertising Initiative (NAI). These regulatory frameworks include restrictions on the use and security of personal information and enforcement mechanisms to verify and ensure compliance.

Review Questions

1. Which one of the following is not part of the three-pronged test used to determine whether a trade practice unfairly injures consumers?

    A. The injury must be substantial.

    B. The injury must not be outweighed by countervailing benefits.

    C. The injury must be directed at a specific group of consumers.

    D. The injury must not be reasonably avoidable.

2. Which one of the following firms was charged by the FTC with failing to conduct required privacy recertifications of its clients?

    A. TRUSTe

    B   Geocities

    C. DesignerWare

    D. Nomi

3. What federal agency has lead responsibility for enforcing the privacy and security obligations of health care providers under HIPAA?

    A. FTC

    B. CFPB

    C. HHS

    D. FCC

4. Your firm was the target of an FTC investigation into unfair trade practices. Rather than engaging in litigation, you negotiated a formal settlement with the agency. What type of document did you most likely sign?

    A. Consent decree

    B. Court order

    C. Negotiated agreement

    D. Merchant agreement

5. Acme Widgets failed to implement reasonable security controls and was the subject of an FTC enforcement action. What criterion did the FTC most likely use to bring this action?

    A. The action was deceptive.

    B. The action was unfair.

    C. The action was both deceptive and unfair.

    D. The action was neither deceptive nor unfair.

6. What firm received the largest privacy-related fine in FTC history?

   A. Snapchat

   B. Facebook

   C. Google

   D. Amazon

7. What industry is subject to the privacy regulations found in FERPA?

   A. Healthcare

   B. Financial services

   C. Education

   D. Brokerages

8. What self-regulatory scheme includes detailed requirements for the protection of credit card information?

   A. NAI

   B. TRUSTe

   C. COPPA

   D. PCI DSS

9. What industry group operates a self-regulatory framework that governs organizations that advertise specifically to children?

   A. Network Advertising Initiative

   B. Better Business Bureau

   C. U.S. Chamber of Commerce

   D. U.S. Department of Commerce

10. Anytown Savings Bank engaged in deceptive practices in promoting its money market accounts to consumers. What federal agency would have jurisdiction over this deceptive practice?

   A. FTC

   B. FCC

   C. CFPB

   D. NCUA

11. When reviewing the website of a potential business partner, you see the following graphic. What term describes this graphic?

    A. Privacy shield

    B. Trust mark

    C. Privacy emblem

    D. Trust shield

12. What law grants the FTC authority to regulate websites that are targeted specifically at children?

    A. COPPA

    B. SOX

    C. GLBA

    D. FERPA

13. If the FTC files a complaint against a company and the company contests that complaint, who oversees the first trial that may take place?

    A. Administrative law judge

    B. FTC commissioners

    C. U.S. District Court judge

    D. U.S. Circuit Court judge

14. In 2014, the FCC reached a settlement with Verizon related to the firm's use of customer information for marketing purposes without consent. What law did the FCC accuse Verizon of violating?

    A. Federal Trade Commission Act

    B. Telecommunications Act

    C. Telemarketing Sales Rule

    D. Broadband Privacy Rule

15. Who is the chief law enforcement officer of a state who may bring enforcement actions against firms under the laws of that state?

    A. Governor

    B. Lieutenant governor

    C. Solicitor general

    D. Attorney general

16. What decision by the EU Court of Justice invalidated the EU/U.S. Privacy Shield?

    A. Schrems II

    B. Colburn I

    C. Riley II

    D. Granger I

17. What federal agency is responsible for the supervision of federally chartered credit unions?

    A. CFPB

    B. FDIC

    C. OCC

    D. NCUA

18. Which one of the following is not an element of the definition of deceptive practices?

    A. There must be a representation, omission, or practice that is likely to mislead the consumer.

    B. The practice must be examined from the perspective of a consumer acting reasonably in the circumstances.

    C. The injury must not be outweighed by countervailing benefits to consumers and to competition.

    D. The representation, omission, or practice must be material.

19. Which one of these firms was charged with an unfair trade practice after installing sensors in retail stores that collected information from mobile devices without consumer consent?

    A. DesignerWare

    B. Wyndham

    C. Snapchat

    D. Nomi

20. What federal regulatory agency has the primary authority to take enforcement actions against unfair and deceptive practices?

    A. Federal Trade Commission

    B. Federal Communications Commission

    C. Federal Regulatory Commission

    D. Department of Commerce

Chapter

4

Information Management

THE CIPP/US EXAM OBJECTIVES COVERED IN THIS CHAPTER INCLUDE:

✓ **Domain I. Introduction to the U.S. Privacy Environment**

- I.C Information Management from a U.S. Perspective
  - I.C.a. Data Sharing and Transfers
  - I.C.d Incident Response Programs
  - I.C.e Workforce Training
  - I.C.g Data and Records Retention and Disposal (FACTA)
  - I.C.j Vendor Management

Protecting personal information requires careful management of that data. Organizations must be aware of all of the business processes and storage locations that handle private information in order to implement appropriate security and privacy controls. The design of appropriate controls also requires a clear understanding of the risks facing sensitive information in the modern cybersecurity landscape.

In this chapter, you will learn about the fundamental practices of data governance, including building a data inventory, appropriately classifying sensitive information, and implementing a data management lifecycle. You'll also learn about the cybersecurity threats facing organizations and best practices for handling security and privacy incidents that arise.

Data Governance

Data governance programs identify, track, and manage sensitive information for an organization, ensuring that data handling practices are consistent with the organization's policies and procedures. This includes building an inventory of sensitive information used by the organization, developing and implementing a robust data classification program, mapping data flows throughout the organization, and managing the full data lifecycle from creation through destruction.

Building a Data Inventory

Organizations often deal with many different types of sensitive and personal information. The first step in managing this sensitive data is developing an inventory of the types of data maintained by the organization and the places where it is stored, processed, and transmitted.

Organizations should consider the following types of information in their inventory (there may be others), the details of which will vary and depend on the organization's scale, scope, and mission:

- *Personally identifiable information (PII)* includes any information that uniquely identifies an individual person, including customers, employees, and third parties. It may be more specifically defined in some laws and contracts, but privacy professionals use it as a broad, sweeping term to refer to any personal information.

- *Protected health information (PHI)* includes medical records maintained by healthcare providers and other organizations who are subject to the Health Insurance Portability and Accountability Act (HIPAA).

- *Financial information* includes any personal financial records maintained by the organization.

- *Government information* maintained by the organization may be subject to other rules, including the data classification requirements discussed in the next section.

Once the organization has an inventory of this sensitive information, it may then begin to take steps to ensure that it is appropriately protected from loss or theft.

Data Classification

Data classification programs organize data into categories based on the sensitivity of the information and the impact on the organization should the information be inadvertently disclosed. For example, the U.S. government uses the following four major classification categories:

- *Top Secret* information requires the highest degree of protection. The unauthorized disclosure of Top Secret information could reasonably be expected to cause exceptionally grave damage to national security.

- *Secret* information requires a substantial degree of protection. The unauthorized disclosure of Secret information could reasonably be expected to cause serious damage to national security.

- *Confidential* information requires some protection. The unauthorized disclosure of Confidential information could reasonably be expected to cause identifiable damage to national security.

- *Unclassified* information is information that does not meet the standards for classification under the other categories. Information in this category is still not publicly releasable without authorization.

Businesses generally don't use the same terminology for their levels of classified information. Instead, they might use more friendly terms, such as Highly Sensitive, Sensitive, Internal, and Public.

Data classification allows organizations to clearly specify the security controls required to protect information with different levels of sensitivity. For example, the U.S. government requires the use of brightly colored cover sheets, such as those shown in Figure 4.1, to identify classified information in printed form.

When dealing with other types of private information, organizations should adapt their classification programs to match their business needs and regulatory requirements. For example, a healthcare provider might design cover sheets similar to those in Figure 4.1 to serve as the top page of a medical chart. The use of these cover sheets prevents a casual observer from viewing any personal information contained in the chart.

Data classifications also help guide the selection of cybersecurity controls to protect data confidentiality, integrity, and availability. Organizations may apply more restrictive controls to information of higher sensitivity levels. For example, the National Institute of Standards and Technology (NIST) publishes NIST Special Publication (SP) 800-53, "Security and Privacy

FIGURE 4.1   Classified information cover sheets

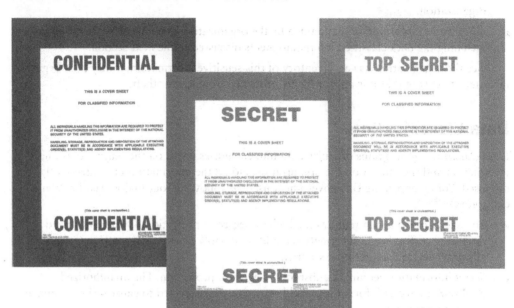

Controls for Information Systems and Organizations," which provides a detailed listing of possible controls that organizations may use to protect security and privacy. NIST 800-53B specifies different types of controls that should be used to protect information deemed low impact, moderate impact, and high impact. For example, Figure 4.2 shows that NIST recommends one control in the Account Management category for information deemed low impact, six additional controls for those deemed moderate impact and two more additional controls for information deemed high impact.

FIGURE 4.2   Account management control listing from NIST 800-53

NIST Special Publication 800-53 (Rev. 4)

Security and Privacy Controls for Federal Information Systems and Organizations

AC-2 ACCOUNT MANAGEMENT

Family: Access Control
Class:
Priority: P1 - Implement P1 security controls first.
Baseline Allocation: Low   Moderate   High

Low	Moderate	High
AC-2	AC-2 (1) (2) (3) (4)	AC-2 (1) (2) (3) (4) (5) (11) (12) (13)

Revision 4 Statements
Control Description
Supplemental Guidance
References

All Controls > AC > **AC-2**

Data Flow Mapping

Data classification and inventory efforts help privacy professionals understand the types of personal information that an organization possesses and where that data resides, but they're not the end of the story. In addition to locating these repositories, privacy professionals should understand how personal information flows throughout the organization.

Data flow mapping efforts provide this insight, tracking the ways that the organization receives, handles, shares, and disposes of sensitive information.

Data flow mapping work produces *data flow diagrams* that serve as artifacts of the work and references for team members seeking to understand how data moves through the organization. These data flow diagrams may vary significantly in their level of technical and process detail. For example, Figure 4.3 shows a data flow diagram from the U.S. government's Cloud.gov site that includes a great deal of technical detail.

Figure 4.4 shows a much higher-level diagram from the U.S. Department of Education that focuses more on business processes and omits technical detail.

There is no right or wrong answer about the appropriate level of technical detail to include in a data flow diagram. The answer depends on the intended use of the diagram and

FIGURE 4.3   Data flow diagram with technical detail

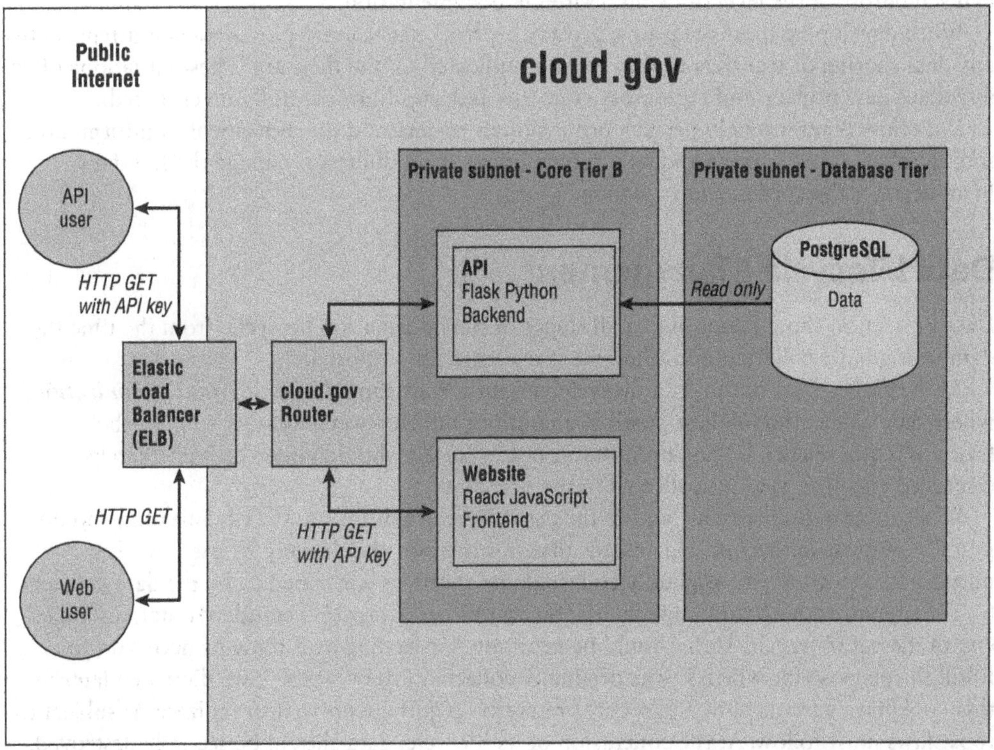

FIGURE 4.4   Data flow diagram without technical detail

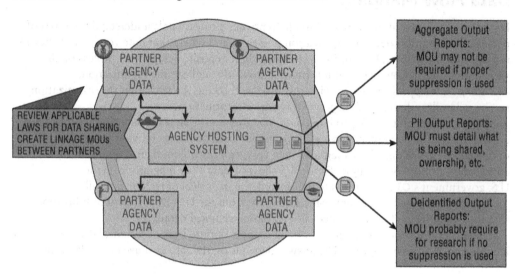

the organization's documentation standards. It is a good idea to develop internal templates and standards for the level of detail desired in documentation.

When developing these diagrams, privacy professionals should pay particular attention to any data sharing or transfers to third parties indicated on the diagram. These situations often introduce new privacy and regulatory concerns and should be carefully investigated.

Data flow diagrams help privacy professionals understand the movement of information through their organizations and also contribute to their ability to manage the full data lifecycle, the subject of our next section.

Data Lifecycle Management

Data protection should continue at all stages of the information lifecycle, from the time the data is originally collected until the time it is eventually disposed.

At the early stages of the data lifecycle, organizations should practice *data minimization,* where they collect the smallest possible amount of information necessary to meet their business requirements. Information that is not necessary should either be immediately discarded or, better yet, not collected in the first place.

While information remains within the care of the organization, the organization should practice *purpose limitation.* This means that information should only be used for the purpose for which it was originally collected and that was consented to by the data subjects.

The organization should implement *data and records retention* standards that guide the end of the data lifecycle. Data should be kept only for as long as it remains necessary to fulfill the purpose for which it was originally collected. Many of the laws discussed later in this book have specific data and records retention requirements that organizations subject to those laws must follow. At the conclusion of its lifecycle, data should be securely destroyed.

The techniques used to destroy data will vary based on the nature of the storage medium and the organization's specific security requirements. Generally speaking, the destruction should be sufficient that a determined adversary would be unable to reconstruct the data, even if they gained access to the destroyed medium.

For example, paper records should be shredded using a cross-cut shredder, incinerated, or pulped. Electronic media may be electronically erased using specialized sanitization software, degaussed using intense magnetic fields, or physically destroyed.

The Fair and Accurate Credit Transactions Act (FACTA) includes specialized guidance for organizations that use consumer reports. The basic requirement of the FACTA Disposal Rule is that covered organizations must take "reasonable measures to protect against unauthorized access or use of the information in connection with its disposal." Organizations are left with significant discretion to interpret this requirement within the context of their business operations, although the law does provide illustrative examples of measures that the FTC considers reasonable. Paraphrased for clarity, some of those examples include the following:

- Implementing policies and procedures that require the burning, pulverizing, or shredding of papers containing consumer information so that the information cannot practicably be read or reconstructed and monitoring compliance with those policies and procedures.

- Implementing policies and procedures that require the destruction or erasure of electronic media containing consumer information so that the information cannot practicably be read or reconstructed and monitoring compliance with those policies and procedures.

- Contracting with a record destruction business to dispose of consumer information after conducting appropriate due diligence. This due diligence may include reviewing an independent audit of the disposal company's operations, obtaining information about the disposal company from several references or other reliable sources, requiring that the disposal company be certified by a recognized trade association or similar third party, reviewing and evaluating the disposal company's information security policies or procedures, or taking other appropriate measures to determine the competency and integrity of the potential disposal company. Customers may request that the vendor provide a certificate of destruction that attests to the disposal of sensitive documents. They may do this to satisfy customer requirements and/or serve as evidence in the event of future litigation.

Workforce Training

Users within your organization should receive regular privacy awareness training to ensure that they understand the types of personal information they may encounter, the regulatory obligations involved with handling that information, the risks associated with your computing environment, and their personal role in minimizing those risks. Strong training programs take advantage of a diversity of training techniques, including the use of *computer-based training (CBT)*.

Not every user requires the same level of training. Organizations should use *role-based training* to make sure that individuals receive the appropriate level of training based on their job responsibilities. For example, a system administrator should receive detailed and highly technical training, whereas a customer service representative requires less technical training with a greater focus on social engineering attacks that they may encounter in their work.

Training should also include content on the specific regulatory requirements facing the organization and the user's role in meeting those requirements. Employees should walk away from training sessions with a strong understanding of their obligations to protect personal information and how they can practically fulfill those obligations in the context of their workday.

Cybersecurity Threats

Cybersecurity threat actors differ significantly in their skills, capabilities, resources, and motivation. Protecting your organization's information and systems requires a solid understanding of the nature of these different threats so that you may develop or select a set of security controls that comprehensively protect your organization against their occurrence.

Before we explore specific types of threat actors, let's examine the characteristics that differentiate different types of cybersecurity threat actors. Understanding our adversary is crucial to defending against them:

Internal Versus external   We most often think about the threat actors who exist outside our organizations: competitors, criminals, and the curious. However, some of the most dangerous threats come from within our own environments. We'll discuss the insider threat later in this chapter.

Level of sophistication/capability   Threat actors vary greatly in their level of cybersecurity sophistication and capability. As we explore different types of threat actors in this chapter, we'll discuss how they range from the unsophisticated "script kiddie" simply running code borrowed from others to the advanced persistent threat (APT) actor exploiting vulnerabilities discovered in their own research labs and unknown to the security community. We will discuss different threat actors in the next section.

Resources/Funding   Just as threat actors vary in their sophistication, they also vary in the resources available to them. Highly organized attackers sponsored by criminal syndicates or national governments often have virtually limitless resources, whereas less organized attackers might simply be hobbyists working in their spare time.

Intent/Motivation   Attackers also vary in their motivation and intent. The script kiddie may be simply out for the thrill of the attack, whereas competitors might be engaged in highly targeted corporate espionage. Nation-states seek to achieve political objectives, whereas criminal syndicates often focus on direct financial gain.

Threat Actors

Now that we have a set of attributes that we can use to discuss the different types of threat actors, let's explore the most common types that security professionals encounter in their work.

Script Kiddies

The term *script kiddie* is a derogatory term for people who use hacking techniques but have limited skills. Often such attackers may rely almost entirely on automated tools they download from the Internet. These attackers often have little knowledge of how their tools and attacks actually work, and they are simply seeking out convenient targets of opportunity.

You might think that with their relatively low skill level, script kiddies are not a real security threat. However, that isn't the case for two important reasons. First, simplistic hacking tools are freely available on the Internet. If you're vulnerable to them, anyone can easily find tools to automate denial-of-service (DoS) attacks, create viruses, make a Trojan horse, or even distribute ransomware as a service. Personal technical skills are no longer a barrier to successfully or destructively attacking a network.

Second, script kiddies are plentiful and unfocused in their work. Although the nature of your business might not find you in the crosshairs of a sophisticated military-sponsored attack, script kiddies are much less discriminating in their target selection. They often just search for and discover vulnerable victims without even knowing the identity of their target. They might root around in files and systems and discover who they've penetrated only after their attack succeeds.

In general, the motivations of script kiddies revolve around trying to prove their skill. In other words, they may attack your network simply because it is there. Secondary school and university networks are common targets of script kiddie attacks because many of these attackers are likely school-aged individuals.

Fortunately, the number of script kiddies is often offset by their lack of skill and lack of resources. These individuals tend to be rather young, they work alone, and they have very few resources. And by resources, we mean time as well as money. A script kiddie normally can't attack your network 24 hours a day. They usually have to work a job, go to school, and attend to other life functions.

Hacktivists

Hacktivists use hacking techniques to accomplish some activist goal. They might deface the website of a company whose policies they disagree with. Or a hacktivist might attack a network due to some political issue. The defining characteristic of hacktivists is that they believe they are motivated by a greater good or cause, even if their activity violates the law.

Their activist motivation means that measures that might deter other attackers will be less likely to deter a hacktivist. Because they believe that they are engaged in a just crusade, they will, at least in some instances, risk getting caught to accomplish their goals. They may even view being caught as a badge of honor and a sacrifice for their cause.

The skill levels of hacktivists vary widely. Some are only script kiddies, whereas others are quite skilled, having honed their craft over the years. In fact, some cybersecurity researchers believe that some hacktivists are actually employed as cybersecurity professionals as their "day job" and perform hacktivist attacks in their spare time. Highly skilled hacktivists pose a significant danger to their targets.

The resources of hacktivists also vary somewhat. Many are working alone and have very limited resources. However, some are part of organized efforts. The hacking group Anonymous, which uses the logo seen in Figure 4.5, is the most well-known hacktivist group. They collectively decide their agenda and their targets. Over the years, Anonymous has waged cyberattacks against targets as diverse as the Church of Scientology, PayPal, Visa and Mastercard, Westboro Baptist Church, and even government agencies.

FIGURE 4.5   Logo of the hacktivist group Anonymous

This type of anonymous collective of attackers can prove quite powerful. Large groups will always have more time and other resources than a lone attacker. Due to their distributed and anonymous nature, it is difficult to identify, investigate, and prosecute participants in their hacking activities. The group lacks a hierarchical structure and the capture of one member is unlikely to compromise the identities of other members.

Hacktivists tend to be external attackers, but in some cases, internal employees who disagree strongly with their company's policies engage in hacktivism. In those instances, it is more likely that the hacktivist will attack the company by releasing confidential information. Government employees and self-styled whistleblowers fit this pattern of activity, seeking to bring what they consider unethical government actions to the attention of the public.

For example, many people consider Edward Snowden a hacktivist. In 2013, Snowden, a former contractor with the U.S. National Security Agency, shared a large cache of sensitive government documents with journalists. Snowden's actions provided unprecedented insight into the digital intelligence gathering capabilities of the United States and its allies.

Criminal Syndicates

Organized crime appears in any case where there is money to be made, and cybercrime is no exception. The ranks of cybercriminals include links to traditional organized crime families in the United States, outlaw gangs, the Russian Mafia, and even criminal groups organized specifically for the purpose of engaging in cybercrime.

The common thread among these groups is motive and intent. The motive is simply illegal financial gain. Organized criminal syndicates do not normally embrace political issues or causes, and they are not trying to demonstrate their skills. In fact, they would often prefer to remain in the shadows, drawing as little attention to themselves as possible. They simply want to generate as much illegal profit as they possibly can.

In its 2019 Internet Organized Crime Threat Assessment (IOCTA), the European Union Agency for Law Enforcement Cooperation (EUROPOL) found that organized crime groups were active in a variety of cybercrime categories, including

- *Cyber-dependent crime*, including ransomware, data compromise, distributed denial-of-service (DDoS) attacks, website defacement, and attacks against critical infrastructure
- *Child sexual exploitation*, including child pornography, abuse, and solicitation
- *Payment fraud*, including credit card fraud and business email compromises
- *Dark web* activity, including the sale of illegal goods and services
- *Terrorism* support, including facilitating the actions of terrorist groups online
- *Cross-cutting crime factors*, including social engineering, money mules, and the criminal abuse of cryptocurrencies

Organized crime tends to have attackers who range from moderately skilled to highly skilled. It is rare for script kiddies to be involved in these crimes, and if they are, they tend to be caught rather quickly. The other defining factor is that organized crime groups tend to have more resources, both in terms of time and money, than do hacktivists or script kiddies. They often embrace the idea that "it takes money to make money" and are willing to invest in their criminal enterprises in the hopes of yielding a significant return on their investments. Some enterprising criminals have even turned their illegal activities into a business model, which includes advertising and selling professional support services for their malicious tools and software, similar to legitimate software and technology firms.

Advanced Persistent Threats (APTs)

In recent years, a great deal of attention has been given to state actors hacking into either foreign governments or corporations. The security company Mandiant created the term *advanced persistent threats (APTs)* to describe a series of attacks that it first traced to sources connected to the Chinese military. In subsequent years, the security community discovered similar organizations and activities linked to the governments of virtually every technologically advanced country.

The term APT tells you a great deal about the attacks themselves. First, these threat actors are capable of developing their own tools and using advanced techniques, and they are not limited to using readily available and prebuilt tools downloaded from the Internet. Second, the attacks are persistent, often occurring over a significant period of time. In some cases, the attacks continued for years as attackers patiently stalked their targets, awaiting the right opportunity to strike.

The APT attacks that Mandiant reported are emblematic of *nation-state attacks*. They tend to be characterized by highly skilled attackers with significant resources. A nation has the labor, time, and money to finance ongoing, sophisticated attacks.

The motive can be political or economic. In some cases, the attack is done for traditional espionage goals: to gather information about the target's defense capabilities. In other cases, the attack might be targeting intellectual property or other economic assets.

Zero-Day Attacks

APT attackers often conduct their own security vulnerability research in an attempt to discover vulnerabilities that are not known to other attackers or cybersecurity teams. After they uncover a vulnerability, they do not disclose it, but rather store it in a vulnerability repository for later use.

Attacks that exploit these vulnerabilities are known as *zero-day attacks*. Zero-day attacks are particularly dangerous because they are unknown to product vendors, and therefore, no patches are available to correct them. APT actors who exploit zero-day vulnerabilities are often able to easily compromise their targets.

Stuxnet was one of the most well-known examples of an APT attack. The Stuxnet attack, traced to the U.S. and Israeli governments, exploited zero-day vulnerabilities to compromise the control networks at an Iranian uranium enrichment facility and likely took years of careful and meticulous planning, software development, testing, and coordination.

Insiders

Insider attacks occur when an employee, contractor, vendor, or other individual with authorized access to information and systems uses that access to wage an attack against the organization. These attacks are often aimed at disclosing confidential information, but insiders may also seek to alter information or disrupt business processes.

An insider might be of any skill level. They could be a script kiddie or very technically skilled. Insiders may also have differing motivations behind their attacks. Some are motivated by certain activist goals, whereas others are motivated by financial gain. Still others may simply be upset that they were passed over for a promotion or slighted in some other manner.

An insider will usually be working alone and have limited financial resources and time. However, the fact that they are insiders gives them an automatic advantage. They already have some access to your network and some level of knowledge. Depending on the insider's job role, they might have significant access and knowledge.

Behavioral assessments are a powerful tool in identifying insider attacks. Cybersecurity teams should work with human resources partners to identify insiders exhibiting unusual behavior and intervene before the situation escalates.

Ransomware

Malicious software comes in many forms. Viruses, worms, Trojan horses, and other types of malware commonly spread over the Internet and through social engineering techniques. In recent years, ransomware attacks have posed a special risk to organizations that process sensitive and critical information.

Ransomware combines traditional malware techniques with the weaponization of encryption technology. After the ransomware takes control of a system, it uses strong encryption to encrypt the contents of that system's hard drive using an encryption key known only to the ransomware author. In some particularly nefarious cases, the ransomware may also reach out to file servers, cloud services, and other accessible storage locations, encrypting their contents as well.

The malware author then demands the payment of a ransom in exchange for the decryption key. Organizations that lack backups of their data find themselves backed into a corner, forced to choose between paying a potentially exorbitant ransom or losing control of their data. A relatively recent and troubling development for privacy professionals is the threat of data disclosure from ransomware criminals if payment demands are not met. Criminals have discovered that some organizations are prepared or resolute enough to not feel compelled to pay a ransom, so they have upped the ante by threating to disclose encrypted and stolen data if the ransom is not paid. These attacks can be particularly devastating to hospitals and other organizations where high availability of data and IT systems is crucial to achieving their mission.

Exam Note

Ransomware is explicitly mentioned in the CIPP/US exam objectives. You should be certain to understand this topic in detail before sitting for the exam!

Incident Response

In the unfortunate event of a data privacy breach, the organization should immediately activate its cybersecurity incident response plan. This plan should include procedures for the notification of key personnel and escalation of serious incidents.

Many technology and privacy professionals use the terms *security event* and *security incident* casually and interchangeably, but this is not correct. Members of a cybersecurity incident response team should use these terms carefully and according to their precise definitions within the organization. The National Institute for Standards and Technology (NIST) offers the following standard definitions for use throughout the U.S. government, and many private organizations choose to adopt them as well:

- An *event* is any observable occurrence in a system or network. A security event includes any observable occurrence that relates to a security function. For example, a user accessing a file stored on a server, an administrator changing permissions on a shared folder, and an attacker conducting a port scan are all examples of security events.

- An *adverse event* is any event that has negative consequences. Examples of adverse events include a malware infection on a system, a server crash, and a user accessing a file that they are not authorized to view.

- A *security incident* is a violation or imminent threat of violation of security policies, acceptable use policies, or standard security practices. Examples of security incidents include the accidental loss of sensitive information, an intrusion into a computer system by an attacker, the use of a keylogger on an executive's system to steal passwords, and the launch of a denial-of-service attack against a website.

 Every security incident includes one or more security events, but not every security event is a security incident.

Computer security incident response teams (CSIRTs) are responsible for responding to computer security and privacy incidents that occur within an organization by following standardized response procedures and incorporating their subject matter expertise and professional judgment.

Phases of Incident Response

Organizations depend on members of the CSIRT to respond calmly and consistently in the event of a security incident. The crisis-like atmosphere that surrounds many security incidents may lead to poor decision-making unless the organization has a clearly thought-out and refined process that describes how it will handle cybersecurity incident response. Figure 4.6 shows the simple incident response process advocated by NIST.

FIGURE 4.6 Incident response process

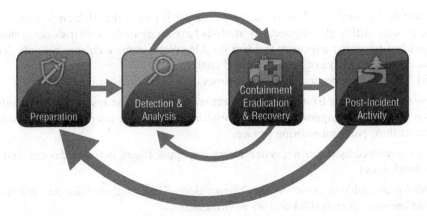

Source: NIST SP 800-61/U.S. Department of Commerce/Public Domain

Notice that this process is not a simple progression of steps from start to finish. Instead, it includes loops that allow responders to return to prior phases as needed during the response. These loops reflect the reality of responses to actual cybersecurity incidents. Only in the simplest of incidents would an organization detect an incident, analyze data, conduct a recovery, and close out the incident in a straightforward sequence of steps. Instead, the containment process often includes several loops back through the detection and analysis phase to identify whether the incident has been successfully resolved. These loops are a normal part of the cybersecurity incident response process and should be expected.

Preparation

CSIRTs do not spring up out of thin air. As much as managers may wish it were so, they cannot simply will a CSIRT into existence by creating a policy document and assigning staff members to the CSIRT. Instead, the CSIRT requires careful preparation to ensure that the CSIRT has the proper policy foundation, has operating procedures that will be effective in the organization's computing environment, receives appropriate training, and is prepared to respond to an incident.

The preparation phase also includes building strong cybersecurity defenses to reduce the likelihood and impact of future incidents. This process of building a defense-in-depth approach to cybersecurity often includes many personnel who might not be part of the CSIRT.

During the preparation phase, organizations may also choose to purchase *cyberinsurance policies* to help manage the risks associated with security and privacy incidents. These policies include protections against the financial impacts associated with those incidents.

Detection and Analysis

The detection and analysis phase of incident response is one of the trickiest to commit to a routine process. Although cybersecurity analysts have many tools at their disposal that may assist in identifying that a security incident is taking place, many incidents are only detected because of the trained eye of an experienced analyst.

NIST 800-61 describes four major categories of security event indicators:

- *Alerts* that originate from intrusion detection and prevention systems, security information and event management systems, antivirus software, file integrity checking software, and/or third-party monitoring services

- *Logs* generated by operating systems, services, applications, network devices, and network flows

- *Publicly available information* about new vulnerabilities and exploits detected "in the wild" or in a controlled laboratory environment

- *People* from inside the organization or external sources who report suspicious activity that may indicate that a security incident is in progress

When any of these information sources indicate that a security incident may be occurring, cybersecurity analysts should shift into the initial validation mode, where they attempt to determine whether an incident is taking place that merits further activation of the incident response process. This analysis is often more art than science and is very difficult work.

Containment, Eradication, and Recovery

During the incident detection and analysis phase, the CSIRT engages in primarily passive activities designed to uncover and analyze information about the incident. After completing this assessment, the team moves on to take active measures designed to contain the effects of the incident, eradicate the incident from the network, and recover normal operations.

At a high level, the containment, eradication, and recovery phase of the process is designed to achieve these objectives:

1. Select a containment strategy appropriate to the incident circumstances.

2. Implement the selected containment strategy to limit the damage caused by the incident.

3. Gather additional evidence as needed to support the response effort and potential legal action.

4. Identify the attackers and attacking systems.

5. Eradicate the effects of the incident and recover normal business operations.

Post-Incident Activity

Security incidents don't end after privacy and security professionals remove attackers from the network or complete the recovery effort to restore normal business operations. Once the immediate danger passes and normal operations resume, the CSIRT enters the post-incident activity phase of incident response. During this phase, team members conduct a lessons-learned review and ensure that they meet internal and external evidence retention requirements.

Lessons-Learned Review

During the lessons-learned review, responders conduct a thorough review of the incident and their response, with an eye toward improving procedures and tools for the next incident. This review is most effective if conducted during a meeting where everyone is present for the discussion (physically or virtually). Although some organizations try to conduct lessons-learned reviews in an offline manner, this approach does not lead to the back-and-forth discussion that often yields the greatest insight.

The lessons-learned review should be facilitated by an independent facilitator who was not involved in the incident response and who is perceived by everyone involved as an objective outsider. This allows the facilitator to guide the discussion in a productive manner without participants feeling that the facilitator is advancing a hidden agenda. NIST recommends that lessons-learned processes answer the following questions:

- Exactly what happened and at what times?
- How well did staff and management perform in responding to the incident?
- Were the documented procedures followed? Were they adequate?
- What information was needed sooner?
- Were any steps or actions taken that might have inhibited the recovery?
- What would the staff and management do differently the next time a similar incident occurs?
- How could information sharing with other organizations have been improved?
- What corrective actions can prevent similar incidents in the future?
- What precursors or indicators should be watched for in the future to detect similar incidents?
- What additional tools or resources are needed to detect, analyze, and mitigate future incidents?

Once the group answers these questions, management must ensure that the organization takes follow-up actions, as appropriate. Lessons-learned reviews are only effective if they surface needed changes and those changes then occur to improve future incident response efforts.

Evidence Retention

At the conclusion of an incident, the CSIRT has often gathered large quantities of evidence. The team leader should work with staff to identify both internal and external evidence retention requirements. If the incident may result in civil litigation or criminal prosecution, the team should consult attorneys prior to discarding any evidence. If there is no likelihood that the evidence will be used in court, the team should follow any retention policies that the organization has in place.

If the organization does not have an existing evidence retention policy for cybersecurity incidents, now would be a good time to create one. Many organizations choose to implement a two-year retention period for evidence not covered by other requirements. This allows incident handlers time to review the evidence at a later date during incident-handling program reviews or while handling future similar incidents.

At the conclusion of the post-incident activity phase, the CSIRT deactivates, and the incident-handling cycle returns to the preparation, detect, and analyze phases.

U.S. federal government agencies must retain all incident-handling records for at least three years. This requirement appears in the National Archives General Records Schedule 3.2, Item 20. See www.archives. gov/files/records-mgmt/grs/grs03-2.pdf for more information.

Building an Incident Response Plan

One of the major responsibilities that organizations have during the preparation phase of incident response is building a solid policy and procedure foundation for the program. This creates the documentation required to support the program's ongoing efforts.

Policy

The incident response policy serves as the cornerstone of an organization's incident response program. This policy should be written to guide efforts at a high level and provide the authority for incident response. The policy should be approved at the highest level possible within the organization, preferably by the chief executive officer. For this reason, policy authors should attempt to write the policy in a manner that makes it relatively timeless. This means that the policy should contain statements that provide authority for incident response, assign responsibility to the CSIRT, describe the role of individual users, and state organizational priorities. The policy is *not* the place to describe specific technologies, response procedures, or evidence-gathering techniques. Those details may change frequently and should be covered in more easily changed procedure documents.

NIST recommends that incident response policies contain these key elements:

- Statement of management commitment
- Purpose and objectives of the policy
- Scope of the policy (to whom it applies and under what circumstances)
- Definition of cybersecurity incidents and related terms
- Organizational structure and definition of roles, responsibilities, and level of authority
- Prioritization or severity rating scheme for incidents

- Performance measures for the CSIRT
- Reporting and contact forms

Including these elements in the policy provides a solid foundation for the CSIRT's routine and crisis activities.

Procedures and Playbooks

Procedures provide the detailed, tactical information that CSIRT members need when responding to an incident. They represent the collective wisdom of team members and subject matter experts collected during periods of calm and ready to be applied in the event of an actual incident. CSIRT teams often develop *playbooks* that describe the specific procedures that they will follow in the event of a specific type of cybersecurity incident. For example, a financial institution CSIRT might develop playbooks that cover

- Breach of personal financial information
- Web server defacement
- Phishing attack targeted at customers
- Loss of a laptop
- General security incident not covered by another playbook

This is clearly not an exhaustive list, and each organization will develop playbooks that describe its response to both high-severity and frequently occurring incident categories. The idea behind the playbook is that the team should be able to pick it up and find an operational plan for responding to the security incident that they may follow. Playbooks are especially important in the early hours of incident response to ensure that the team has a planned, measured response to the first reports of a potential incident.

 Playbooks are designed to be step-by-step recipe-style responses to cybersecurity incidents. They should guide the team's response, but they are not a substitute for professional judgment. The responders handling an incident should have appropriate professional expertise and the authority to deviate from the playbook when circumstances require a different approach.

Documenting the Incident Response Plan

When developing the incident response plan documentation, organizations should pay particular attention to creating tools that may be useful during an incident response. These tools should provide clear guidance to response teams that may be quickly read and interpreted during a crisis situation. For example, the incident response checklist shown in Figure 4.7 provides a high-level overview of the incident response process in checklist form. The CSIRT leader may use this checklist to ensure that the team doesn't miss an important step in the heat of the crisis environment.

FIGURE 4.7   Incident response checklist

Action	Completed
Detection and Analysis	
1. Determine whether an incident has occurred	
1.1 Analyze the precursors and indicators	
1.2 Look for correlating information	
1.3 Perform research (e.g., search engines, knowledge base)	
1.4 As soon as the handler believes an incident has occurred, begin documenting the investigation and gathering evidence	
2. Prioritize handling the incident based on the relevant factors (functional impact, information impact, recoverability effort, etc.)	
3. Report the incident to the appropriate internal personnel and external organizations	
Containment, Eradication, and Recovery	
4. Acquire, preserve, secure, and document evidence	
5. Contain the incident	
6. Eradicate the incident	
6.1 Identify and mitigate all vulnerabilities that were exploited	
6.2 Remove malware, inappropriate materials, and other components	
6.3 If more affected hosts are discovered (e.g., new malware infections), repeat the Detection and Analysis steps (1.1,1.2) to identify all other affected hosts, then contain (5) and eradicate (6) the incident for them	
7. Recover from the incident	
7.1 Return affected systems to an operationally ready state	
7.2 Confirm that the affected systems are functioning normally	
7.3 If necessary, implement additional monitoring to look for future related activity	
Post-Incident Activity	
8. Create a follow-up report	
9. Hold a lessons learned meeting (mandatory for major incidents, optional otherwise)	

Source: NIST SP 800-61/U.S. Department of Commerce/Public Domain

The National Institute of Standards and Technology publishes a Computer Security Incident Handling Guide (SP 800-61) that contains a wealth of information that is useful to both government agencies and private organizations in developing incident response plans. The current version of the guide, NIST SP 800-61 revision 2, is available online at nvlpubs. nist.gov/nistpubs/SpecialPublications/NIST. SP.800-61r2.pdf.

Data Breach Notification

Organizations may also have a responsibility under national and regional laws to make public notifications and disclosures in the wake of a data breach. This responsibility may be limited to notifying the individuals involved or, in some cases, may require notification of government regulators and/or the news media.

In the United States, every state has a data breach notification law with different requirements for triggering notifications. The European Union's GDPR also includes a breach notification requirement. The United States lacks a federal law requiring broad notification for all security breaches but does have industry-specific laws and requirements that require notification in some circumstances.

The bottom line is that breach notification requirements vary by industry and jurisdiction, and an organization experiencing a breach may be required to untangle many overlapping requirements. For this reason, organizations experiencing a data breach should consult with an attorney who is well versed in this field. You will learn more about various breach notification laws elsewhere in this book as we cover the various federal, state, and international statutes that apply to different industries and geographic jurisdictions.

Vendor Management

Many risks facing an organization come from third-party vendors with whom the organization does business. These agreements are of particular importance when dealing with cloud vendors that will directly handle personal information on behalf of the organization.

Vendor risks may be the result of relationships that arise somewhere along the organization's supply chain, or they may be the result of other business partnerships. Organizations may deploy some standard agreements and practices to manage these risks. Commonly used agreements include the following:

- *Master service agreements (MSAs)* provide an umbrella contract for the work that a vendor does with an organization over an extended period of time. The MSA typically includes detailed security and privacy requirements. Each time the organization enters into a new project with the vendor, it may then create a *statement of work* (SOW) that contains project-specific details and references the MSA.

- *Service-level agreements (SLAs)* are written contracts that specify the conditions of service that will be provided by the vendor and the remedies available to the customer if the vendor fails to meet the SLA. SLAs commonly cover issues such as system availability, data durability, and response time.

- *Data processing agreements (DPAs)* outline how personal data will be processed by the vendor on behalf of the organization. DPAs typically include requirements for data protection, compliance with relevant data protection laws, and the rights of data subjects.

- A *memorandum of understanding (MOU)* is a letter written to document aspects of the relationship. MOUs are an informal mechanism that allows the parties to document their relationship to avoid future misunderstandings. MOUs are commonly used in cases where an internal service provider is offering a service to a customer that is in a different business unit of the same company.

- *Business partnership agreements (BPAs)* exist when two organizations agree to do business with each other in a partnership. For example, if two companies jointly develop and market a product, the BPA might specify each partner's responsibilities and the division of profits.

Organizations will need to select the agreement type(s) most appropriate for their specific circumstances. These agreements take on particular importance when the vendor will be involved in the handling of sensitive information on behalf of the organization. In those cases, organizations should include specific contract language that obligates the vendor to meet the organization's privacy and security expectations.

Organizations operating under some regulatory frameworks may need to follow the vendor management practices required by those standards. For example, the Health Insurance Portability and Accountability Act (HIPAA) requires the creation of a business associate agreement (BAA) that obligates the vendor to comply with HIPAA's security, privacy, and breach notification rules. Similarly, the Payment Card Industry Data Security Standard (PCI DSS) requires that organizations subject to PCI DSS work only with service providers that are certified as compliant with PCI DSS requirements.

Vendor Cybersecurity Incidents

Vendors may experience cybersecurity incidents of their infrastructure and systems and organizations, and they should include this possibility in their own vendor management and cybersecurity incident response plans.

Vendor agreements should clearly spell out the vendor's obligations to report known or suspected security incidents to the customer and create SLAs for incident response and notification. Organizations should also have a 24-hour contact method for reporting potential cybersecurity incidents.

Summary

Privacy professionals are able to best serve their organizations when they have a strong understanding of the personal information handled by the organization. This should include an inventory of the types and locations of sensitive personal data as well as data flow diagrams that trace the movement of that data within the organization and between the organization and third parties. Data governance programs provide a framework for these activities and include the use of data classifications to specify the appropriate controls for different categories of sensitive information.

Organizations should have a documented incident response plan that describes how the organization will react in the event of a privacy or security breach. These plans should include detailed playbooks that describe the appropriate triage actions for first responders as well as the follow-up actions to contain, eradicate, and recover as the response unfolds.

Exam Essentials

Understand strong data governance practices. Organizations should build an inventory of personal information as part of their privacy programs. This inventory should then serve as the basis for a data lifecycle management process that monitors and secures sensitive information from the time it is first collected until it is disposed. Sensitive information should be assigned classifications that assist employees in understanding the appropriate security and privacy controls for that data.

Know the impact of data sharing and transfers. Data flow diagrams show all the ways that data moves throughout an organization and how it is transferred and shared with third parties. Privacy professionals should understand these transfers and know the impact of regulatory requirements on data transfer and sharing relationships. HIPAA requires the implementation of a BAA for these relationships, whereas PCI DSS requires the use of certified service providers.

Explain appropriate data and records retention and disposal practices. Organizations should retain personal information only for as long as it is necessary to fulfill the purposes for which the information was obtained. At the conclusion of this period, personal information should be securely disposed through appropriate physical or electronic destruction procedures or the use of a qualified destruction contractor.

Understand the cybersecurity threat landscape. A variety of threat actors jeopardize the security of sensitive information. These include insiders, script kiddies, hacktivists, criminal syndicates, and advanced persistent threats. These attackers use a wide variety of tools and techniques to compromise the security of personal information, including the use of ransomware to render information inaccessible to authorized users, or by threatening to disclose information if ransom conditions are not met.

Describe proper incident-handling procedures. Organizations should adopt a formal, written incident response plan that describes how they should react in the event of a cybersecurity or privacy incident. This plan should address the key incident response phases of preparation; detection and analysis; containment, eradication, and recovery; and post-incident activity.

Explain appropriate methods of workforce training. Employees who may encounter personal information in the course of their work should receive ongoing training about their privacy obligations. This training should include detailed information on how they should handle personal information. It should also include information on any regulatory obligations they must consider when making decisions regarding personal information.

Understand vendor management practices. Organizations should develop vendor management programs that track the vendors handling personal information on their behalf and maintain appropriate agreements with and monitoring of those vendors. Vendor relationships should include clearly documented responsibilities for cybersecurity incident response.

Review Questions

1. Jen is the data classification manager for a hospital system and is assigning data into categories. Which one of the following categories would be the most directly applicable to a patient's medical record?

   A. PII

   B. Financial information

   C. PHI

   D. Government information

2. Which one of the following statements about data flow diagrams is incorrect?

   A. Data flow diagrams should always show details of the technical environment.

   B. Data flow diagrams should show internal processes that handle sensitive information.

   C. Data flow diagrams should map the sharing and transfer of information to third parties.

   D. Data flow diagrams contribute to the ability of privacy professionals to manage the data lifecycle.

3. Which one of the following laws includes specific requirements for the destruction of information contained within consumer reports?

   A. FACTA

   B. HIPAA

   C. GLBA

   D. SOX

4. Which of the following statements about workforce privacy training are incorrect? (Select all that apply.)

   A. All employees should receive the same information during privacy training.

   B. Privacy training should take place on a regular basis.

   C. Training should include content on regulatory requirements.

   D. Individuals completing training should understand their role in protecting privacy.

5. Which one of the following cybersecurity threats would likely have access to the most sophisticated attack tools?

   A. Insider

   B. Hacktivist

   C. Script kiddie

   D. APT

6. What type of malicious software uses encryption to render data inaccessible to authorized users?

   A. Virus

   B. Worm

   C. Ransomware

   D. Trojan horse

7. Kelly is investigating a situation where an employee's computer was infected with malware and that malware was used to steal the employee's password. What term best describes this situation?

   A. Event

   B. Adverse event

   C. Social engineering

   D. Incident

8. Which of the following are common sources of security alerts that may indicate a need for an incident response effort? (Select all that apply.)

   A. Third-party monitoring services

   B. Intrusion detection systems

   C. Security information and event management systems

   D. File integrity checking software

9. Which one of the following is not an objective of the containment, eradication, and recovery phase of incident response?

   A. Limit the damage caused by an incident.

   B. Identify the attackers and attacking systems.

   C. Recover normal business operations.

   D. Detect a potential security incident.

10. Who is the most effective person to lead a lessons-learned session in the wake of a cybersecurity incident?

    A. Independent third party

    B. Chief privacy officer (CPO)

    C. Chief information officer (CIO)

    D. Incident response team leader

11. Which one of the following laws includes a data breach notification requirement that applies to many different categories of personal information?

    A. GDPR

    B. HIPAA

C. GLBA

D. FERPA

12. Gwen is entering into a long-term relationship with a consulting firm that will provide project-based services to her organization. She would like to have an overarching agreement with the organization that includes general terms. What type of agreement is most appropriate for this situation?

A. SOW

B. BPA

C. MOU

D. MSA

13. Referring to the scenario in question 12, after the overarching agreement is signed, what instrument would Gwen use to document the requirements of a specific project engagement?

A. SOW

B. BPA

C. MOU

D. MSA

14. Justin is the privacy officer for a healthcare organization that maintains patient records. The organization's marketing group would like to use those records to send solicitations to individuals for a new fitness center that the organization is opening. What principle should Justin be most concerned might be violated?

A. Data minimization

B. Purpose limitation

C. Separation of duties

D. Least privilege

15. What type of cybersecurity attacker is least likely to have access to advanced tools?

A. APT

B. Insider

C. Script kiddie

D. Hacktivist

16. During which phase of the incident response process does the organization create incident response policy and procedures?

A. Detection and analysis

B. Containment, eradication, and recovery

C. Preparation

D. Post-incident activity

17. Tonya is concerned that her organization frequently suffers ransomware attacks, so she is developing a detailed process that the organization should follow when one of these incidents occurs. What term best describes the document that Tonya is creating?

    A. Procedure

    B. Policy

    C. Strategy

    D. Playbook

18. What term is used to describe cybersecurity exploits for which there is not yet an effective corrective measure?

    A. Zero-day

    B. Ransomware

    C. Script

    D. Malware

19. Which one of the following is not an acceptable method for the disposal of paper records containing personal information?

    A. Shredding

    B. Incineration

    C. Degaussing

    D. Use of a third-party disposal firm

20. Rob is concerned that individuals in his organization are unsure of the appropriate cybersecurity controls to apply to different types of information. Which one of the following practices would best address this need?

    A. Data destruction

    B. Data flow mapping

    C. Data classification

    D. Data lifecycle management

Chapter 5

Private Sector Data Collection

THE CIPP/US EXAM OBJECTIVES COVERED IN THIS CHAPTER INCLUDE:

✓ **Domain II. Limits on Private-Sector Collection and Use of Data**

- II.A. Cross-Sector FTC Privacy Protection
  - II.A.a The Federal Trade Commission Act
  - II.A.b FTC Privacy Enforcement Actions
  - II.A.c FTC Security Enforcement Actions
  - II.A.d The Children's Online Privacy Protection Act of 1998 (COPPA)
  - II.A.e Future of Federal Enforcement (Data brokers, Big Data, IoT, AI, unregulated data)
- II.B. Healthcare/Medical
  - II.B.a Health Insurance Portability and Accountability Act of 1996 (HIPAA)
  - II.B.b Health Information Technology for Economic and Clinical Health (HITECH) Act of 2009
  - II.B.c The 21st Century Cures Act of 2016
  - II.B.d Confidentiality of Substance Use Disorder Patient Records Rule
- II.C. Financial
  - II.C.a The Fair Credit Reporting Act of 1970 (FCRA)
  - II.C.b The Fair and Accurate Credit Transactions Act of 2003 (FACTA)
  - II.C.c The Financial Services Modernization Act of 1999 ("Gramm–Leach–Bliley" or GLBA)
  - II.C.d Red Flags Rule

The United States regulates information privacy in the private sector through a complicated patchwork of legislation, regulation, and self-regulation. Privacy enforcement in the private sector is perhaps the most complex and important area of expertise for privacy professionals. The Federal Trade Commission (FTC) plays a lead role in privacy protection in the private sector, but the FTC's role is not comprehensive. Additional federal laws regulate privacy for specific industries such as healthcare, finance, education, telecommunications, and marketing. Together with industry best practices, this regulatory environment provides the backbone of consumer privacy protection for U.S. companies. This chapter first covers federal privacy regulations applying across the private sector and then delves into industry-specific privacy rules.

FTC Privacy Protection

The Federal Trade Commission (FTC) is the government agency broadly responsible for consumer protection. The FTC is where individuals and businesses can turn to file complaints about companies, business practices, and identity theft. The FTC's mandate falls under the FTC Act and other laws that the agency enforces or administers. Among its most important activities, the FTC can bring actions against third parties according to Section 5 of the FTC Act, which prohibits "unfair and deceptive trade practices."

General FTC Privacy Protection

The United States does not have a single comprehensive privacy law like the European Union's General Data Protection Regulation (GDPR), discussed in Chapter 9, "International Privacy Regulation." The United States also lacks a single agency responsible for privacy enforcement; private-sector companies often engage in self-regulated privacy practices by publishing privacy notices and policies detailing what information they collect from consumers and how they use that information. The FTC has the ability to initiate enforcement actions based on these privacy policies. The FTC often decides whether or not to initiate an enforcement action by examining the difference between a company's stated privacy practices and actual business conduct.

As you learned in Chapter 3, "Regulatory Enforcement," the FTC has broad authority to enforce privacy rules under the Federal Trade Commission Act as well as degrees of shared authority for rulemaking and enforcement established in additional legislative acts. In addition to enforcement actions, the FTC helps to monitor and improve U.S. private sector privacy practices with proactive strategies. For example, the FTC conducts regular studies of national private sector privacy practices, issues regular reports on enforcement actions, and offers educational programming such as workshops, events, and online materials.

The FTC helps develop new privacy rules by playing an advisory role to lawmakers. FTC personnel regularly testify before Congress and comment on legislative and regulatory proposals that impact consumer privacy. The FTC also works with international partners and organizations on global privacy and accountability issues.

Review from Chapter 3

The FTC has the authority to investigate businesses for unfair and deceptive practices and to issue complaints against businesses that lead to civil penalties if ignored. A business may appeal an FTC complaint successively to an administrative law judge, the FTC Commission, and the Federal District Court. In practice, the FTC settles most investigations with informal agreements or with more formal consent decrees that carry penalties if violated. These examples are the main menu of possible FTC enforcement actions.

The Children's Online Privacy Protection Act (COPPA)

In 1998, the United States enacted the Children's Online Privacy Protection Act (COPPA) to provide special privacy protections for children under the age of 13. Young children may be more vulnerable than adults online because they may be more easily manipulated into sharing private data and can't meaningfully provide consent for data collection. As awful as it is to contemplate, children may also fall victim to online child predators. Under COPPA, businesses operating websites used by children have additional requirements to control data collection on children. This includes requirements for privacy notices, affirmative parental consent, and more. These protections not only enhance privacy—and therefore safety—for children but also allow parents to distinguish legitimate child-oriented online services from bad actors.

COPPA Scope

COPPA is intended to regulate operators of online services that collect data about children under the age of 13. Online services include websites, mobile apps, smart devices, and so on. We refer to these collectively as "online services" in this chapter. COPPA applies to online operators that specifically design online services for children under 13 years old and those that know that children under 13 use their services online. For the purposes of this section, a child is a person under the age of 13. Specifically, COPPA applies to the following:

- Online services intended for children that gather, use, and share children's data
- General online services where the operator knows they are gathering, using, and sharing children's data
- Online services that knowingly collect children's personal information from *another* online service or website targeted at children

As with most legislation enforced by the FTC, COPPA usually applies only to commercial websites and *not* to nonprofit or government websites. There are exceptions in cases where nonprofit websites are operated for the commercial benefit of their members.

COPPA Requirements

When it comes to children's personal data, COPPA's privacy and security requirements are intended to provide extra protections and more control for parents. Under COPPA, personal information is defined broadly. Like other categories of PII for adults, COPPA's definition of personal information protects data such as Social Security numbers, full names, and home addresses. But when it comes to children, COPPA also applies to any screen names or other online identifiers, geolocation data, any media of a child's image or voice, and phone numbers.

COPPA also protects *any* other information collected from the child that is combined with any personal information as defined earlier. For example, the name of a child's elementary school is not explicitly listed as protected data. However, if a website collects a child's photo *and* the name of the elementary school, it becomes possible to identify, or even locate, the child. In this example, the name of the school also becomes protected personal information under COPPA.

COPPA grants specific rights to parents and guardians of children under 13. Parents and guardians have the right to approve the collection and use of personal information by any service under COPPA. Parents may also revoke that consent and require an operator to delete any personal data obtained from their children. Parents also have the right to approve the collection and use of personal data *only* as necessary to use the online service. Parents cannot be required to also approve the use of personal data by third parties, such as advertisers, as a condition of service except when a third party is a necessary part of the service.

If an online service is subject to COPPA, then the operators must meet several privacy and security requirements under the law to protect children's personal information. These include the following:

Privacy policies   COPPA requires that online service operators publish complete privacy policies that meet COPPA requirements. Policies must include details about all the personal information the service collects, including how it is collected and used.

They must also include details about any third party with access to personal data via the service (such as advertising services), along with contact information for those third parties. Finally, policies need to articulate the rights of parents and guardians, along with instructions for parents to act on those rights.

Parental notification   Parents must be notified directly before any online service can collect personal information on their children. If an online service makes any substantive changes to its practices, then the operator must provide an updated notification to any parents who previously agreed to data collection. This notice must explain the consent process; detail the information the service intends to collect; and provide a link to the privacy policy as well as assurance that any data collected, including contact data, will be deleted if parental consent isn't granted.

Parental consent   The online service is required to get approval from parents for the use and collection of personal information. COPPA details specific formats that are acceptable for parental consent, such as a signed form. Online services are also required to confirm the identity of the parent.

Parental control   Online services must maintain procedures to enable the other parental rights mentioned earlier. These include the ability for parents to view any personal information collected, revoke any previous consent, restrict the online service from further use of their information, and have personal information deleted.

Information security   COPPA requires operators to implement information security programs to maintain the confidentiality, security, and integrity of children's personal information. Such a program must include reasonable steps to protect against any unauthorized access to children's data and procedures to delete data when it is no longer needed.

COPPA Enforcement

The FTC enforces COPPA and may seek fines of up to $43,280 for each violation. Penalties vary depending on the severity of the offense, the negligence of the operator, and the operator's records of previous violations. COPPA may also be enforced by states and some other agencies that regulate specific industries, such as the Department of Transportation (DOT).

In 2019, the FTC secured a landmark judgment against Google-owned YouTube. The FTC found that YouTube knowingly collected children's personal information without following regulations under COPPA. This case is important because YouTube didn't previously consider itself within the scope of COPPA because YouTube content is crowdsourced social media and not centrally managed. This judgment helps to affirm COPPA's application to emerging social media companies.

Future of Federal Enforcement

The future of federal enforcement will continue to build on core directives of the FTC to protect consumers and encourage competition. According to the FTC's "Comment on the Future of Privacy" in 2018, the FTC sees a future of continued enforcement of unfair and deceptive trade practices with respect to privacy and security. However, the explosion of information technologies has birthed new industries that present new challenges for regulators.

In the Internet age, the FTC now must contend with applying regulations to new types of businesses that cross the boundaries of traditional industries. Several breakthrough technological capabilities have enabled these new business models. Examples include the following:

Big Data   People generate massive amounts of data online. Web browsing, communications, e-commerce transactions, business operations, and even government activities are all conducted online and generate data. It is now possible to harvest a lot of this information. *Data brokers* are companies that acquire and gather datasets from disparate online sources so that it can be resold.

Artificial Intelligence (AI)   For big data to be useful, it must be analyzed to develop insights. With access to massive datasets that constantly update, there's no way humans performing manual analysis can keep up. AI is a term used to describe powerful computing technology that is able to perform cognitive tasks that, until recently, only humans could perform. Famous examples of AI in action occurred when IBM's supercomputers, named Deep Blue and Watson, defeated human champions in both chess and the game show, *Jeopardy.*

Machine Learning (ML)   The term *machine learning* is often confused with AI. In fact, ML is considered to be a part of AI. ML actually refers to a category of algorithms that allow computers to measure outcomes and make improvements without human intervention. For example, an AI system could be programmed to try different layouts for an e-commerce website. ML makes it possible for the AI to "learn" which layout leads to sales and then apply that layout.

Internet of Things (IoT)   IoT refers to many well-known smart devices, such as lightbulbs, thermostats, and security cameras, that can all be controlled from a smartphone. Ubiquitous Internet connectivity and the shrinking size of computers has made it possible to put tiny computers inside everything from vacuums to automobiles. IoT devices may also leverage many of the other technologies described here. A self-driving car, for example, may be programmed by an AI system analyzing big data on traffic patterns and employing ML to make rapid improvements while the car drives.

For example, the rapid innovations in AI allow for the rapid processing of massive quantities of data that cross jurisdictional and industrial boundaries. AI enables new types of businesses, such as brokers of big data or massive datasets harvested across trillions of online transactions for billions of people. In 2012, the federal government began to anticipate the need to address the challenges of regulating these emerging privacy issues when the Obama administration issued a report proposing a Consumer Privacy Bill of Rights. Derived from *traditional fair information practices*, this document aimed to empower consumers by giving them more control over how businesses handle their data, by restricting collection of their personal data and by ensuring that their data will only be used for the agreed purpose. The Consumer Privacy Bill of Rights doesn't have the force of law, and compliance is voluntary. It formed the backbone for a proposed approach to new privacy legislation from the Obama administration in 2015, but that legislation stalled. Subsequent federal legislation derived from these principles has continued to flounder in Congress. After Obama's term in office ended, the Consumer Privacy Bill of Rights was removed from the White House website by the new administration. As you will learn in Chapter 9, however, several states are enacting laws that embrace principles similar to this document.

Also in 2012, the FTC issued a report titled "Protecting Consumer Privacy in an Era of Rapid Change." This report included a series of recommendations for regulations and called out specific areas of concern for privacy in the Internet age, including the need to consider the following:

- Do-not-track mechanisms and disclosure of Internet tracking practices
- Implications of data collection enabled by mobile devices, such as geolocation data
- Large platforms that are able to consolidate big data from across many services

The privacy challenges emerging from these technologies have only grown since 2012. Today, for example, *digital advertisers* may purchase data from social media platforms, Internet search providers, online retailers, and other online services. Because individuals can be tracked across the Internet, digital advertisers can often connect all of this big data back to an individual and, using AI, perform sophisticated analyses of individual behaviors to use in automatically displaying Internet ads sculpted for that person's interests.

This is clearly a powerful technology. However, consumers are a few steps removed from the advertiser and less able to control the use of their data. Consumers may not even know how their data is being used. A social media company, for example, may be able to use AI to deduce a person's likes and dislikes based on information shared by the person's friends, *even if that person doesn't participate in that company's services at all*. All this data may be collected, analyzed, interpreted, and even bought and sold automatically by systems using AI. These practices may even create new classes of *unregulated data* that are not well covered by existing privacy legislation.

Cambridge Analytica Scandal

In the leadup to the 2016 presidential election, operatives working for the Trump campaign hired a company called Cambridge Analytica to provide detailed psychological profiles of voters. Cambridge Analytica harvested data from millions of Facebook users by building an app for Facebook that requested access to a user's Facebook profile. Once a user granted access, Cambridge Analytica was able to access all the data from that user's profile as well as their friends' profiles. Users were never told how their data was being used, and the friends did not even give permission.

The Trump campaign was able to employ digital advertising technologies to micro-target campaign messages to individual voters based on their unique preferences. Many privacy advocates saw this as an invasion of privacy intended to manipulate the electorate. From a statutory perspective, this sort of activity is very difficult for regulators to manage. As mentioned in Chapter 3, the FTC heavily penalized Facebook in 2019 for its deceptive privacy practices, but the actions of the Trump campaign and Cambridge Analytica remain largely unregulated.

The emerging IoT industry illustrates these challenges well. Self-driving cars gather and use massive quantities of data to improve complex AI systems that can calculate lifesaving braking maneuvers at 70 miles per hour. A system like this crosses all sorts of boundaries. Could the data be used to target consumers for advertising or political campaigns? Self-driving cars collect data on all the "dumb" cars around them. How should the privacy of other motorists be protected?

The implications for enforcement are huge. AI can process, transform, analyze, and transfer data at scales well beyond the abilities of human regulators to monitor. Such data transactions may also dodge privacy and security regulations in multiple ways. For example, AI may be able to *deduce* an individual's personal information without actually collecting it, thus avoiding requirements for privacy notifications or consent. AI systems may also avoid regulation because big data collection doesn't necessarily respect jurisdictional boundaries. Firms may be based in a country with lax data protection laws but collect data from users across the world, even if those users' nations have stricter data privacy laws.

Each year, the FTC provides public reports detailing enforcement actions and emerging topics in privacy and security. In 2020, for example, the FTC provided a report on the use of artificial intelligence to address some of the challenges discussed above. The report recommends, for example, that businesses employing AI

- Inform consumers about how they use AI.
- Explain any decisions impacted by AI that affect consumers.
- Work to remove bias, discrimination, and stereotypes from any decisions made by AI.
- Make sure that AI models are based on good statistical principles.
- Hold a human-run organization accountable for the decisions made by AI.

FTC Annual Reports

Annual and special FTC reports are available online. The report on AI mentioned earlier is available at www.ftc.gov/news-events/blogs/business-blog/2020/04/using-artificial-intelligence-algorithm.

The FTC, along with other federal agencies with responsibility for privacy enforcement, is approaching these challenges both by extending existing enforcement authority and by supporting new legislation. The FTC regularly seeks judgments that extend and apply the doctrine prohibiting unfair and deceptive trade practices to new technologies and industries. The FTC also advocates with Congress for increased rule-making authority under existing laws and advises lawmakers on developing new privacy legislation to address emerging challenges for privacy enforcement.

Medical Privacy

Personal medical information enjoys special protections under the law. The importance of doctor–patient confidentiality has long been ensconced in medical practice. Patients are more likely to be honest and forthcoming if they can trust their doctors to keep their medical information private. Armed with more information, doctors are better able to treat their patients and may even save more lives. Medical privacy extends the principles of doctor–patient confidentiality to protect the medical information that patients disclose in the process of receiving care.

Medical privacy is important in many ways beyond the trust relationship between patients and care providers. If private medical information is revealed irresponsibly, the patient may suffer embarrassment, job loss, financial consequences, and more. Consider, for example, a person seeking treatment for addiction. What would happen if their condition were to become public? At the same time, some patient data must be shared in order to provide medical care. Providers, hospitals, pharmacies, insurance companies, and others must all collaborate to provide access to treatment.

This section explores the federal legislation that provides the framework for medical privacy. It is important to note that medical privacy legislation only protects certain types of information in specific circumstances. For example, a doctor is bound by confidentiality when a patient reveals a medical concern. If that patient shares the same concern with their barber, the barber is *not* bound by any sort of confidentiality. On the other hand, medical privacy rules are also often enhanced by stricter state laws. When working with medical data, privacy professionals need to know what data is protected and under what circumstances.

The Health Insurance Portability and Accountability Act (HIPAA)

In 1996, Congress passed the *Health Insurance Portability and Accountability Act (HIPAA)*. HIPAA was enacted to improve several aspects of the healthcare system, including the sharing of data among providers and insurers, the process of switching health plans, and more. HIPAA also set important standards for privacy and security of medical information.

HIPAA privacy and security rules apply to *protected health information (PHI)*. PHI includes medical information pertaining to patient health that is collected by healthcare providers for medical records, conversations with healthcare providers, individual medical information stored by health insurance companies, information used in healthcare billing or payment, and more. HIPAA also protects electronic personal health information (ePHI). ePHI includes any PHI stored or transmitted electronically.

HIPAA Scope

HIPAA is complex piece of legislation that regulates privacy across a wide range of healthcare-related activities. As mentioned earlier, not all medical information is protected by HIPAA under all circumstances. HIPAA applies to certain *covered entities* and to certain healthcare *transactions*. When a covered entity conducts a covered transaction, that entity and the transaction itself are both regulated under HIPAA. HIPAA covered entities fall into three broad categories:

Health insurance plans   This category includes health insurance companies, HMOs, employer health plans, and government health programs, such as Medicare, that cover healthcare costs.

Healthcare clearinghouses   These organizations help to manage the sharing of healthcare information by converting healthcare data into formats that can be read by differing health information systems.

Healthcare providers   Providers include doctors, hospitals, mental health professionals, dentists, long-term care facilities, pharmacies, and more.

HIPAA also extends to third-party *business associates* of covered entities if they meet certain conditions. A business associate is any third-party individual or organization that works with a covered entity to fulfill healthcare-related functions and that has access to PHI or ePHI. HIPAA requires covered entities to have written agreements with any third parties, called *business associate agreements (BAAs)*, that require the business associate to conform with HIPAA.

These types of organizations are subject to HIPAA and therefore covered entities if they engage in healthcare transactions that are regulated under HIPAA. HIPAA covers quite a broad set of healthcare-related transactions that include everything from health insurance claims to medical referrals. HIPAA does more than regulate the privacy of these transactions. Under the law, HHS administers specific standards for conducting these transactions electronically. In addition to protecting patient privacy, these standards attempt to add some uniformity and definition that all covered entities must use in common. These standards help reduce medical errors, increase oversight and accountability, enable medical research, and increase the speed of transactions. Any organization that falls into any of the categories listed *and* that engages in any of these common healthcare-related transactions is subject to the provisions of HIPAA.

There are some specific exceptions under HIPAA. Some records are not covered under HIPAA, even for covered entities. These include personnel records for employees, academic records covered by the Family Education Rights and Privacy Act (FERPA), and information that has been properly anonymized so that it could not be used to identify a patient.

HIPAA-Covered Transactions

According to the federal government's guidance for HIPAA, the following transactions are covered by HIPAA: "payment and remittance advice, claims status, eligibility, coordination of benefits, claims and encounter information, enrollment and disenrollment, referrals and authorizations, and premium payments." You can read more about HIPAA at www.cms.gov/ Regulations-and-Guidance/Administrative-Simplification/Transactions/TransactionsOverview.

HIPAA Privacy Requirements

The HHS Centers for Medicare & Medicaid Services (CMS) provides the rules and standards for organizations subject to HIPAA. In the year 2000, HHS established the HIPAA *Privacy Rule* that lays out guidelines for protecting the privacy of PHI. The Privacy Rule does the following:

▪ Requires the implementation of information privacy practices

▪ Limits use and disclosure of data without patient authorization

▪ Gives patients additional rights with respect to their medical information, including the right to view and correct their medical records

All HIPAA-covered entities are subject to the Privacy Rule. The HHS Office of Civil Rights (OCR) is responsible for implementing and enforcing the Privacy Rule and may impose monetary penalties for violations. Let's take a closer look at the specific provisions of the rule and its enforcement.

Information Privacy Practices

The Privacy Rule requires covered entities to implement standards and practices to safeguard PHI. These standards and practices must be contained in written *privacy policy and procedures* documentation. These must be consistent with the Privacy Rule. Covered entities are required to retain any records related to their privacy policies and related activities, such as complaints or public notices, for six years.

A privacy *policy* differs from a privacy *notice*. A privacy policy generally refers to an organization's internal practices for protecting information privacy. A privacy notice is published by an organization to inform the consumers about how it collects, uses, retains, and shares personal data.

Other privacy safeguards include the requirement to designate a privacy official responsible for the privacy policy, implementing a process for addressing privacy complaints, training employees on privacy practices, and implementing reasonable privacy safeguards. Safeguards may be physical, administrative, or technical. For example, safeguards may include ensuring all filing cabinets are appropriately locked (physical), only allowing need-to-know personnel to possess a key to the filing cabinets (administrative), or providing an electronic checkout system for accessing files (technical). Covered entities cannot retaliate against anyone for filing a privacy complaint or ask patients to waive any rights under the Privacy Rule as a condition of care or coverage.

Use and Disclosure

The Privacy Rule aims to protect patient privacy to the greatest extent possible while allowing for information sharing as necessary for the provision of healthcare services and to maintain public health and safety. The Privacy Rule is therefore intended to block covered entities under HIPAA from using PHI for practices such as selling PHI to advertisers or sharing PHI with prospective employers.

The Privacy Rule regulates both *use* and *disclosure* of PHI. According to HIPAA, use of PHI regulates how PHI is handled within an organization. Regulations relating to use help ensure that PHI is only used for intended purposes and that access to PHI is not intentionally or inadvertently abused. HIPAA defines use of PHI as

> . . . the sharing, employment, application, utilization, examination, or analysis of such information within an entity that maintains such information.

Rules that regulate disclosure are intended to prevent organizations from sharing PHI with third parties. If PHI is shared with third parties by any means, it is considered a disclosure. It is important to remember that not all disclosures are illegal under HIPAA. The Privacy Rule, rather, regulates when and how disclosures may be made. HIPAA defines disclosure as follows:

> Disclosure means the release, transfer, provision of access to, or divulging in any manner of information outside the entity holding the information.

The Privacy Rule has specific requirements detailing how covered entities may use and disclose PHI. These requirements are intended to ensure that patients know how their PHI is used and shared, that PHI is only used to provide healthcare services (with limited exceptions), and that patients must provide authorization before their PHI can be used for anything else.

Without a patient's explicit authorization, covered entities may only disclose PHI to designated parties for a few specific purposes, including the following:

- To the patients themselves

- As necessary to deliver healthcare services (treatment, billing, running a clinic, etc.)

- By informal permission of the patient—for example, a patient allowing another person to pick up prescriptions

- If, in the process of sharing PHI in an authorized way, other PHI is disclosed incidentally

- For activities in the public interest (the rule defines 12 specific activities that qualify, including, for example, disclosures required by law, essential government functions, and serious threats to health and safety)

- Limited sharing for research and public health purposes

For any other use or disclosure of PHI, the covered entity must obtain written authorization from the patient. As mentioned earlier, covered entities may not require patients to waive this right in exchange for services. Authorizations can't be written too broadly. For example, a provider can't ask an individual to grant blanket permission to share data for any purpose. Authorizations must be written so that they are easily understood and must specify the PHI to be disclosed, to whom, and for what purpose.

As mentioned at the beginning of this section, the goal of the Privacy Rule is to keep PHI as private as possible while allowing for necessary sharing. Even when PHI is shared in a permitted way or with patient authorization, the Privacy Rule includes an important principle to further improve privacy across all uses and disclosures. This is the principle of *minimum necessary* usage and sharing. This means that covered entities should keep access to patient data to need-to-know personnel, redact unnecessary information when disclosing data for permitted purposes, keep track of where all PHI is stored and make sure extra copies aren't floating around, and generally default to keeping data private and restricted unless explicitly permitted. As part of their privacy policies and procedures, covered entities must document their practices for managing and disclosing PHI.

Generally speaking, any use or disclosure of PHI not explicitly allowed by the law under the conditions described here is considered a breach. Breaches may be caused intentionally, such as when a healthcare organization is the victim of a cyberattack. Unauthorized uses and disclosures may also be accidental, such as when healthcare information is inadvertently disclosed to the wrong party. In the case of an accidental use or disclosure of PHI, the law may not define the event as a breach in the first place, depending on the circumstances and if there's only low risk to patients.

Naturally, breaches put patients at risk, but breaches also create risks and obligations for healthcare organizations. Breaches usually trigger further requirements for healthcare organizations to notify patients and the HHS department. A breach in itself may not constitute a HIPAA violation, but breaches may certainly bring increased regulatory scrutiny and, potentially, investigations by government oversight agencies.

 HIPAA's rules for breach notifications were modified by the Health Information Technology for Economic and Clinical Health (HITECH) Act. Breach notification rules are discussed in greater detail in the next section on the HITECH Act.

Individual Rights

The Privacy Rule offers individuals certain rights related to their PHI. As a foundation to these rights, individuals first have the right to know how a covered entity manages their data. Covered entities are therefore required to publish a *Privacy Notice* that explains how PHI is used and shared, the covered entities' obligations to protect patient privacy, the privacy practices in place, and patient privacy rights. These Privacy Notices provide an important vehicle for OCR enforcement because they allow investigators to determine whether an organization's behavior differs from its published Privacy Notice. These Privacy Notices must be conveyed directly to an individual if an organization has a direct treatment relationship with that person. Privacy Notices must also be posted wherever healthcare services are delivered and available by request. Organizations need to make a good-faith effort to obtain a written acknowledgment from patients that they've received the Privacy Notice.

Patients have the general right to access and review their medical records. This includes any health information used for medical care, paying for healthcare, complaints, and other elements of the medical record. There are a few important exceptions to this right:

- Psychotherapy notes
- Information gathered for legal actions
- Lab results specifically restricted by the Clinical Laboratory Improvement Amendments (CLIA)
- Circumstances in which a covered entity believes allowing the patient access to medical records may cause that person to harm themselves or others

Additional patient rights include the right to request corrections to medical records, to get a list of any entities to whom their PHI has been disclosed, and to request restrictions on the disclosure of PHI.

Additional Considerations

The Privacy Rule covers a few other issues in addition to laying out privacy practices and patient rights. The Privacy Rule designates specific organizational types to illustrate which parts of an entity are subject to the Privacy Rule. For example, organizations may be "hybrid entities," where only part of the business is a covered entity. The rule clarifies organizational obligations for the Privacy Rule for affiliated entities, shared healthcare arrangements, and health maintenance organizations (HMOs).

The rule allows patients to designate *personal representatives* who are treated the same as the patient with respect to privacy. Parents are considered personal representatives for their minor children unless parental rights have been legally revoked.

The Privacy Rule also addresses *preemption*, an important legal concept we covered in Chapter 2, "Legal Environment." States may enact additional privacy protections for PHI that are more stringent than HIPAA, and many states have done so. However, state laws may not preempt HIPAA by creating exceptions or less stringent regulations. HIPAA recognizes that states need to make use of health information in some cases, however, and makes some allowances for states to use PHI without patient consent. For example:

- State requirements to report health information for record-keeping (such as births and deaths)

- States' use of PHI for certain public health purposes, such as reporting vital statistics or enforcing public health regulations

- State requirements to report information about health plans for oversight purposes

Finally, the same exceptions apply to the Privacy Rule as apply to HIPAA generally. First, the Privacy Rule only applies to HIPAA-covered entities. The exceptions are described earlier and include, as a reminder, records covered under FERPA, employment records, and deidentified information.

HIPAA Privacy Enforcement

The OCR works with covered entities to encourage voluntary compliance whenever possible. For example, if an organization is made aware of a violation, it is typically allowed 30 days to make a correction. In this situation, the OCR does not impose a fine as long as the violation wasn't due to willful neglect. If the violations are not corrected through voluntary compliance, the OCR may impose fines. OCR penalties may range from $100 all the way up to $50,000 per violation. For repeated violations of the same HIPAA provision, fines may accrue up to a maximum of $1.5 million per year. If an organization violates multiple provisions, fines could be even higher. These penalties may vary based on the seriousness of the violations, the level of negligence of the offender, and any record of previous violations.

An individual who intentionally breaks the Privacy Rule by stealing or sharing PHI may also be subject to criminal prosecution by the Department of Justice (DOJ). Criminal penalties also vary, beginning at a fine of up to $50,000 and up to 1 year in prison and topping out at fines of up to $250,000 and up to 10 years in prison. The penalties increase if the offense was intended for personal gain or malicious harm. Note that enforcement is handled either through civil penalty or criminal prosecution, not both. If the DOJ handles enforcement via criminal prosecution, the OCR does not impose civil penalties.

Use of Online Tracking Technologies by HIPAA-Covered Entities and Business Associates

In 2022, HHS released a guidance document titled "Use of Online Tracking Technologies by HIPAA Covered Entities and Business Associates." This guidance clarifies how HIPAA-regulated entities may use online tracking technologies that collect a broad range of data about user activities. These technologies include cookies, scripts, and pixels used on websites and mobile apps. Although this data can be beneficial for user experience and service provision, it also presents significant privacy and security risks, particularly in the healthcare sector where sensitive health information is involved.

The reason this becomes complicated is that organizations typically rely on third-party vendors to provide these tracking technologies. Depending on the circumstances, that might constitute a disclosure of PHI to the vendor. HHS provides different guidance to covered entities depending upon the specific circumstances:

- In cases where the tracking technology is used on web pages that authenticate users, the tracking technology generally does have access to PHI, and the vendor should be considered a business associate.

- In cases where tracking technology is used on unauthenticated web pages, the tracking technology generally does not have access to PHI, and the vendor does not need to be considered a business associate unless the page does have access to PHI. HHS provides three examples of unauthenticated pages that may have access to PHI:

  - Login and registration pages that collect user information
  - Pages that address specific symptoms or health conditions
  - Pages that allow patients to search for doctors or schedule appointments

---

HIPAA Security Requirements

The HIPAA *Security Rule* is similar to the Privacy Rule in that it was established by HHS to provide an information security framework for the implementation of HIPAA. The Security Rule applies to covered entities and business associates in the same way as the Privacy Rule, and it is also enforced by the OCR. However, the Security Rule applies only to ePHI, whereas the Privacy Rule applies to all PHI. The Security Rule is intended to implement the protections of the Privacy Rule to ePHI by providing standards for data security.

The HIPAA Security Rule states that it is intended to safeguard the "confidentiality, integrity, and availability" of PHI. To accomplish this, covered entities and business associates must attempt to foresee cybersecurity threats as well as risks of any other unauthorized PHI disclosure to a reasonable degree. Organizations must protect information, put controls in key places to address those threats, and include employee training in information security practices.

The Security Rule's requirements for confidentiality are intended to protect against unauthorized access as described by the Privacy Rule. This is a good example of a way in which the Security Rule supports the application of the Privacy Rule to ePHI. Similarly, the other terms in the four general rules detailed earlier are designed to support the Privacy Rule by making sure data isn't improperly destroyed, is available for authorized access, and isn't inadvertently disclosed to the wrong parties.

The Security Rule also requires that covered entities and business associates implement appropriate data controls. However, the specific information security controls may vary from organization to organization, depending on the scale, function, resources, and capabilities of the organization. The Security Rule handles the wide variety of data security strategies by requiring all covered entities to complete a regular risk analysis that identifies information risks and the probability and severity of each of those risks. Organizations are then allowed to implement security controls that respond appropriately to the unique risks they face. These controls must include an information security management program that identifies personnel responsible for the program, appropriate employee training, controlled access to ePHI, ongoing program evaluation, physical security to facilities and workstations, and technological controls to monitor and protect data.

See Chapter 4, "Information Management," for a deeper dive into the information management and incident response principles.

HIPAA Security Enforcement

The Security Rule has other aspects in common with the Privacy Rule. In general, the Security Rule, as with all aspects of HIPAA, preempts state laws. The OCR manages enforcement as it does with the Privacy Rule. In fact, OCR enforcement actions commonly address violations of both rules when the violation involves ePHI.

In one example, the OCR investigated a Georgia healthcare provider named Athens Orthopedic. In 2016, Athens Orthopedic suffered a large data breach, and the hacker stole PHI that impacted more than 208,000 people. After a lengthy investigation, the OCR determined that Athens Orthopedic had long been negligent in applying both the Privacy and Security Rules. Athens failed to comply with requirements such as conducting risk analyses, implementing BAAs, and training employees on the Privacy Rule. In September 2020, Athens entered into a resolution agreement with OCR that included a $1.5 million fine, as well as a plan to correct violations and to submit to ongoing monitoring. Even though Athens Orthopedic was hacked by a criminal, the organization was found at fault for failing to implement the required privacy and security protections that may have prevented the breach.

Exam Tip

The HIPAA Privacy and Security rules are important to understand for the exam. We recommend reviewing these provisions in detail.

The Health Information Technology for Economic and Clinical Health Act

The Health Information Technology for Economic and Clinical Health (HITECH) Act was passed in 2009 in order to improve healthcare by bringing health systems up to date with modern technology. For this reason, the HITECH Act provides incentives for healthcare organizations to use *electronic health records (EHRs)* and penalties that serve as disincentives for organizations that don't adopt EHRs. The scope of the HITECH Act is aligned with HIPAA, and the HITECH Act applies to covered entities and transactions. Although the main purpose of the HITECH Act was to speed up innovation in healthcare, the act included important updates to HIPAA related to privacy.

Along with encouragement to adopt EHR, the HITECH Act provides additional privacy and security requirements for PHI, including requirements to notify victims about data breaches involving their information. *The Breach Notification Rule* is usually triggered when any unsecured PHI is used or disclosed in any way not authorized by the law. HHS uses four primary factors to determine whether an authorized use or disclosure constitutes a breach. To determine whether a breach has occurred, an organization must evaluate the following:

- The type of information involved and whether individual patients may be identified. If, for example, the data is fully anonymized and the information can't be assigned to any individual, then the information may not be PHI in the first place.

- The parties who used or accessed the information. Malicious actors, such as cybercriminals, may present far more risk to patients than an accidental disclosure to the wrong doctor.

- The likelihood that PHI was actually shared. For example, if an organization was able to show that an email containing PHI was deleted before being read, then there is a lower risk of a breach.

- How well PHI is secured. Organizations may mitigate risk through technological, physical, and administrative controls. For example, a breach is unlikely if the data is appropriately encrypted and are therefore unviewable.

Covered entities must notify victims within 60 days of knowing about a data breach to explain the breach and any steps victims should take to protect themselves. If the breach affects more than 500 individuals in a given state, then the covered entity is also required to notify media outlets, usually in the form of a press release.

Covered entities are also required to notify HHS of any breaches. If the breach affects more than 500 people total, then HHS must be notified within 60 days. Breaches that affect fewer people may be reported annually. Finally, business associates must notify the covered entity of any breaches within 60 days. Once the covered entity has been notified of a breach by a business associate, the covered entity is responsible for the rest of the notification requirements. Importantly, covered entities can't merely claim they made all appropriate notifications after a breach—they have to prove it. Covered entities must therefore maintain documentation or other evidence to demonstrate that they fulfilled the notification requirements outlined by the HITECH Act.

Exam Tip

Many regulations include rules for notification timelines that vary depending on the scale of a breach. For example, the HITECH Act allows a covered entity only 60 days to notify individuals of a breach and applies additional rules if the breach affects over 500 people in a state. For the exam, it is helpful to recall conditions that trigger different notification timelines as well as the timelines themselves.

Not all unauthorized uses and disclosures of PHI are considered *breaches* under the law. As mentioned in the HIPAA section earlier, there are circumstances when unauthorized disclosures aren't due to negligence and don't present much risk to patients. In these instances, the law does not consider the events to be breaches and notification requirements are not triggered. There are three types of use and disclosure that are not subject to the breach notification rule, because these circumstances don't meet the rule's definition of a breach:

- If an employee of a covered entity or business associate accidentally accesses PHI but was acting in good faith.

- If more than one person authorized to access the *same* PHI accidentally share with one another.

- If the covered entity or business associate has good reason to believe that no unauthorized parties will be able to retain the information. If, for example, the disclosed data were fully encrypted and there was no way the information could be viewed, then the breach notification rule would not apply.

In addition to breach notification rules, the HITECH Act adds business associates to the HIPAA directly, rather than only through agreements with covered entities. This means that the OCR can pursue enforcement actions directly against business associates just as it does with covered entities. The HITECH Act increases fines for HIPAA violations to up to $1.5 million, as was the case in the example of Athens Orthopedic described earlier. Finally, the act adds to the HIPAA Privacy Rule by requiring individual authorization for the use of PHI in marketing, providing the ability for individuals to revoke authorizations for disclosure, and requiring healthcare organizations to maintain records of any PHI disclosures that may be viewed by patients upon request.

The 21st Century Cures Act

The 21st Century Cures Act was passed in 2016 in order to improve the development of treatments, devices, and drugs for serious illnesses, including addiction. This act attempts to further improve efficiency in both the development and delivery of treatment by encouraging the adoption of more standardized EHRs. This act has several provisions with privacy implications.

This act also sets up a framework that allows healthcare providers to share with family members or caregivers certain information about mental health and substance abuse treatments for adults. These guidelines are issued by HHS and provide instructions for how such sharing may be conducted with respect to HIPAA. The 21st Century Cures Act refers to this as the "compassionate" sharing of information. As with other provisions of this act, this provision is intended to speed the development and delivery of treatment.

The act penalizes *information blocking*. Information blocking occurs when an organization prevents appropriate sharing of electronic health information. Information blocking can inhibit the development of medical devices and treatments. Penalties for information blocking may be as high as $1 million per violation.

The 21st Century Cures Act adds privacy protections for individuals participating in medical research. The act exempts federal government medical research information that could identify an individual from Freedom of Information Act (FOIA) requests. The act also makes it easier for researchers to view medical information remotely while protecting the identity of individuals. Finally, this act offers increased confidentiality for research participants by creating "certificates of confidentiality" issued by the National Institutes of Health (NIH). These additional privacy provisions improve medical research because they make it more likely that individuals will choose to participate.

Confidentiality of Substance Use Disorder Patient Records Rule

By the 1970s, the government faced growing public concerns related to drug addiction. Many recreational drugs had been designated as illegal narcotics and banned, and in 1971, President Nixon first declared a "war on drugs." The government moved to combat drug trafficking and drug sales and implemented more antidrug education programs. There was also renewed focus on treatment for people suffering from substance use disorder. Social and legal risks presented barriers to anyone seeking treatment. There was, and remains, a strong social stigma against becoming known as an "addict." Sufferers may face consequences in their jobs and relationships. Furthermore, in the context of the war on drugs, law enforcement was more focused on prosecuting drug-related crimes. Also, at that time, HIPAA had not yet been implemented, and patients had reason to fear that their medical treatment records might be used against them in criminal or civil court.

In 1975, Congress sought to mitigate both of these risks to those seeking treatment by implementing the Confidentiality of Substance Use Disorder Patient Records Rule. This rule has since been updated several times by Congress. In most cases, it has been amended to align with new federal privacy laws, such as HIPAA.

The rule appears in U.S. law as 42 CFR Part 2. It is often referred to colloquially as just "Part Two."

The rule applies to any records related to alcohol and substance abuse treatment that could possibly identify an individual patient. The rule also restricts information that may expose a patient to any criminal charges. Any substance abuse treatment program that receives federal funding is subject to this rule.

Most discourses of patient information require patient consent with few exceptions. Such exceptions include research, medical emergencies, audits, child abuse, reporting crimes that occur at the treatment program itself, and information shared in response to a legal court order. Violations can be penalized, with fines of up to $500 for a first offense and up to $5,000 for repeat offenses. Violators of this rule may also be subject to criminal prosecution.

Financial Privacy

Personal financial information is often a very private matter for individuals and yet essential for conducting business. Financial information is used to help people buy homes, pay for college, insure their property, get a job, and more. Banks, insurance companies, creditors, and even universities must use personal financial information to open accounts, complete transactions, evaluate credit applications, and run many aspects of their businesses.

In the United States, a series of key federal regulations govern the financial sector. These include regulations for consumer credit reporting, banking and insurance, and even investment services. In general, financial institutions are not subject to the FTC Act as mentioned earlier because they are regulated separately, as described in this section.

Privacy in Credit Reporting

Credit reports have a huge impact on people's lives. Consumers depend on positive credit ratings to buy homes and cars, and sometimes even to get jobs. Credit reporting firms amass huge amounts of private financial, tax, and employment data on individuals that could be damaging if made public. Banks and other financial services businesses also rely on accurate evaluations of creditworthiness to make sound investment and credit decisions. As we saw after the subprime mortgage crisis of 2008, it is also in the public interest to ensure fair and accurate credit reporting for both lenders and borrowers. Federal legislation regulates credit reporting through two principal legislative acts: the Fair Credit Reporting Act (FCRA) and the Fair and Accurate Credit Transactions Act (FACTA).

The Fair Credit Reporting Act (FCRA)

In 1970, the United States enacted FCRA. In the years leading up to 1970, consumer credit reporting became an increasingly common tool used by businesses in making decisions that affected people's lives. Credit reporting information was more often shared broadly between businesses, and third-party brokers of this information began to emerge. FCRA enacted regulations to improve accuracy and trust in credit reporting while giving consumers some visibility into their own credit reports.

FCRA Scope

The FCRA only regulates *consumer reporting agencies (CRAs)*, not broader commercial credit rating organizations. Unsurprisingly, a *consumer* reporting agency is any agency that provides consumer reports about individual consumers. In determining the applicability of the FCRA to a given agency, the key question is therefore, "What constitutes a consumer report?" According to the FCRA, a consumer report must first be actually "furnished" to a customer and used for the purpose of making decisions about an individual related to extending credit, insurance coverage, or employment. This means that information helping to inform credit decisions about an individual must be communicated to a third party, for a fee, to be considered a consumer report. The types of information that make something a consumer report under the FCRA are as follows:

- Creditworthiness
- Credit standing
- Credit capacity
- Character
- General reputation
- Personal characteristics
- Mode of living

If an organization sells reports including this information, as described earlier, then the organization fits the definition of a consumer reporting agency and is subject to the requirements of the FCRA. The most well-known examples of CRAs are the three biggest consumer credit reporting agencies in the United States: Equifax, Experian, and TransUnion.

CRAs must honor certain consumer rights and follow specific regulations. FCRA regulations specify the requirements for maintaining accurate reports, for determining when CRAs can share credit reports, and for properly managing information used in the reports. The FCRA also regulates how consumer reports may be used once purchased from a CRA.

The FCRA grants certain rights to make sure consumers know how CRAs collect and use their information to make decisions about extending credit. The FCRA gives consumers the right to request access to their consumer reports, including credit scores, and to be told if anything in their reports has been used to make unfavorable decisions. A notice of an unfavorable decision must include the following:

- Contact information for the CRA that provided the credit report
- An explanation that the CRA only furnished the information and did not play a decision-making role
- An explanation of consumer rights, including the right to access the credit report and credit score and to dispute inaccurate information

The FCRA also grants consumers limited control over the information in credit reports by giving consumers the right to dispute anything in their consumer report that is incorrect. If information is found to be incorrect, CRAs are required to correct that information. Finally, individuals also have some rights to control access to their consumer reports. Consumers have the right to give consent before their reports may be shared with employers, to implement security freezes on their reports to limit disclosure, and to seek damages from businesses that violate their rights.

CRAs are subject to requirements under the FCRA that are consistent with these consumer rights. For example, the law limits how consumer reports can be used without consent of the consumer, requires CRAs to make sure information in credit reports is accurate and fair to the best of their knowledge, prohibits the use of outdated information (usually 7–10 years is the limit), and provides means for consumers to exercise the rights mentioned earlier, such as the right to dispute the accuracy of information in a report.

The FCRA also regulates any entity that receives consumer reports from CRAs to make decisions about consumers. These users of consumer reports could be banks, car dealerships, employers, advertisers, or anyone else using a consumer report to make a judgment about an individual. Users of consumer reports must also make a reasonable effort to use only accurate, current, and complete reports; notify consumers whenever they make an unfavorable decision based on a consumer report; and only use consumer reports as allowed under the law by providing certification to a CRA that they have a legitimate legal reason to use the consumer report. Consumer reports may always be shared with written permission from a consumer. Without consumer consent, reports may only be shared for limited other "permissible purposes," including these:

- In response to court orders or other mandatory legal requests
- To review a consumer's application for insurance underwriting or financial services, such as a credit card
- When the information is needed to complete a transaction initiated by the consumer
- To evaluate a consumer's existing accounts or services to verify ongoing eligibility
- To review a consumer's application for certain government licenses or benefits where financial responsibility is a legal criterion
- For use by prospective investors and insurers to evaluate risk when deciding whether to invest in consumer debt
- For use in setting appropriate levels of child support payments
- For use by insurance and credit firms to screen consumers in advance of offering products and services

As you can see, the permitted uses under the FCRA are broad and allow for many scenarios under which organizations may use credit reports without the express permission of the consumer. Consumer credit report information isn't really in the control of consumers. Rather, such information is owned by creditors who furnish the information to CRAs. Consumer rights are granted to ensure that consumers are informed about the information and use of their credit reports and to give consumers some ability to ensure the accuracy of their credit reports.

FCRA Enforcement

Enforcement authority for the FCRA is shared by the FTC, the Consumer Financial Protection Bureau (CFPB), and states' attorneys general. Any of these entities can exercise their jurisdictional authority to investigate FCRA violations and seek damages. Penalties may include damages paid to consumers, punitive damages to punish violators, and recovering of legal costs related to enforcement litigation.

Fair and Accurate Credit Transactions Act (FACTA)

The Fair and Accurate Credit Transactions Act (FACTA) was passed in 2003. FACTA updates the FCRA with additional protections intended to respond to the increasing need to protect consumers from identity theft in the digital information age. FACTA provides several important provisions to allow consumers to monitor their credit reports for fraud and address any fraudulent data. FACTA also strengthens the obligations of organizations managing credit reporting to detect and prevent identity fraud. The most well-known provision of FACTA guaranteed everyone the right to free credit reports each year. Prior to FACTA, CRAs could charge consumers for access to their credit reports.

FACTA allows consumers to place fraud alerts on their credit reports that must be included on any credit report. Potential creditors are required to verify an applicant's identity before extending credit. Fraud alerts are active for 90 days and may be extended up to 7 years if identity theft has indeed taken place. The act also enhances consumer rights to dispute inaccurate information on a credit report by allowing consumers to trigger an investigation into disputed data by the CRA.

In addition to enhancing consumer rights to control fraud in their credit reports, FACTA provides other protections against identity theft. All merchants are required to partially mask credit card numbers on receipts and transaction records, and Social Security numbers must be similarly redacted by consumer request. Any users of credit records must dispose of paper and electronic records when no longer needed. FACTA also requires higher standards and more disclosure from CRAs to ensure that information is accurate and to tell consumers specifically how they calculate credit scores.

FACTA modifies other aspects of the FCRA as well. FACTA clarifies preemption rules in relation to states, exempts certain communications involving employers, further protects medical information, and creates an entity to offer educational programs for financial literacy.

Gramm–Leach–Bliley Act (GLBA)

The Financial Services Modernization Act of 1999 is more commonly known as the Gramm–Leach–Bliley Act (GLBA) after the names of the lead lawmakers who sponsored the legislation. GLBA establishes broad federal regulation to improve information privacy and security for the financial services industry.

Exam Tip

This act may appear on the exam under the name "GLBA" *or* its official name, the "Financial Services Modernization Act of 1999."

GLBA Scope

If a business is *significantly engaged* in offering financial services, then it is considered a *financial institution* and is regulated under GLBA. The standard of significant engagement hinges principally on two factors: the formality of offering financial services and the frequency of offering financial services. For example, if a barber occasionally allows a good customer to come back and pay later, then the barber probably does not meet the standard. However, if the barber starts a formal credit program as a regular service, then the barber would be significantly engaged in offering financial services.

Financial services and products may include obvious products like credit cards and bank loans. Less obvious activities include collecting debts, loan servicing, check-cashing services, tax services, and higher education institutions that offer student loans. Firms that manage investments for others are also included.

As a federal statute, GLBA preempts state laws with less stringent requirements. As with other federal laws, states are free to enact regulations with stronger requirements as long as those requirements don't contradict the provisions of the GLBA. As discussed in Chapter 8, "State Privacy Laws," many states have enacted laws with stricter requirements than GLBA. However, when states do enact privacy laws with stricter provisions than GLBA, many state laws offer exemptions for institutions or data regulated under GLBA. In these cases, financial institutions are exempt from some of the more stringent provisions of state privacy laws and may continue to comply with GLBA. For example, the California Consumer Protection Act (CCPA) includes an exemption for "personal information collected, processed, sold, or disclosed pursuant to the federal Gramm–Leach–Bliley Act." Note that this provision does not exempt financial institutions themselves from the CCPA. Such exemptions reduce compliance burdens on financial institutions operating in multiple states.

GLBA Privacy Requirements

The GLBA *Privacy Rule* is intended to protect consumer privacy both by better informing consumers about how their financial information is used and by regulating the use of consumer information by financial institutions. Financial institutions must share their privacy notices with customers when they first begin a business relationship and provide updated privacy notices every year thereafter.

As with privacy notice requirements under other legislation, the notice must describe privacy policies and disclose how customer information is collected, used, and shared. The notice must also inform customers about any third parties that may access their data. Unlike COPPA, customers are merely *informed* about third-party information sharing and not given the right to explicitly *consent* to third-party sharing. The privacy notice must also reference the information security practices in place to protect customer data as described in the GLBA Safeguards Rule (see the next section).

GLBA also recognizes a legal difference between *customers* and *consumers*. Customers have an ongoing regular relationship with a financial institution. For example, an account holder at a bank would be a customer. Consumers, however, may only conduct isolated transactions with a financial institution, such as cashing a check at a bank or visiting a bank's website. For *customers*, financial institutions must provide their full privacy notices with all the details listed in GLBA when the customer relationship begins and then annually thereafter. For *consumers*, the financial institution only needs to provide a summary privacy notice that includes instructions for finding the full notice.

GLBA Safeguards Requirements

The GBLA *Safeguards Rule* provides a framework for financial institutions' obligations for protecting information security. The rule requires financial institutions to implement organized information security programs with the goals of safeguarding customer information security and confidentiality. The requirements for safeguards echo those of other similar laws discussed in this chapter. Financial institutions are required to attempt to anticipate threats as well as risks of any unauthorized information access or disclosure. These organizations must implement appropriate measures to protect against these threats and risks. When considering the risk of unauthorized access, the Safeguards Rule emphasizes protecting against scenarios where the consumer may be harmed as a result.

Under GLBA, information security programs must include designated personnel to manage information security, ongoing assessment of risks and the controls in place to minimize those risks, and assessment of any third-party partners to make sure those partners can meet the standards of the financial institution's information security program.

GLBA also offers guidance on the types of controls financial institutions should consider for lowering their risk. GLBA emphasizes three categories of information security controls: workforce training, securing of information systems, and ongoing monitoring of information systems for problems. As companies consider information risk, GLBA is concerned not only with safeguards that reduce the risk of cyberattacks but also with the risk of data loss or exposure due to failures in information systems or procedures or human mistakes.

 Real World Scenario

The Role of the Privacy Professional: A Case Study

Many of the federal laws described in this chapter require private organizations to implement privacy programs and to notify customers about those programs. Privacy professionals are often called on to create privacy programs and related notices that proactively comply with all applicable regulations. Privacy professionals must therefore understand principles of jurisdiction (explained in Chapter 2, "Legal Environment") and scope to determine which laws apply to their business. Healthcare providers must comply with HIPAA, colleges that receive federal funding must comply with FERPA and GLBA, and so on. Privacy professionals will typically try to construct a unified privacy policy that complies with all applicable laws rather than building standalone privacy programs for each statute.

It is instructive for aspiring privacy professionals to consult examples from industry. Microsoft has a well-developed privacy notice that addresses many regulations that apply to Microsoft products and services:

`privacy.microsoft.com/en-us/privacystatement`

As a simple exercise, review the main headings covered by the Microsoft privacy statement. As of this writing, these include the following:

- Personal data we collect

- How we use personal data

- Reasons we share personal data

- How to access and control your personal data

- Cookies and similar technologies

- Products provided by your organization—notice to end users

- Microsoft account

- Other important privacy information:

  - Security of personal data

  - Where we store and process personal data

  - Our retention of personal data

  - California Consumer Privacy Act

  - Advertising

  - Collection of data from children

  - Preview or free-of-charge services

  - Changes to this privacy statement

  - How to contact us

The statement goes on to provide product-specific privacy information for various Microsoft products and services. The core list of contents is relatively short and written in plain language (as is the whole statement). Although privacy statutes aren't mentioned by name, this privacy statement is obviously responding to several regulations at once. For example, multiple regulations such as HIPAA, GLBA, and many self-regulation programs require companies to disclose how they collect, use, and share personal information.

The section on children's data clearly responds to COPPA, and the statement even provides notice of changes to Microsoft's practices, in keeping with the spirit of rules such as GLBA.

The Microsoft privacy statement represents the notice to customers about how Microsoft's privacy program operates. The statement itself is, of course, only the public side of what is certainly a broad and deep internal privacy and security program. Behind the statement, Microsoft's privacy program most likely includes many of the requirements discussed in this chapter, such as these:

- Designated personnel in charge of the program
- Role-based training across Microsoft's vast workforce
- Physical, administrative, and technological controls
- Regular assessment and monitoring of the privacy program
- Protocols to monitor for both intentional and accidental breaches
- Incident response procedures to notify customers and appropriate authorities as required in case of a breach

Privacy professionals are likely to play key roles in developing such privacy programs and the related notices to the public. It is useful to review privacy notices provided by industry leaders such as Microsoft in order to see how companies connect the dots between many seemingly disparate statutes to create coherent programs and statements. Privacy professionals collaborate with IT security professionals, risk management offices, legal counsel, and other key experts to develop, manage, and monitor this sort of program. Providing a comprehensive program that satisfies all applicable regulations at once (when possible) offers many benefits. Organizations are able to achieve compliance more efficiently, provide clearer training to employees, and more clearly disclose their practices to the public.

Red Flags Rule

The Red Flags Rule adds obligations for financial institutions or any creditor to proactively monitor consumer data for identity theft by watching for "red flags." The rule requires covered institutions to have a written plan for monitoring for these red flags. The rule doesn't specify which factors should be monitored as red flags. Instead, the rule directs businesses to independently identify red flags that are appropriate to monitor on behalf of customers.

In addition to identifying red flags, the rule requires a written plan for protecting consumers from identity theft and must include procedures to "detect, prevent and mitigate identity theft." The rule also requires that these procedures include a process for validating the legitimacy of any consumer changes of home address and to notify consumers if an address in any credit report information is significantly different from the consumer's real address. This helps to detect identity fraud.

The Red Flags Rule was first created under FACTA in 2003 and enforced, like the FCRA and FACTA, by the FTC, the CFPB, and states' attorneys general. However, in 2011, the Dodd–Frank Act transferred enforcement responsibility for the Red Flags Rule to the Securities and Exchange Commission (SEC) and the Commodity Futures Trading Commission (CFTC) for any entities they regulate.

Exam Tip

The Red Flags Rule provides a good example of shared regulatory authority. The SEC enforces this rule for any entities in its scope of authority. The FTC, as well as the CFPB, also enforce the rule for any organizations under their jurisdictions.

Consumer Financial Protection Bureau

Enacted in 2008, the *Dodd–Frank Wall Street Reform and Consumer Protection Act (Dodd–Frank Act)* renovated the way the federal government regulated the financial industry and added new federal agencies. Of these new agencies, the Consumer Financial Protection Bureau (CFPB) is most significant for privacy regulation.

The CFPB has significant responsibility for regulating the financial sector. Dodd–Frank centralized rulemaking authority for both GLBA and the FCRA/FACTA under the CFPB. In addition to rulemaking, the Dodd–Frank Act gave the CFPB shared authority, along with the FTC, for enforcement against financial institutions based on unfair and deceptive trade practices. Dodd–Frank adds another enforcement principle to the doctrine on unfair and deceptive practices: *abusive* practices. Following the Dodd–Frank Act, these enforcement principles are known as unfair, deceptive, or abusive acts (UDAAPs). The definitions of unfair and deceptive practices were discussed in Chapter 3.

Abusive practices are defined by Dodd–Frank and enforceable by the CFPB. An abusive practice is any act that "materially interferes with the ability of a consumer to understand a term or condition of a consumer financial product or service." Practices are also considered abusive if they exploit consumer misunderstanding, consumers who are unable to understand the terms, or a consumer relying on a third party that may be exploiting them.

Remember that acts that generate enforcement actions may constitute any combination of unfair, deceptive, or abusive practices. An enforcement action may be initiated for a violation of one of these principles, two of them, or all three.

Online Banking

The emergence of online banks offering credit, investment, and other financial services has significantly expanded the sphere of regulatory enforcement for all financial privacy regulations. In addition to complying with any financial privacy regulations, online

banking activities may be subject to FCC regulations related to telemarketing and electronic marketing, described later in this chapter.

Educational Privacy

The education sector is subject to regulations designed specifically to protect student privacy. Student academic records may impact a person's chances of getting a job, getting into graduate school, and more. In the context of AI and big data, as discussed earlier in this chapter, academic records may be used inappropriately in combination with other data to discern even more private information that, in turn, can be exploited for advertising, to stigmatize individuals, or to influence other adverse decisions about a person.

Family Educational Rights and Privacy Act (FERPA)

The Family Educational Rights and Privacy Act (FERPA) of 1974 defines protected academic information and creates a framework to keep that information private and secure. FERPA helps to protect students while removing barriers to risk-taking in education by reducing the chance that a person might be stigmatized by underperforming in a challenging academic program.

FERPA Scope

FERPA applies to any academic records maintained by education institutions receiving federal funding from the U.S. Department of Education. FERPA applies to almost every college and university, as well as most public elementary, junior, and high schools, because almost all of these organizations receive federal funding. Many private elementary, junior, and high schools don't seek any funding from the Department of Education and are therefore not regulated under FERPA.

FERPA is very broad in defining the scope of the records it protects. FERPA protects any records that are maintained by an educational institution that pertain directly to a student. FERPA also applies to any third parties working on behalf of the educational institutions, such as providers of information systems that contain student grades. FERPA also has a very broad definition of what is considered a "record" under the law. FERPA protects records in any format, whether they are on paper, in email, in a database, or captured on video. FERPA record types commonly include the following:

- Grades and transcripts
- Class rosters
- Course schedules
- Health records for minors
- Financial information for higher education students
- Disciplinary records

FERPA excludes law enforcement records and some application data. Because FERPA applies only to students of an educational institution, application data from students who never became enrolled students is not covered under FERPA. For enrolled students, applications become part of the educational record. Data collected after students graduate is not considered educational records. Finally, individual notes, memory aids, and the sort created by teachers are classified as "sole possession" records and not considered part of the academic record under FERPA as long as they aren't shared.

FERPA Requirements

FERPA protects privacy by requiring certain protections and rights with respect to academic records. These rights and protections are granted to students if they are over 18 or attending a higher education institution. If a student is under 18 and attending elementary, junior, or high school, FERPA grants its protections and rights to the parent or guardian.

FERPA forbids schools from sharing information from a student's academic record without consent from the student or parent. Students or parents also have the right to view their educational records and challenge anything they think is inaccurate.

Academic records can be disclosed if the student or parent consents to the disclosure or if the data are sufficiently anonymized. FERPA-covered information may also be disclosed in case of an imminent threat to health or safety. Schools may also share academic information, without authorization from the student or parent, when sharing with other educators with a "legitimate educational interest," another school at which the student is also enrolled or applying, financial aid providers, educational research entities, and accreditation bodies and as required by law enforcement.

Educational Technology

Educational technology companies often handle data falling under FERPA. For example, most schools use third-party providers to run information systems functions, including grades, transcripts, and course scheduling, room assignments, and more. In most cases, educational institutions craft contracts with these providers, designating them as "school officials." Such contract language helps accomplish two goals for the school. First, it makes the third party effectively part of the school under FERPA and thus allows the school to share student records with the third party. Second, it makes the third party subject to FERPA in its own right.

Telecommunications and Marketing Privacy

Businesses leverage troves of personal data in order to advertise goods and services. At a minimum, advertisers seek contact information to reach consumers by postal mail, phone call, text, fax, email, and anywhere online. Regulations in this area are structured to permit reasonable advertising and marketing efforts, as long as those activities aren't unduly harmful to consumers.

The regulations around telecommunications and marketing have evolved with technology to address concerns arising from new capabilities that may not have been regulated by previous laws. Still, regulation lags behind technological innovation, and lawmakers do not have settled strategies for protecting consumer privacy in the digital age.

Telephone Consumer Protection Act (TCPA) and Telemarketing Sales Rule (TSR)

In 1991, the U.S. Congress passed the Telephone Consumer Protection Act (TCPA). This act directs the FCC to regulate unsolicited sales and marketing phone calls. The TCPA was updated in 2012 to add the authority for regulating autodialers and robocalls. The history of enforcement rulings under the TCPA also confirms that the act applies to text messages.

The FCC and FTC have worked together to reconcile the rules promulgated by the TCPA with the Telemarketing Sales Rule (TSR) of 1995. The TCPA and TSR contain similar core regulations. The TSR adds some key provisions, so these requirements are discussed more fully under the TSR.

One important difference between the TCPA and TSR relates to their differing *subject matter jurisdiction* (see Chapter 2). Even though the TSR is regulated jointly by the FTC and FCC, it was the FTC that issued the TSR. Therefore, the TSR is subject to the jurisdiction of the FTC Act. Financial institutions, for example, are not regulated under the FTC Act. However, the FCC has jurisdiction over all telemarketing activities across industry and has updated its rules to be as consistent as possible with the TSR.

The *Established Business Relationship (EBR) Exemption* provides an exception from most of the provisions of the TCPA and the TSR (discussed next) if organizations are calling or texting existing customers. A customer is defined as an individual who has completed a purchase or other transaction with an organization within the last 18 months.

Telemarketing Sales Rule

The FTC implemented the Telemarketing Sales Rule (TSR) in 1995 as part of the guidelines for regulating industry under the Telemarketing and Consumer Fraud and Abuse Prevention Act. The TSR regulates sales and marketing phone calls and text messages.

Scope

The TSR applies to firms that carry out telemarketing activities. The rule defines telemarketing activities as the use of interstate telephone calls intended to get consumers to buy goods or services, or to make donations to charity.

There are some exemptions to the TSR. Financial services, for example, are not regulated by either the FTC or the FCC and are usually exempt. There are also exemptions for non-profits, airlines, and long-distance phone service providers. Certain insurance and investment sales activities are also exempt. Finally, specific telephone calls are exempt that include consumer-initiated calls in response to ads, mailings, and business-to-business calls. As with the TCPA, the TSR exempts calls to consumers with whom the caller has an existing business relationship.

Requirements

The TSR requirements are intended to ensure that telemarketers are up front and honest and that sales calls are not unduly harassing, and to give consumers some control over the calls. Telemarketers may only make calls between 8 a.m. and 9 p.m., must use a valid caller ID, and must connect consumers to a live person within two seconds. They must identify themselves and the call as a sales call and offer full disclosure of goods, services, costs, and any other conditions of the sale. Telemarketers are also prohibited from misrepresenting any of this information to consumers. Finally, the TSR only permits the use of automated calls (robocalls) with the direct written permission of the recipient. The most well-known require-ment of the TSR is the national Do-Not-Call registry, discussed in detail next.

Do-Not-Call Registry (DNC)

The National Do-Not-Call (DNC) registry helps prevent unwanted sales and marketing calls to consumers. The DNC allows consumers to register their phone numbers in a national database maintained by the federal government. If a phone number is listed in the DNC, most direct marketing to that number is forbidden.

Scope

The DNC applies based on the nature of specific phone calls. With some limited exceptions, it doesn't matter what type of organization is making these calls. The DNC forbids any interstate phone calls to consumers made for sales or marketing purposes.

There are some important exceptions, including political groups, charities, some nonprofit organizations, and surveys. The DNC also allows businesses to call their existing customers. If a charitable organization is exempt, it doesn't necessarily mean that telemarketers hired by charities are exempt. If a telemarketing firm calls consumers for a charity, then consumers may opt out of those calls, and the telemarketer would be subject to the DNC for any further calls related to that charity. It is important to note that the DNC is rather strict about whether nonprofits can be considered exempt. To be exempt, a nonprofit must not exist to promote profit for others. For example, a nonprofit national group that exists to promote restaurant supply sales would likely *not* be exempt under the rule.

Certain phone calls made by for-profit organizations may also be exempt. The principle behind these exemptions is whether or not the calls are really for sales or marketing pur-poses. If an organization *never* makes any telemarketing calls, then its calls may be exempt if the calls are informational in nature or fit one of the exemptions listed earlier (such as political calls, charity, or surveys) or they are calling existing customers or others who have granted authorization in writing.

Finally, there is a Safe Harbor provision in the DNC rule that exempts telemarketers from penalties if they violate the DNC accidentally. To qualify for this exemption, the telemarketer must show that a call made in error was a true accident and not just the result of sloppy or negligent implementation of the DNC rule by demonstrating that they have

- Made the call by accident
- Documented procedures for following DNC rules
- Employee training on these procedures
- A maintained list of phone numbers specific to the company that they aren't allowed to call
- An updated national DNC list
- A process for monitoring and enforcing their own procedures

Requirements

Telemarketers are responsible for maintaining updated records on phone numbers listed in the DNC. Telemarketers must pay the government to download a current DNC list and ensure that it is updated at least every 31 days. Telemarketers must also obtain written permission from a consumer to call any number listed in the DNC.

Enforcement

Legally speaking, the DNC exists as a set of rules under the TSR, enforced jointly by the FTC, FCC, and states. As a part of the TSR, the FTC or FCC may apply penalties of up to $43,280 per call. States may also seek penalties for violation of state-level DNC lists. States may fine violators up to $25,000 per call.

> The penalty amount comes from the maximum civil penalty for any violation of section 5 of the FTC Act.

In 2020, the FTC and the state of Ohio fined Globex Telecom $1.9 million for providing voice over Internet Protocol (VoIP) capabilities to engage in telemarketing that violated the DNC. Globex Telecom was, in fact, providing telemarketing services for another company that was scamming consumers with fake credit cards. Even though Globex wasn't the company offering the scam, it was still liable under the DNC. This case is also interesting because it marks the FTC's first action against a VoIP marketing firm and confirms that the FTC has the ability to enforce regulations even if the technology used to make these calls changes.

The Junk Fax Prevention Act (JFPA)

The Junk Fax Prevention Act was added to the TCPA as an amendment in 2005. The act prohibits sending unsolicited advertisements to fax machines. The JFPA also acknowledges that faxes may be sent from a computer, from another fax machine, or from another multi-function device. Regardless of how a fax is sent, the act applies to all documents received by a fax machine.

The JFPA does allow for faxes sent with the consent of the recipient and under the EBR exemption described earlier. Recipients must be able to opt out for free at any time. Any faxes sent under the EBR exemption must also contain sender contact information and instructions for opting out. Violations of the JFPA may incur penalties from $500 per page up to $1,500 per page, if the violation was willful. There are no exceptions for accidental faxes.

Controlling the Assault of Non-solicited Pornography and Marketing (CAN-SPAM) Act

The regulations we've discussed apply only to unwanted commercial telephone calls. Until relatively recently, advertisers were free to flood consumers' email inboxes with unwanted commercial messages. Email solicitations were largely unregulated and could also market products that were offensive to many, including pornography. In 2003, the federal government passed the Controlling the Assault of Non-solicited Pornography and Marketing (CAN-SPAM) Act in order to provide consumers with some protection and control related to unsolicited commercial email.

Scope

The CAN-SPAM Act regulates all commercial messages, not only mass email marketing programs. *Commercial* messages under the act include any advertising messages and promotions for services or products. Many emails contain a mix of content that may not all be commercial. Most commonly, business email content that is not commercial in nature may be considered *transactional or relationship* content under the act. Transactional or relationship content may pertain to existing transactions or update customers on order status, for example.

The act considers the *primary purpose* of a message to determine whether the sender is in violation. If a reasonable person would probably think a message's primary purpose is commercial, then the act applies, even if the message covers other topics. The act applies to messages sent to consumers as well as messages sent to other businesses. It applies to all "electronic messages," not only email. Facebook messages, for example, are also subject to the CAN-SPAM Act.

Because the CAN-SPAM Act regulates commercial electronic messages, it applies to all senders of such messages. This means that businesses and individuals are both subject to the law. If a business employs another firm, such as a marketing firm, to send out email messages on its behalf, then *both* the marketing firm and the business are responsible for complying with the CAN-SPAM Act.

Requirements

The CAN-SPAM Act requirements are focused on requiring businesses to be honest and transparent in email and to give consumers the opportunity to opt out of email marketing from businesses.

Senders of commercial messages must inform recipients of the advertising purpose of the message, identify the sender, and share the sender's physical location. Senders are also prohibited from deceiving recipients about any of this information through techniques such as false email aliases or fake email subject headings.

Senders are required to create a simple way for recipients to opt out of receiving future messages. Every message must provide a clear notice about how to use the opt-out process and is not allowed to charge for opting out. A sender must allow recipients to exercise the right to opt out for up to 30 days after sending a message. Once a sender receives an opt-out request, they have 10 days to cease all commercial messages to that recipient and are prohibited from selling the email recipient's email address to others.

Enforcement

The CAN-SPAM Act is enforced mainly by the FTC. However, several other federal agencies and U.S. states may also pursue enforcement actions under the CAN-SPAM Act. Although there is no private right of action for individuals under the CAN-SPAM Act, there are limited rights for Internet service providers (ISPs) to seek civil damages if they have been harmed financially as the result of CAN-SPAM violations.

CAN-SPAM enforcement may even include criminal prosecution if the sender is using stolen or hacked computing equipment or email accounts, falsifying email metadata to cover up violations, or committing other egregious acts.

Exam Tips

- Be familiar with all the obligations this act imposes on senders of commercial messages related to opt-out requests, including the time limits involved in allowing opt-outs, acting on opt-outs, and keeping an individual's email address private following an opt-out.

- The CAN-SPAM Act provides a good example of federal preemption because it does not allow states to enforce any stricter statutes. For example, the CAN-SPAM Act prevents states from passing laws requiring recipients to opt in to receive commercial messages.

Special Rules for SMS Marketing and the Wireless Domain Registry

The FCC has rules in place to ban sending commercial advertising wirelessly to mobile phones without obtaining specific consent from a recipient in advance. These rules are designed to prevent advertisers from spamming cell phones with text messages, thus clogging cellular networks and incurring charges for mobile subscribers. This rule applies to messages sent directly to mobile phones using technologies like SMS text messaging. It does not apply, for example, to email messages that recipients may happen to read via email apps on their smartphones.

The difficulty is that senders may not know which messages are being routed to email domains and which are being routed to domains used to distribute SMS messages to mobile phones. Mobile service providers maintain specific domain names that are dedicated to messaging to mobile devices, but message senders need a way to know which domains these are so that they can avoid sending to those domains without prior consent.

For this reason, the FCC created the *Wireless Domain Registry* of Internet domain names that are used to distribute messages to mobile devices, primarily as SMS text messages. Mobile service providers are required to submit updated domain names to the list and to report any updates or changes within 30 days. Senders of any commercial electronic messages are required to maintain an updated copy of the list.

Anyone sending commercial electronic messages must either exclude these domains from their messages or comply with the FCC's rules to procure prior and specific consent from recipients before sending. The Wireless Domain Registry is a service provided to help senders avoid inadvertently violating the rules.

Telecommunications Act and Customer Proprietary Network Information

In 1996, the Telecommunications Act represented a historic reform to federal laws that regulate communications businesses. This act provided sweeping changes to a wide variety of regulations. With respect to privacy regulation, the Telecommunications Act implements rules for customer proprietary network information (CPNI).

CPNI refers to metadata information that communications companies collect about subscriber telephone calls. CPNI includes data about phone calls such as call dates and times, length of calls, callers' network provider, and the phone numbers on both ends of incoming and outgoing calls. In addition to phone call data, CPNI includes data about the subscriber, such as the carrier services used (such as long-distance or conference calling) and billing details.

Clearly, this information is very personal to many people. The rules for CPNI are intended to limit the unauthorized sharing of CPNI, improve information security, and ensure that subscribers know how their information is collected, used, and disclosed.

Scope

Regulations around CPNI apply to telecommunications carriers. The Telecommunications Act's definition of a carrier is quite simple: any business that charges a fee for providing telecommunications services to the public. CPNI rules also apply to VoIP providers, which the act defines as service providers that connect real-time voice communications to or from traditional telephone networks, Internet-protocol devices, and end-user devices over broadband.

It doesn't matter if the carrier is a small or large business. Regardless of scale, all carriers are required to file an annual report with the FCC certifying their compliance with CPNI handling rules.

Requirements

The Telecommunications Act empowers the FCC to make rules for regulating the use and sharing of CPNI by telecommunications providers. The rules permit carriers to use CPNI internally to communicate with customers about their existing services and provide general customer service. Carriers may also use CPNI for billing and collections, to prevent identity theft or other forms of fraud, to respond to court orders, or if there is a real emergency need. Outside of these limited allowed uses, carriers are required to obtain consent before sharing an individual's CPNI.

The FCC requires carriers to implement safeguards to protect their subscribers' personal information. These include security controls to prevent criminals from posing as subscribers. Service providers must verify customer identities by checking a photo ID if in person or by using passwords online and over the phone. As with other regulations for safeguarding information discussed in this chapter, the FCC's rules also require appropriate employee training on these safeguards, and carriers must keep records of any outside sharing of CPNI along with documentation of subscriber consent.

CPNI rules include robust notification requirements for carriers. Carriers must inform customers about how to exercise their rights to opt out of information sharing. Carriers must also notify customers of any significant changes to their account information, such as names, passwords, or addresses, in order to help detect intrusions. In the case of a data breach involving CPNI, carriers must first notify law enforcement agencies within seven days of learning about the breach and then notify any affected subscribers.

 CPNI does not include SMS text messages. The FCC classifies text messages as "information services" rather than telecommunications services. Text messages are therefore not regulated as CPNI.

Cable Communications Policy Act

The Cable Communications Policy Act (CCPA) of 1984 was a sweeping overhaul of federal laws applying to cable television providers. This act is an example of a congressional move toward simplifying and reducing regulations to encourage the growth of the cable industry through increased competition and consumer choice. The act includes key privacy provisions that protect consumer information.

Scope

The CCPA and its privacy provisions apply to "cable television system operators." These are cable companies that use a cable system to deliver their services. The act applies to companies that deliver services through third-party partners, any entity that owns a significant stake in a cable company, and any company helping to run cable systems. Modern streaming video services provided over the Internet are not usually in scope because these services do not meet the law's definition of providing cable service.

Requirements

In general, cable companies are not allowed to collect any personally identifiable information (PII) from subscribers without first obtaining consent in writing. Cable companies may, however, collect PII without additional consent if needed either to deliver their services to the customer or to detect any attempts to steal cable services.

The rules for information disclosure under the act are a bit of a patchwork. Most disclosure of PII requires advance consent; some PII may be disclosed without consent, and some PII may be shared as long as the subscriber has the chance to opt out.

Cable companies may disclose customer PII in order to provide services or to prevent theft of services, just like when collecting information. Cable companies may disclose information in response to court orders as well, as long as they notify the customer of the order. In these cases, subscribers are not asked for consent, nor may subscribers opt out. However, cable companies may share customer names and addresses (but not information about viewing habits) provided that they first give subscribers a chance to opt out.

As with other information privacy regulations, this act requires cable companies to provide customers with a privacy notice when they first sign up for service and annually thereafter. The notice must inform subscribers about what PII is collected, along with how, when, and how often that PII may be used or shared in the future. Cable companies must also give subscribers access to all PII they've collected and allow subscribers to request corrections of any inaccurate information. Cable companies must destroy PII when it is no longer needed.

Enforcement

Although the FCC is the regulator generally overseeing the Cable Communications Policy Act, regulatory authority is shared among all sorts of governmental authorities at the local and national levels. The act also provides consumers with a *private right of action*. Individuals may pursue civil litigation against a cable company in the federal district court system. Plaintiffs may seek to recover actual damages as well as punitive damages, along with court costs.

Video Privacy Protection Act (VPPA) of 1988

The Video Privacy Protection Act (VPPA) was passed in 1988, back in the days when customers still went to video stores to rent movies to watch at home. The VPPA was designed to protect an individual's video rental or purchase history from potentially embarrassing disclosure. Even though the VPPA was enacted before online streaming services took over the home video industry, its provisions still impact streaming media regulations because courts have begun to interpret the VPPA as applicable to streaming video services as well.

Scope

VPPA applies to any PII collected from a consumer during transactions to rent, buy, or subscribe to the services or products of a *videotape service provider*. Such providers include anyone involved in providing audio/video materials for rental or purchase. Those who deliver audio video materials are also considered videotape service providers under the law.

Requirements

Any PII collected by a videotape service provider may only be shared with the customer, with written consent from the customer, in response to a court order, or as needed to conduct regular business, such as billing operations. Much like the sharing provision of the CCPA, the videotape service providers are also allowed to share customer names and addresses—and nothing else—as long as they give the customer a chance to opt out.

When the VPPA was first drafted in 1988, the act was unclear on what constituted written consent from a consumer. In 2012, Congress amended the act to clarify consent and to explicitly allow electronic consent, as long as that electronic consent is not buried in other user agreements. The consumer may give ongoing consent for up to two years and must be able to withdraw consent at any time.

Enforcement

The VPPA also provides a Private Right of Action and enables individuals to sue videotape service providers for violations. Consumers may seek actual and punitive damages along with court costs. Finally, the VPPA preempts state law only if a state law allows or even requires *more* disclosure than is permitted by the VPPA. State and local laws, however, may enact and enforce stricter protections against the disclosure of PII.

Driver's Privacy Protection Act (DPPA)

The Driver's Privacy Protection Act of 1994 (DPPA) was enacted to prevent states from releasing personal information from their state Departments of Motor Vehicles (DMV) driver's licensing databases. Prior to the DPPA, states could sell or share DMV data without restriction. For example, this information was used by extremists to track and harass providers and patients of abortion services. Such data could also be accessed by stalkers or to locate celebrities.

Scope

The DPPA applies to all states in the United States and requires that they protect the following personal information found in driver records:

- Name
- Address
- Telephone number
- Social Security number
- Driver identification number
- Photograph
- Height, weight, gender, and age
- Medical/disability information
- Fingerprints

Requirements

The DPPA prohibits states from indiscriminately sharing DMV data. The DPPA still allows states to share DMV data for several permissible purposes, including sharing with government agencies, in cases of vehicle theft, for managing motor vehicle records and titles, to conduct "the normal course of business" for DMV operations, for criminal or civil legal proceedings, for research purposes (as long as personal information remains private), for insurance, to notify owners of vehicle impounds, for authorized investigations, for employer license verification, and for tolls. States are also permitted to authorize DMV data sharing for other purposes as long as "such use is related to the operation of a motor vehicle or public safety." All other disclosures of DMV data are permitted only with the written consent of the license holder. States may still sell or transfer DMV data to third-party entities, but those third parties are also subject to the DPPA's provisions.

Enforcement

The DPPA provides individuals with a private right of action, allowing them to sue anyone who obtains, discloses, or uses information from their driver's record in a manner inconsistent with the DPPA. Courts may award actual damages, punitive damages, reasonable attorneys' fees, litigation costs, and other relief deemed appropriate by the court.

Digital Advertising and Data Ethics

Digital advertising continues to reshape the marketing industry. Digital advertisers are able to collect massive data sets on consumers, often through data brokers, by tracking individuals' online activities across websites. Advertisers are able to construct profiles of individual behaviors and employ artificial intelligence to predict consumer preferences or influence decisions about consumers. Consumers are often unaware that information about their online activities is being collected and sold.

Many regulations at the state and federal levels require businesses to disclose their privacy practices in some form, but these requirements vary widely by jurisdiction. Many privacy advocates support the notion that businesses should adopt ethical approaches to managing personal information regardless of jurisdiction. Industry self-regulatory frameworks offer common codes of ethics to meet this need.

The International Chamber of Commerce's (ICC's) *Advertising and Marketing Communications Code* (`https://iccwbo.org/publication/icc-advertising-and-marketing-communications-code/`) is one commonly used self-regulatory framework. The ICC code rests on core principles that help marketing and communications businesses to disclose their practices. The core principles require that "all marketing communication should be legal, decent, honest and truthful." The ICC *Advertising and Marketing Communications Code* provides detailed instructions to help businesses implement the core principles and disclose their practices. Self-regulatory frameworks may help businesses build trust with consumers and, at the same time, support compliance with many privacy laws.

Web Scraping

Web scraping is the process of automatically extracting information from websites. This technique is widely used across various industries for purposes such as market research, price comparison, sentiment analysis, and data aggregation. By leveraging web scraping, organizations can gather large volumes of data quickly and efficiently, providing valuable insights and competitive intelligence.

Web scraping involves using bots or software programs to load web pages, extract the desired data, and store it in a structured format, such as a database or spreadsheet. Although web scraping can be an incredibly powerful tool, it also comes with legal and ethical considerations. Websites may have terms of service that prohibit scraping, and unauthorized scraping can lead to technical restrictions, legal actions, or damage to the website's infrastructure.

Organizations performing web scraping must ensure compliance with applicable laws and regulations, such as the Computer Fraud and Abuse Act (CFAA) in the United States, which can penalize unauthorized access to computer systems. Ethical web-scraping practices include respecting restrictions placed on websites by their owners and avoiding actions that would disrupt the normal functioning of the website.

Summary

Privacy protection across the private sector in the United States is provided by a complicated and interrelated set of laws, agencies, and court decisions. Information privacy professionals need to be familiar with these legislative acts as well as the agencies that provide guidance and enforcement. In general, federal regulation of the private sector is an ever-shifting balance of individual privacy rights, business interests, encouraging innovation, and encouraging competition in the market. Many of these regulations support these goals by allowing businesses to use personal data but requiring disclosure to customers, privacy programs that include safeguards, and some abilities for customers to see and correct their personal data.

Privacy professionals must be able to understand the requirements of these various laws in order to lead organizations into compliance. As discussed in the case study on Microsoft's privacy statement, privacy professionals often accomplish this goal by helping organizations build comprehensive privacy programs along with a unified public privacy notice. Such a program seeks to satisfy requirements for all applicable privacy statutes in a coherent and unified way.

Privacy regulation of the private sector represents a balance of competing imperatives. These include the rights of private citizens, the need to promote consumer choice as a tool to encourage competition in free markets, the use of personal data necessary to conduct business, and the need for governmental entities to access personal data for regulation, law enforcement, and national security.

Exam Essentials

Distinguish the role of the FTC in private sector data protection.   Some sectors are regulated under industry-specific laws. For example, the financial, communications, and education sectors all operate under regulations targeted to their sector. The FTC, however, provides general regulatory authority across industry based on section 5 of the FTC Act. Section 5 grants the FTC broad authority to enforce privacy rules as derived from its authority to regulate unfair and deceptive trade practices.

Identify the basic principles of privacy and security programs.   Many private sector regulations include rules that require organizations to implement privacy and security programs to safeguard information. Many of these requirements are very similar. They require a person to be in charge of the program; the program must be written down, communicated to consumers, and (often) regularly assessed. Most of these programs have goals that include safeguarding personal information from cyberthreats as well as unauthorized access via technical, physical, and administrative controls.

Differentiate the various forms of consent.   Many private sector regulations provide some individual control over the collection, use, and/or sharing of personal information by allowing people to make choices about how their information is managed. Some regulations, such as COPPA, require businesses to obtain express written consent in advance in order to collect, use, or share personal information. Other regulations allow information collection and sharing unless people opt out.

Recognize extra protections for vulnerable populations.   Privacy laws usually strike a balance between supporting businesses and protecting consumers. However, this balance often tips in favor of consumers when it comes to more vulnerable people. For example, COPPA adds special protections for children and regulatory burdens for businesses, and the 21st Century Cures Act adds protections for people with substance use disorders.

Understand how laws regulating advertising have evolved.   Beginning with mailing addresses and telephone numbers, businesses have long used personal information to bombard consumers with unsolicited advertising. Regulations have evolved to regulate the use of private data for marketing via phone, fax, text messages, and email. Many of these laws are now being interpreted by the court system as applicable to newer channels that include social media and Internet advertising. For the exam, it will be helpful to understand which privacy provisions were added by which regulations.

Know the exceptions.   Each major piece of privacy legislation contains important exemptions that usually grant additional rights to individuals or extra leeway to businesses. For the exam, it is important to understand the logic behind exceptions for individual laws. Exemptions that allow businesses to use personal information without consent often include responding to court orders and using information as needed to conduct business or detect fraud.

Review Questions

1. Which one of the following problems was the Red Flags Rule *primarily* designed to help detect?

   A. A data security breach

   B. Consumer identity theft

   C. Unauthorized access to information by an employee of a financial institution

   D. Inaccurate information contained in a consumer credit report

2. The Dodd–Frank Act created which federal agency empowered with broad enforcement authority for financial privacy regulations?

   A. The Bureau of Consumer Protection

   B. The Commodity Futures Trading Commission

   C. The Consumer Financial Protection Bureau

   D. The Securities and Exchange Commission

3. NetBank is a new online financial institution that has engaged a marketing firm for a telephone advertising campaign without bothering to check the National Do Not Call Registry. NetBank may be investigated by which agency?

   A. FTC

   B. CFPB

   C. FCC

   D. HHS

4. eMaps, Inc., has been investigated for failing to perform an annual review of its privacy policy and procedures as promised in its privacy notice. eMaps enters into an agreement to perform its annual reviews as promised and submits to annual monitoring by the government. This enforcement action is most likely which of the following?

   A. An FTC civil complaint

   B. An FTC consent decree

   C. A civil ruling resulting from a private right of action

   D. A penalty imposed by the Office of Civil Rights

5. Soomin's 11-year-old son is working at the family computer when she notices her son uploading a picture and typing in his mother's cell phone number. When she asks why, he says he has just registered for a video game he wants to play online. Soomin is immediately suspicious. The online video game provider is most likely violating which of the following?

   A. The COPPA requirement to post a privacy notice clearly explaining how data is collected, used, and stored

   B. The VPPA requirement to avoid disclosing video or video game viewing information without consent

    C. The COPPA requirement to obtain express parental consent before collecting PII on children under 13 years old

    D. The rules for protecting CPNI that include the mother's cell phone number

6. MediRecs Co. provides secure server space to help healthcare providers store medical records. MediRecs would best be described under HIPAA as which of the following?

    A. Service provider

    B. Business associate

    C. Covered partner

    D. Covered entity

7. Which of the following is not a regular role for the FTC to play in privacy protection?

    A. Providing programs of public education and information about privacy compliance

    B. Taking enforcement actions to address violations of the FTC Act

    C. Advising lawmakers on new privacy legislation

    D. Adjudicating legal appeals to state-level enforcement actions of individual state privacy laws

8. Dimitri cashed a paycheck at County Bank three months ago, but he doesn't have an account there and hasn't been back since. Under GLBA, County Bank should consider Dimitri as which of the following?

    A. Customer

    B. Consumer

    C. Visitor

    D. No relationship with the bank

9. Under what circumstances might an organization be able to call consumers without regard to the National Do Not Call Registry (DNC)?

    A. The organization is a business that conducts telemarketing calls for advertising but always verbally asks customers if their number is on the DNC before proceeding.

    B. The organization is a business that normally makes calls for advertising but ignores the DNC if the call in question is not intended for sales purposes.

    C. The organization is a business that conducts telemarketing calls for advertising, but the call in question was made by accident because the business forgot to download an updated DNC list last month.

    D. The organization is a business calling recent customers to advertise new products.

10. Which of the following *best* describes FACTA's primary purpose?

    A. To reduce predatory behaviors by creditors

    B. To regulate unsecured credit offers

    C. To protect people from identity theft

    D. To enable consumers to choose which credit reporting agency handles their credit reports

11. Under HIPAA, which of the following is *not* an acceptable reason to share PHI without the consent of the patient?

A. Limited records were provided to the CDC for a study on infectious diseases.

B. Patient contact information was shared with a third-party debt collector.

C. A patient verbally directed their spouse to pick up a prescription.

D. A patient's diagnosis was shared with a prospective employer as part of a preemployment background check.

12. Which of the following is *not* a common feature of information security safeguards required by private sector privacy and security regulations?

A. A documented information security program or policy

B. Designated personnel with responsibility for information security

C. Employee training on information security practices

D. An information security forensics team to analyze cyberattacks

13. In addition to regulating unfair and deceptive practices, the Dodd–Frank Act prohibits financial institutions from engaging in another set of business practices known as which of the following?

A. Abusive

B. Negligent

C. Harmful

D. Wrongful

14. Bella is a senior at Planeville College. She is about to complete her bachelor of arts degree and is applying to graduate schools in her area. Planeville College may legally release her transcripts to which of the following parties without her express consent? (Choose all that apply.)

A. The graduate schools where Bella is applying

B. Bella's legal guardians

C. A state research study on graduation and retention rates

D. The foundation providing Bella's scholarship funds

15. Under HIPAA, patients have the right to view all of the following in their medical files except:

A. Psychotherapy notes

B. Medical diagnoses

C. Treatment records

D. Billing records

16. Mary is collecting background information on a potential client. Which of the following types of information would most likely cause this to be considered a consumer credit report? (Choose all that apply.)

    A. Educational background

    B. General reputation

    C. Marital status

    D. Mode of living

17. Sandy is an information privacy professional at a large health information clearinghouse in Nevada that has just suffered a breach of PHI impacting 800 Nevadans. What are the notification requirements Sandy should follow?

    A. Notify victims within 60 days, and notify HHS in an annual report.

    B. Notify HHS within 60 days, and provide notice to victims as part of the required annual privacy notice.

    C. Notify HHS, and place a prominent notice in local media outlets within 60 days.

    D. Notify victims and HHS, and place a notice in prominent local media outlets within 60 days.

18. What may be the most important *current* impact of VPAA regulation?

    A. Protecting historic records of video viewing habits from unwanted disclosure

    B. The extension of VPAA privacy protections to DVD sales and rentals

    C. Implications for movie theaters

    D. The emerging applicability of VPAA privacy protections to streaming media

19. Mark is a chef starting a new restaurant. He messages all his friends on his favorite social media platform to invite them to book a table at his restaurant. As a side note, Mark also provided an update on his family and said he looked forward to catching up. Should Mark's message be regulated under CAN-SPAM, and why?

    A. Yes, because the message mentioned a commercial topic.

    B. No, because the message was also about catching up with friends.

    C. Yes, because the primary purpose was commercial even though Mark mentioned personal topics as well.

    D. No, because Mark was messaging over social media and not via email.

20. CureSearch is a medical research firm that analyzes electronic results from new medical drug trials. Assuming that the information sharing is appropriate under the law, which piece of legislation most likely allows CureSearch to readily access the study results?

    A. HIPAA

    B. HITECH

    C. The 21st Century Cures Act

    D. The Confidentiality of Substance Use Disorder Patient Records Rule

Chapter 6

Government and Court Access to Private Sector Information

THE CIPP/US EXAM OBJECTIVES COVERED IN THIS CHAPTER INCLUDE:

✓ **Domain III. Government and Court Access to Private-Sector Information**

- III.A. Law Enforcement and Privacy
  - III.A.a Access to Financial Data
  - III.A.b Access to Communications
  - II.A.c The Communications Assistance to Law Enforcement
- III.B. National Security and Privacy
  - III.B.a Foreign Intelligence Surveillance Act of 1978 (FISA)
  - III.B.b USA Patriot Act of 2001
  - III.B.c The USA Freedom Act of 2015
  - III.B.d The Cybersecurity Information Sharing Act of 2015 (CISA)
- III.C. Civil Litigation and Privacy
  - III.C.a Compelled Disclosure of Media Information
  - III.C.b Electronic Discovery

The U.S. government routinely seeks access to personal information to support criminal investigations, national security, and civil litigation processes. However, U.S. citizens are guaranteed certain rights under the Constitution that limit the government's power to interfere in their lives. The Fourth Amendment to the U.S. Constitution protects U.S. citizens from "unreasonable searches and seizures" by federal agencies without a legal warrant. The Fourth Amendment covers "persons, houses, papers, and effects." Although such sweeping language may seem at first to guarantee broad privacy protection from federal authorities, the legal picture is much more complicated.

Over the years, Supreme Court decisions have further defined the reasonable expectation of privacy individuals enjoy under the Constitution. In some cases, Court rulings have revealed conditions in which the Fourth Amendment does not protect individual privacy. In other situations, the obligations of the government are unclear. In many of these instances, the federal government has enacted legislation to address questions left open by the Constitution relating to the government's authority to conduct searches. This chapter further explores the laws governing the federal government's ability to access personal information.

Law Enforcement and Privacy

In 1976, the Supreme Court took up a case where the defendant, Mitchell Miller, argued that federal prosecutors should not be allowed to use evidence in court from certain financial records. The evidence, microfilm of checks and deposit slips, had been acquired directly from Miller's banks in response to a subpoena *duces tecum* (request to present evidence). Miller argued that these records were his private papers and protected by the Fourth Amendment. In this case, Miller argued, law enforcement would have needed a search warrant in order to obtain the records.

The Supreme Court disagreed in the landmark *United States v. Miller* ruling. The Court's ruling asserted that the financial records in question did not belong to Miller. Instead, these records belonged to the banks as part of the records financial institutions must maintain to do business. This ruling means that the Constitution does not prevent financial institutions from responding to a properly authorized subpoena.

Furthermore, this ruling had implications for establishing the limits of constitutional privacy protection generally, not only for financial records. This ruling gave rise to an understanding of constitutional privacy protection known as the *third-party doctrine*. This doctrine means that once a person voluntarily turns certain information over to a third party for transactions, the individual is usually no longer considered the owner of that information. Constitutional protections, therefore, may not apply.

Access to Financial Data

Because the Constitution does not automatically protect the privacy of personal information once given to third parties, the federal government has enacted legislation to control government access to financial data. This legislation attempts to balance individual privacy with law enforcement needs. This section will explore two legislative acts with a direct bearing on law enforcement and financial privacy.

Right to Financial Privacy Act (RFPA) of 1978

Following the *Miller* Supreme Court ruling, the legislature saw the need to offer some regulation and guidance on how federal authorities can access financial data. The RFPA lays out the process federal authorities must follow to request customer data from a financial institution and grants certain privacy rights to the customers of financial institutions. The RFPA does not provide the same level of privacy protection for financial records held by banks as the Fourth Amendment. The act does, however, prevent unfettered government access without due process.

RFPA Scope

The RFPA regulates requests for customer records between the federal government and private financial institutions. The act applies to the entire federal government, including federal law enforcement agencies. The RFPA does not apply to state or local governments or any private organizations.

The RFPA applies when the federal government requests customer information from financial institutions. The RFPA borrows the definition of *financial institutions* from the Consumer Credit Protection Act (CCPA), discussed in Chapter 5, "Private Sector Data Collection." Finally, the RFPA provides rights for customers to protect their data. Under the act, a *person* may be an individual *or* a group of up to five people who do business in some form with a financial institution.

There are many exceptions to the RFPA that permit financial institutions to share customer information with the federal government without regard to RFPA requirements. For example, disclosures may be made to *supervisory agencies* or government agencies that regulate financial institutions themselves. These agencies include the Securities and Exchange Commission (SEC), the Federal Deposit Insurance Corporation (FDIC), the Consumer Financial Protection Bureau (CFPB), and more. These agencies may examine financial records because they are regulating the financial institutions themselves and not investigating customers. Other exceptions in the RFPA permit disclosures in order to avoid conflicts with other laws and statutes, such as the Internal Revenue Code. Disclosures may also be made if the information does not identify specific customers, in response to appropriate court orders, and in certain emergency situations related to national security. Finally, customer financial information may be disclosed when a bank files a suspicious activity report (SAR). SARs are discussed in the section on the Bank Secrecy Act.

RFPA Requirements

The act requires that requests for protected information be made with appropriate authority, for a good reason, and with appropriate documentation. The RFPA further requires the government to notify customers of requests and give them the chance to object before obtaining their financial information.

The act prohibits the disclosure of customer information to federal agencies unless the financial records are "reasonably described." This means that federal agencies may not just go fishing for information without specificity. The request and the disclosure must also be authorized in one of the following ways:

Customer Authorization   The customer may authorize the disclosure voluntarily with a specific written statement.

Administrative or Judicial Subpoena   The government may obtain an appropriate judicial or administrative subpoena or summons to obtain customer financial information. The customer must receive a copy on or before the date the subpoena is served on the bank and has the opportunity to challenge it.

Search Warrant   A federal agency may also obtain information from a bank through a search warrant. In this case, the customer must be notified no later than 90 days after a warrant is issued, unless a court authorizes a further delay in notification.

Formal written Request   An agency may also make a formal written request directly to a bank. These requests must follow specific rules and operate much like a subpoena. These requests are discussed in more detail next.

The last of these is the most permissive criteria for federal agencies. The RFPA, however, regulates these requests to ensure fairness and provide some individual rights. Government agencies may only make such a request if the information cannot be obtained through a subpoena process, and requests must satisfy several requirements:

- Requests must be made in accordance with the legal authority granted to the specific agency making the request.
- They must have a plausible belief that the requested information is "relevant to a legitimate law enforcement inquiry."
- The government must provide the customer with a copy of the request. This copy must be sent to the customer on or before the date the request is sent to the bank, and the copy must include instructions enabling the customer to object to the requested disclosure.

For subpoenas or formal written requests, customers have 10 days to object. If the request was mailed, then the customer is allowed 14 days from the date of mailing. Customers may be required to argue their challenge in court and may choose to use a lawyer. Federal agencies are not required to track customers down to ensure they receive a copy of the request. The law requires only that the notice be sent to a customer's last known address.

Exam Tip

For the exam, pay special attention to time periods specified by any regulation. One such example from the RFPA is the period allowed for a customer to object to a requested disclosure or subpoena. The customer is allowed 10 days from receiving notice of the request. However, if the request was mailed, then the customer is allowed 14 days from the date of mailing.

RFPA Enforcement

The RFPA provides for a *private right of action* that allows plaintiffs to pursue civil damages in a U.S. district court. If a customer believes their rights under the RFPA have been violated, they have three years from the date of that violation to bring a complaint forward in court. Individual federal agencies that violate the statute could be liable for civil penalties of $100 per violation, actual damages, or potential punitive damages (if the court thinks the violation was intentional), as well as the plaintiff's legal costs. Individual employees of the federal government could also face disciplinary consequences if they are found to have knowingly violated customer rights. Finally, a district court may impose additional sanctions against a federal agency, such as requiring the destruction of any records that have been obtained illegally.

Bank Secrecy Act of 1970

Unlike the RFPA, the Bank Secrecy Act (BSA) was not formulated to protect individual privacy. On the contrary, the BSA was established to help federal law enforcement agencies combat money laundering. Criminals may use money laundering schemes to hide profits from illegal activities, finance terrorism, evade taxes, and more. The BSA requires financial institutions to monitor, document, and retain records and to report suspicious activities around financial transactions. The BSA creates a paper trail and monitoring system that allows federal investigators to connect the financial dots as money changes hands.

Exam Tip

The BSA is also known as the Currency and Foreign Transactions Reporting Act. It is a good idea to be familiar with both names for the exam.

BSA Scope

The BSA applies to organizations defined as *financial institutions*. The BSA uses a unique definition for financial institutions rather than drawing on one from another law. This definition includes more organizations than one might expect. Banks, credit unions, brokerages, and investment firms are certainly included. But so are currency exchanges, any organization offering credit cards, any business offering traveler's or cashier's checks, precious metal or jewelry dealers, pawnbrokers, travel agencies, telegraph companies, vehicle sales companies, gambling operations, and even the U.S. Postal Service.

This broad definition of financial institution intends to cover all the avenues criminals might use to hide the transfer of wealth. For example, a criminal may use ill-gotten cash to buy gems, sell those gems for cash, and deposit the cash in a legitimate bank account. The definition of financial institutions in the BSA makes such transactions more easily traceable by law enforcement.

BSA Requirements

The BSA requires financial institutions to create and maintain records of financial transactions and to monitor accounts and transactions for signs of money laundering. Banks are obligated to report certain types of transactions or suspicious activity to the government.

Under the BSA, financial institutions must keep most financial transaction records for at least five years in case these records need to be made available for law enforcement. The information that must be retained includes records of account statements, checks, deposits, certificates of deposit, credit, and more. The BSA is also specific about what information must be preserved in the record for each of these types of transactions.

Financial Institutions must have an Anti-Money Laundering (AML) program in place. The AML program must include procedures and controls for compliance, periodic third-party assessment, identified personnel responsible for the program, and appropriate staff training. Finally, the BSA was modified by the USA-PATRIOT Act in 2001. After this modification, all banks must implement a customer identification program (CIP) as part of their AML program. The CIP requirement compels banks to have procedures for identifying customers, as the law puts it, "to the extent reasonable and practicable." The CIP must include procedures for obtaining and verifying identifying information from customers that includes their name, date of birth, address, and an appropriate identification number, such as a taxpayer ID number.

For an example of corporate compliance with the AML requirement, see Bank of America's website describing its AML program:

```
investor.bankofamerica.com/index.php/corporate-
governance/anti-money-laundering
```

In addition to retaining records and monitoring transactions for possible signs of money laundering, financial institutions must actively report certain customer activity to the U.S. Treasury Department's Financial Crimes Enforcement Network (FinCEN).

Currency Transaction Report (CTR)   A financial institution is required to notify FinCEN of any transaction activity that totals more than $10,000 in a given day for a customer. This could occur through multiple transactions, different accounts, and different physical locations. If any combination of deposits or withdrawals totals $10,000 per day or more, the financial institution must file a CTR within 15 days. A CTR does not often indicate illegal activity, but it does ensure additional government oversight for large movements of cash.

Suspicious Activity Report (SAR)   Financial institutions are required to file an SAR whenever they have reason to notice financial activity that might indicate money laundering or other violations of the law. In addition to whatever triggers may be specifically identified in an institution's AML program, the BSA lays out a few conditions, such as large transactions and any abuse by company insiders.

Importantly, the BSA prohibits financial institutions from notifying customers when filing an SAR. Because the SAR contains personal financial records pertaining to an identifiable customer, this makes the SAR an important exception to the RFPA described in the previous section.

Although the CTR and SAR are the most well-known reporting requirements of the BSA, the act has other reporting requirements as well. Examples include the Report of International Transportation of Currency or Monetary Instruments (CMIR) and the Report of Foreign Bank and Financial Accounts (FBAR).

BSA Enforcement

The Bank Secrecy Act is enforced by the U.S. Treasury Department. Several federal agencies involved in regulating the financial sector may bring enforcement actions. FinCEN often takes the lead in investigating violations. Civil penalties may be assessed against banks or individuals for violations of different provisions of the act, such as a failure to keep records or a failure to file a required report. It is important to remember, however, that the BSA is intended to prevent money laundering and other financial crimes. An investigation into BSA violations may turn up criminal offenses as well.

Access to Communications

The Fourth Amendment protects citizens from warrantless searches and seizures involving "their persons, houses, papers, and effects. . . ." Clearly, the Fourth Amendment protects the privacy of communications conducted by mail, as was the case in the late 18th century.

However, the Constitution was written long before the advent of modern communications technologies. It was less clear whether the same privacy protections applied to electronic communications that were conducted via telephone or, later, via digital computing technologies.

In the 1960s, the FBI collected enough evidence to arrest and prosecute a man named Charles Katz for running an illegal interstate gambling operation. Katz was using public phone booths to place his illegal bets, and the FBI bugged those phone booths. After his arrest, Katz argued that the evidence collected was inadmissible under his Fourth Amendment rights because it had been collected without a search warrant. Katz argued his case to the Supreme Court. The Court ruled decisively for Katz and established the precedent that the Fourth Amendment indeed protects oral communications intended to be private, no matter how those conversations are conducted.

In the *Katz v. United States* case, the government argued that Katz was using public phone booths and therefore the conversations were not technically private. The Court disagreed with this argument and enshrined the legal standard that if an individual is in a situation with a "reasonable expectation of privacy," then they are protected by the Fourth Amendment.

Katz is viewed as overturning the precedent set by the landmark 1928 *Olmstead v. United States*, discussed in Chapter 1, "Privacy in the Modern Era."

Although the Supreme Court has ruled that the Fourth Amendment protects oral communications and, more broadly, electronic communications, it is important to keep the *third-party doctrine* in mind. If any communications records are held by third parties, such as communications service providers, then those records are no longer the property of the individual and not protected by the constitutional guarantee of an individual's right to privacy.

Electronic Communications Privacy Act (ECPA)

The Electronic Communications Privacy Act (ECPA) of 1986 commonly refers to a collection of three legislative titles. First, the federal rules around telephone surveillance that were first enacted by the Wiretap Act of 1968 generally protect the privacy of oral communications. Second, the Stored Communications Act (SCA) generally protects digital communications, such as email. Finally, the ECPA regulates technologies for collecting data about communications, known as *pen registers* and *trap-and-trace devices*. These three components of the ECPA are identified as Titles I, II, and III of the law. Taken on the whole, the ECPA represents the primary legislation regulating the ability of the federal government to eavesdrop on U.S. citizens' communications.

Title I: Wiretaps

Title I of the ECPA, known as the *Wiretap Act*, prohibits spying on real-time communications without consent. Although the Wiretap Act was originally designed to protect the privacy of telephone conversations, it applies to any oral conversations conducted by "wire, oral, or electronic communication." Because the law applies to all oral communication, it also regulates the use of hidden recording devices. There are a few important categories of exceptions to the Wiretap Act:

- The law provides an exception for communications service providers that unavoidably overhear some oral communications in the normal course of business.

- Legal eavesdropping by the government is permitted as authorized by appropriate laws, such as the Foreign Intelligence Surveillance Act (FISA), discussed later in this chapter.

- Law enforcement may also intercept communications with appropriate court orders, such as a warrant.

- Communications may be intercepted or recorded with the consent of only one party in the communication.

Exam Tip

Some state privacy laws are stricter than the federal EPCA and require all parties to a conversation to consent before wiretapping may begin. For the exam, it helps to pay attention to whether questions are referring to state or federal laws. State privacy laws are discussed further in Chapter 8, "State Privacy Laws."

Title II: Stored Communications Act (SCA)

As discussed earlier in this chapter, the *third-party doctrine* generally holds that information is no longer protected by the Fourth Amendment once it is turned over to a third party. Because most digital communications, such as email, actually reside on third-party computer services, this is especially problematic. Therefore, Title II extends privacy protections to digital communications that are typically stored on servers owned by service providers. The SCA prohibits unauthorized access to any files stored by service providers as well as information about customers.

The SCA prohibits anyone from unauthorized access to personal electronic communications held by service providers. Information about communications, such as email headers and timestamps, are also protected. Government law enforcement agencies may only access stored electronic communications with appropriate legal authorization, such as a search warrant. The SCA provides a level of protection similar to that provided by the Fourth Amendment.

The SCA includes several exceptions. A category of these exceptions is intended to allow service providers to conduct their business. For example, service providers are allowed to access and disclose communications as necessary to provide service, to forward communications to the intended destination, and with the permission of the originator or intended recipient of the communications. There are also exceptions allowing service providers to disclose communications to the government if they have reason to believe that the disclosure pertains to an emergency that threatens serious physical danger.

CLOUD Act

The *Clarifying Lawful Overseas Use of Data (CLOUD) Act*, enacted in 2018, addresses legal challenges surrounding access to data stored abroad. It amends the SCA to enable U.S. law enforcement agencies to compel U.S.-based technology companies to provide data stored on servers, regardless of the data's physical location. This act resolves jurisdictional issues that previously hindered access to critical information stored in other countries.

Title III: Pen Registers and Trap-and-Trace Devices

Finally, the ECPA regulates the use of technologies that track metadata about communications. These technologies don't usually record the content of a communication but track information about that communication. For example, they may track phone numbers for outgoing and incoming calls, the date and time of communications, and so forth. Typically, *pen registers* (or dialed-number recorders) are devices that track information on outgoing communications, and *trap-and-trace* devices track information on incoming communications. In our age of digital communications, both of these functions may be performed by software or network technologies.

These technologies do not track the content of communications and enjoy somewhat less privacy protection under the law. In general, the law prohibits anyone, including government agencies, from using these technologies to track communications unless authorized by another law (such as FISA) or court order.

The ECPA represents federal legislation and does not preempt state laws. Many states have more stringent requirements for disclosure than ECPA. For example, the ECPA requires only one party to a conversation to consent to intercepting or recording a conversation. Eleven states, however, have laws that require all parties to a conversation to consent before a conversation can be intercepted or recorded.

The Communications Assistance for Law Enforcement Act (CALEA)

CALEA is another law intended to assist law enforcement rather than to enhance individual privacy. CALEA requires companies that manufacture telecommunications devices and telecommunications carriers to enable authorized government surveillance. CALEA requires telecommunications companies to make government wiretapping capabilities baked-in features of their products and services. CALEA also requires that telecommunications companies provide reasonable assistance and consulting to law enforcement.

CALEA enables law enforcement to pursue legally authorized surveillance consistent with laws such as the Fourth Amendment and the ECPA. CALEA does not create new privacy rules or lower the legal bar for authorizing law enforcement to conduct searches. Rather, CALEA helps law enforcement carry out legal searches and prevents telecommunications carriers and manufacturers from designing products and services in a way that impedes law enforcement.

There are important limitations to CALEA. It does not authorize the government to perform mass surveillance of U.S. citizens. Therefore, CALEA further makes telecommunications companies responsible for ensuring that these capabilities don't inadvertently reveal private communications that are not covered by whatever legal process authorizes a given search. Furthermore, CALEA does not allow the government to require carriers or manufacturers to implement specific features or technologies, nor may the government prohibit specific features or technologies. If, for example, the FCC were to develop a government spyware app for smartphones, manufacturers could not be compelled to install it. Finally, telecommunications companies may not be compelled to help the government decrypt any encrypted communications. There is an exception when the company itself provided the encryption and already has decryption information available to disclose.

Apple Takes on the FBI

CALEA has been criticized both for failing to adequately support law enforcement and for giving the government too much power to invade privacy. This controversy was thrust into the public sphere after a 2016 terrorist shooting killed 14 people in San Bernardino, CA. The gunmen were killed by the police, and an iPhone was recovered from one of the attackers. The FBI ordered Apple to help decrypt the phone, relying on the All Writs Act of 1789. Apple refused, and an extensive legal battle ensued where initial court judgments sided with Apple.

The FBI eventually dropped the case before it was fully litigated, but the case brought new controversy around CALEA. Although the All Writs Act does empower law enforcement to order assistance from companies, there is a Supreme Court precedent holding that, where an existing federal statute is in force, that statute trumps the All Writs Act.

Because CALEA does not compel Apple to help law enforcement break encryption, law enforcement advocates raised concerns. Some began to lobby for amendments to CALEA to give more power to law enforcement to compel cooperation from telecommunications companies, especially to prevent terrorism. On the other hand, many privacy advocates hold that CALEA gives the government too much surveillance power as it is. Even though CALEA includes due process requirements, some privacy advocates feel the technological capabilities CALEA requires could be too easily exploited by the government.

National Security and Privacy

The statutory approach to regulating privacy while protecting national security is a study in contrast. The government needs to gather as much intelligence as possible to discover and prevent terrorist acts. Private citizens, on the other hand, have established rights to privacy under the Fourth Amendment and other laws. This tension is not dissimilar from the tensions surrounding the needs of law enforcement and individual rights in other areas of law.

When it comes to national security and preventing terrorism, however, the stakes are much higher. To combat foreign powers or root out terrorism, intelligence gathering must be conducted in secret. Intelligence must sometimes be gathered quickly, and the consequences of missing something may be far more deadly than in a regular criminal investigation. When it comes to preventing terrorism, lawmakers have leaned toward granting more power to the government than they would allow for regular law enforcement activities.

This area of law is not without controversy. Critics worry that the government may exploit fear of terrorism in the national imagination to erode individual rights. Government watchdogs worry that extraordinary powers to spy on Americans may be misused beyond the national security context to target activists or political opponents. The debate continues as lawmakers work to balance our national security with our constitutional freedoms.

Foreign Intelligence Surveillance Act (FISA) of 1978

In the mid-1970s, the nation was rocked by the Watergate scandal. Public trust in the government, already eroded by the controversies surrounding the Vietnam War, declined even further. Lengthy investigations revealed that President Nixon had been spying illegally on his political opponents. Worse, the investigation revealed that the president had secretly directed federal agencies to spy on Americans for his own political purposes. Richard Nixon became the first president in U.S. history to resign from office.

In the ensuing years, the United States wrestled with how to rebuild trust in the federal government through appropriate regulation. Legislators saw the need for statutory oversight and accountability so that a powerful president would never again be able to exploit the immense power of the presidency to violate constitutional rights. At the same time, such oversight could not unduly curtail the government's ability to conduct legitimate intelligence-gathering activities, which must often be kept secret to protect national security.

In 1977, Senator Ted Kennedy introduced the Foreign Intelligence Surveillance Act (FISA) to provide a legal framework to manage government spying. FISA limits surveillance to appropriate foreign targets and sets legal processes for due process and oversight. FISA keeps most of these processes secret for national security reasons but ensures that no single federal office has the power to authorize government surveillance without oversight. Principle features of FISA include the following:

Surveillance of Foreign Powers   FISA was designed to help the government track foreign agents spying on the United States. Under FISA, the government may authorize surveillance activities without meeting the standard set by the Fourth Amendment, as long as the surveillance targets are not "United States persons." FISA's definition of "United States person" refers to individuals who may be protected by the U.S. Constitution. The definition includes U.S. citizens, legal aliens, permanent U.S. residents, and even U.S. corporations. Federal law enforcement agencies may obtain authorization for surveillance under FISA if they have probable cause to think the surveillance target is an agent of a foreign power, even if there's no reason to believe actual criminal activity has occurred.

Authorization for Specific Forms of Surveillance   When FISA was first passed, it included rules to authorize the government to conduct electronic surveillance, such as wiretapping. In the years since, FISA has been amended to include the ability to authorize pen registers, trap-and-trace devices, clandestine physical entry and search, and the ability to request some financial records. FISA only authorizes government surveillance if pursuing foreign intelligence is a "significant" purpose of the investigation.

The Foreign Intelligence Surveillance Court (FISC)   The FISC is a special court established for the purpose of overseeing FISA intelligence-gathering activities. FISC exists in parallel to the public U.S. judicial system but operates in secret. The chief justice of the Supreme Court appoints 11 district court judges to serve as the FISC justices. The U.S. attorney general's office must apply to the FISC for secret warrants that permit the government to conduct surveillance under FISA. FISC warrants may last for 90 days, for 120 days, or for up to one year before they must be reauthorized by the FISC.

Authority for Warrantless Surveillance   The U.S. attorney general may also authorize surveillance without a FISC warrant for up to one year if the surveillance is only targeted at foreign powers and there is "no substantial likelihood" that the surveillance will pick up communications of U.S. persons. The U.S. attorney general must certify that the investigation meets FISA requirements and share a sealed copy of that certification with the chief justice.

Surveillance of U.S. Persons Acting as Agents of Foreign Powers   Of course, U.S. persons, including full U.S. citizens, may also be working as spies for a foreign power. In this case, the Fourth Amendment still applies, and the government must show probable cause to believe criminal activity is involved in obtaining authorization for surveillance. Importantly, FISA notes that U.S. persons enjoy the First Amendment right to free speech and that the exercise of free speech alone cannot constitute a probable cause of criminal activity. FISA was designed during the Cold War era, and this provision had special significance. Many U.S. persons exercised their First Amendment rights to criticize the U.S. government and to support socialist or other pro-USSR political beliefs. Under FISA, such speech alone cannot be used as grounds to make a U.S. person the target of government surveillance.

Minimization Principle   FISA provides sweeping authority for secret government surveillance. It is not difficult to imagine the temptation for law enforcement to use intelligence gathered under FISA for criminal investigations. If this were permitted, FISA could become a massive loophole allowing the government to bypass individual rights established by laws such as the EPCA. FISA requires the U.S. attorney general to implement *minimization procedures* to ensure that any intelligence gathered and retained pertains only to the intended investigation and avoids collecting incidental information on U.S. persons. If, for example, the government had a hidden microphone in a restaurant, the minimization procedures may require the creation of a transcript that shares only conversations with the surveillance target.

FISA has been amended many times over the years, most often to expand the government's authority for surveillance. For example, FISA originally authorized surveillance if collecting foreign intelligence was the "primary purpose" of the investigation. After the 9/11 terrorist attacks, the USA-PATRIOT Act lowered that threshold to "significant purpose." The USA-PATRIOT Act also allowed roving wiretaps, which target an individual without requiring the government to specify which devices they plan to surveil for the warrant.

FISA Amendments Act Section 702

Until 2008, FISA required federal intelligence agencies to obtain a warrant from the FISC to authorize wiretapping. Warrant applications had to name specific foreign targets and show probable cause. In the years following 9/11, the U.S. intelligence community rapidly scaled up counter-terrorism operations. The intelligence community and the Bush Administration advocated for the ability to conduct mass surveillance to monitor communications of non-U.S. persons abroad to try to detect and prevent terrorist attacks from potentially unknown actors. In 2008, FISA was amended to expand the government's power to conduct surveillance on non-U.S. persons located outside of the United States. This amendment is known as Section 702.

Section 702 allows the government to obtain a certification, rather than a warrant, from FISC to conduct surveillance. These certifications allow the government to conduct broad surveillance for up to a year. Certifications may be resubmitted and renewed annually thereafter. Certifications issued under Section 702 allow the government to conduct surveillance on categories of people without naming specific targets or showing probable cause. To receive such a certification, the government only needs to show that the surveillance targets are non-U.S. persons who are not on U.S. soil for a legitimate foreign intelligence-gathering purpose. The government also must present documented procedures, including minimization procedures, for safeguarding against the incidental collection or dissemination of information on U.S. persons.

Critics of Section 702 are concerned that this provision grants overly broad surveillance powers to U.S. intelligence agencies with too little oversight. Section 702 enables the U.S. government to collect massive amounts of communications data. Even though the law requires that such wiretapping may only target non-U.S. persons who are not on U.S. soil, the indiscriminate mass collection of communications data is likely to include the personal information of U.S. persons. Despite the requirements for safeguarding against the inadvertent collection of information on U.S. persons, many privacy advocates believe that

Section 702 is ripe for abuse. Parts of the National Security Agency's controversial mass data collection programs, made public by Edward Snowden, were authorized by Section 702.

USA-PATRIOT Act

Following the 9/11 terrorist attacks, the federal government made it an urgent priority to identify and remedy shortcomings in U.S. intelligence services to help prevent future attacks. Following 9/11, the government enjoyed a short period of near-unanimous bipartisan support for initiatives combatting terrorism. Legislation that would previously have been seen as invasive to privacy suddenly became possible. The government moved quickly to introduce legislation to greatly increase the power of the federal government to conduct surveillance and to enable interagency cooperation within the intelligence community. As a result, Congress enacted the Uniting and Strengthening America by Providing Appropriate Tools Required to Intercept and Obstruct Terrorism Act of 2001 (USA-PATRIOT Act, or Patriot Act).

The Patriot Act updated and expanded law enforcement powers in many different statutes, including FISA. This expansive law included provisions that created new criminal offenses related to terrorism, statutes to help victims of terrorist acts, and new powers to help law enforcement combat money-laundering operations that finance terrorism. However, the most controversial provisions of the Patriot Act concerned privacy. Title II of the Patriot Act contains three provisions that allowed the government so much surveillance power that the legislature made the provisions temporary.

> Although these three provisions are broadly associated with the Patriot Act, they actually update the government's authority under FISA and the ECPA, described earlier.

Section 206: Roving Wiretaps

Before the Patriot Act, the government was required to be very specific about wiretapping targets when applying for warrants, even when conducting surveillance under FISA. The government was required to specify exactly which devices, phone numbers, or networks were targeted for wiretapping. The Patriot Act, however, authorized *roving wiretaps* that authorize surveillance of any devices or communications associated with an individual. This was meant to help law enforcement track surveillance subjects even when the target used so-called burner phones—that is, frequently switched phones to elude wiretapping.

Section 206 of the Patriot Act expired in March 2020 and, as of this writing in 2024, has not yet been renewed.

Section 207: The "Lone Wolf" Provision

As discussed earlier, FISA provides a means for the government to authorize the surveillance of foreign powers. Known foreign terrorist organizations are generally considered to be foreign powers, and FISA may be used to authorize surveillance against them. However, FISA did not have a provision for intelligence gathering against a single individual engaged in terrorism if that individual wasn't linked to some sort of foreign power. This provision enabled the government to authorize surveillance under FISA against a single individual—a "lone wolf"—if the government has good reason to believe that the target is involved in international terrorism.

Section 207 of the Patriot Act expired in March 2020 and, as of this writing in 2024, has not yet been renewed.

Section 215: Business Records Provision

Perhaps the most controversial part of the Patriot Act, section 215, allowed the government to apply to the FISC to order a business to share records of any "tangible things" if that investigation is targeted at gathering foreign intelligence. This power to order the production of business records was most concerning to privacy advocates because it allowed federal law enforcement to circumvent the rights and protections afforded to U.S. persons under several other laws. Federal agencies could request the production of anything they deemed relevant to gathering foreign intelligence. This meant that the government could demand information held by third parties without a subpoena or specific warrant and without notifying individuals or giving them the chance to object in court.

In 2013, a young computer specialist named Edward Snowden was working as a contractor with the National Security Agency (NSA) when he became perhaps the most famous whistleblower in the world of privacy. Snowden revealed that the NSA used Section 215 to conduct mass surveillance of Americans for years. The NSA purportedly used the power of the Patriot Act to order access to phone records, text message records, and even email accounts for millions of people. The government has since stated that it has halted this practice for a variety of technical compliance reasons, but Snowden's revelations remain a source of intense controversy.

Section 215 of the Patriot Act expired in March 2020 and, as of this writing in 2024, has not yet been renewed.

National Security Letters

National Security Letters (NSLs) are a form of administrative subpoena used to order the production of business records. NSLs may also include a *gag order*. A gag order legally prohibits the recipient of an NSL, such as an Internet service provider (ISP), from disclosing the government's order. This allows the government to collect private records of U.S. persons with little oversight or public accountability. NSLs have been used to collect stored email and electronic information, phone and text message data, and even web browsing histories. Privacy advocates find this practice controversial because it is difficult to protect against potential abuses of power by government agencies.

NSLs had been in limited use under FISA before the Patriot Act, but Title V of the Patriot Act expanded the use of NSLs. The Patriot Act set a very low bar for authorizing NSLs and made it relatively easy for agencies such as the FBI to obtain and serve these letters. The government's use of these letters soared, and their constitutionality has been challenged in court. Over the years, courts have ruled against the government in several cases, finding the government's use of these letters has sometimes violated the Fourth Amendment, and that gag orders have sometimes violated the First Amendment. In response to these rulings, Congress has periodically attempted to resolve these constitutional issues by updating the rules for using these letters. However, the use of NSLs remains legally problematic.

The Future of the Patriot Act

When it was passed in 2001, Sections 206, 207, and 215 of the Patriot Act were intended to be temporary. Congress wanted the opportunity to reconsider these sweeping governmental powers after the fervor following the devastating attacks of 9/11 had receded. In the following years, Congress continually reauthorized these provisions, but always with revisions that generally enhanced privacy protections and always for another temporary period of time. The most recent large-scale reauthorization was accomplished in 2015 via the USA-FREEDOM Act, discussed next.

However, as of this writing, these three provisions have lapsed and currently sit in legislative limbo. Ongoing investigations may continue to use surveillance techniques authorized by these provisions—but not new investigations. Congress was set to renew these provisions in March 2020, and both the U.S. Senate and House passed some version of a reauthorization. However, the final bill was derailed before it could be negotiated between the two chambers of Congress. Today, the provisions remain expired, and the future of these government surveillance powers remains uncertain.

The USA Freedom Act of 2015

In 2015, the controversial provisions of the Patriot Act were set to expire unless reauthorized by the U.S. Congress. Legislators faced a very different political landscape than they had in 2001 when the Patriot Act was first enacted. Edward Snowden's revelations about the NSA's secret mass surveillance of Americans were fresh, and the public had become increasingly concerned that government agencies had twisted the intent of the Patriot Act to spy on Americans rather than to combat terrorism.

At the same time, federal law enforcement agencies argued that the Patriot Act's expanded surveillance powers had become critically important in the fight against terrorism and could not be allowed to expire. As a compromise, the legislature passed the USA Freedom Act. The Freedom Act reauthorized the expiring provisions of the Patriot Act but included several reforms to curtail government overreach and better protect privacy. These changes were intended to end the NSA's program of mass data collection on Americans, to better protect constitutional rights, and to make legal actions under FISA more transparent to the public.

The name USA-FREEDOM Act stands for the "Uniting and Strengthening America by Fulfilling Rights and Ensuring Effective Discipline Over Monitoring Act."

Several of the most well-known changes the USA Freedom Act made to more controversial Patriot Act provisions included the following:

- Prohibited bulk data collection by requiring the request to list specific search parameters called *selection terms*. Selection terms narrow the request by naming criteria such as specific phone numbers, email addresses, or accounts.

- Subjected requests for pen registers and trap-and-trace devices under FISA to the selection-terms requirement as well.

- Reformed the NSL process by requiring that NSLs specify selection terms, put some restrictions on the government's ability to impose gag orders, and created a process for recipients to object to an NSL or to a gag order in an NSL.

- Strengthened FISA *minimization* requirements to reduce the accidental collection or disclosure of personal information not directly relevant to an investigation.

- Restricted the U.S. attorney general from authorizing requests for business records without applying to the FISC unless there is an emergency.

- Added legal advisers, called *amicus curiae* (friends of the court), to help FISC interpret the legality of requests from the U.S. attorney general.

- Increased transparency by requiring the U.S. attorney general to report regularly to Congress on activities authorized under FISA and requiring periodic review of FISA orders for possible declassification.

Even though the USA Freedom Act added several new requirements to better protect individual privacy rights, Congress was still uncomfortable with making these governmental powers permanent. The USA Freedom Act extended the revised provisions of the Patriot Act only through the end of 2019. As mentioned earlier, the Patriot Act and USA Freedom Act provisions have lapsed, and there has been no progress toward reauthorizing them.

The Cybersecurity Information Sharing Act of 2015

Private companies often hold key information about cyber threats that is of great value to federal law enforcement agencies. If private companies share their intelligence on cyber threats with the government, then federal agencies can assemble disparate information from all over the private sector as well as their own intelligence-gathering operations. By combining information on cyber threats, the government would be better able to track and defend against cyberattacks.

There are, however, barriers for private companies when it comes to sharing cyber-threat information. For example, private companies do not want to risk any details of their internal operations becoming public, lest that information benefit the competition or affect stock prices. Additionally, private sector companies do not want to reveal information that suddenly lands that company in the middle of legal action, such as an FTC or antitrust investigation.

The Cybersecurity Information Sharing Act (CISA) of 2015 removes legal barriers that discourage companies from cooperating. CISA both empowers private companies to implement their own cyber-defense mechanisms and provides ways for companies to share cyber-threat information with the government without endangering themselves.

CISA authorizes private companies to implement their own cyber-defense program to monitor and defend against cyber threats. Companies are allowed to share information that comes from monitoring their own internal IT systems in accordance with CISA. CISA also protects companies from any liabilities under other laws, such as the EPCA, that result from cyber-threat monitoring, as long as the cybersecurity program is conducted as authorized by CISA.

With a cyber-defense and monitoring program in place, private companies are more likely to detect cyber threats in the first place. For clarity, CISA defines *cyber-threat indicators* that may be shared with the government. The law further implements several other provisions that help reduce barriers that may prevent companies from sharing these cyber-threat indicators with the government:

- Private companies are required to remove PII before sharing, so the government only receives data in an anonymized state unless the personal information is related directly to the cyber threat itself.

- CISA reduces liability for companies by exempting them from antitrust liabilities or loss of attorney-client privilege related to sharing.

- The information shared is still designated as proprietary to the company and is exempted from federal and state Freedom of Information request laws.

CISA also permits the government to share nonclassified cyber-threat intelligence with private companies. This, in return, helps to bolster the private companies' cyber-defense programs. Sharing in both directions is voluntary under CISA. Importantly, CISA only protects companies from liability for disclosures that would be otherwise prohibited when information is shared only according to CISA's strict protocols. CISA, therefore, offers a form of *safe harbor* from certain liability under very specific circumstances. Well-known conduits for CISA-compliant information sharing are the Information Sharing and Analysis Centers (ISACs). ISACs are industry-specific, nonprofit organizations that coordinate with federal authorities, such as the Department of Homeland Security, to facilitate information under the CISA safe harbor.

Civil Litigation and Privacy

Any litigation process usually requires parties to share information. They may disclose their own information to make their cases, of course. They also often demand to see information from the other side as well. This process of sharing information is called *discovery*. Information requested during litigation may be subject to privacy rules and may require special handling or authorization. Privacy and disclosure requirements contained in important privacy regulations are described throughout this book. There are a few special rules related to sharing information for legal proceedings that apply to the news media and to the disclosure of electronic information in litigation.

Compelled Disclosure of Media Information

The U.S. Constitution protects the news media in two ways. First, the First Amendment includes language to ensure freedom of the press and prevents the government from interfering with the news media. Second, the Fourth Amendment has been used to argue for protecting the privacy of journalists. The media often reports information from confidential sources, and journalists feel an obligation to protect those sources from prosecution. Otherwise, few people would come forward to share information in the public interest. Whistleblowers, for example, fall into this category. If a person has been party to unsavory or illegal behavior, they may be willing to come forward and expose the enterprise only if they do not fear prosecution themselves.

Naturally, law enforcement authorities would benefit if they could compel reporters to reveal the identities of confidential sources. In addition, prosecutors could probably gather important evidence from records held by the media. In the past, investigators have used search warrants to try to compel media organizations to turn over information. The Supreme Court has also ruled that the Constitution does not protect journalists from duly authorized search warrants.

The key Supreme Court ruling that journalists must turn over information in response to a search warrant stems from the Court decision in *Zurcher v. Stanford Daily*. In 1978, reporters from the Stanford University student newspaper, *Stanford Daily*, had covered a story about a student demonstration and took pictures of the demonstrators. The district attorney investigating the demonstrators served the *Stanford Daily* with search warrants to obtain photographs and other information about the demonstrators. The paper argued in the Supreme Court that they were protected from responding to such warrants by both their First and Fourth Amendment rights.

The Supreme Court ruled against the newspaper and upheld the search warrants. Following the *Zurcher* decision, the legislature became concerned that a free press required additional protections under the law. In 1980, Congress passed the *Privacy Protection Act* (PPA) in order to better protect journalistic privacy.

The PPA prohibits law enforcement from using a warrant to search news media personnel, the homes of journalists, news media facilities, and journalistic records. The PPA protects information held by journalists from searches, as long as the materials "have a purpose to disseminate to the public. . . ." The PPA divides journalistic materials into two categories: "work product materials" and "documentary materials." The term *work product materials* generally refers to anything authored by a journalist, and the term *documentary materials* generally refers to information collected by a journalist.

The PPA protects both categories of material from law enforcement searches. In order to compel a journalist to disclose confidential information covered under the PPA, a court may issue a *subpoena duces tecum*, which would order the journalist to appear in court and bring the relevant documents. This type of court order is unlike a search warrant. Warrants require law enforcement to show probable cause, may be served without notice, and do not give the subject any chance to object. Subpoenas, however, do not require probable cause but do require notification in advance, and subjects have the opportunity to challenge the subpoena in court.

There are some exceptions to the PPA, including these:

- Situations where law enforcement is investigating the journalist as a suspect in a crime.

- Cases where an immediate search might be necessary to help law enforcement prevent death or serious injury.

- Situations where law enforcement has good reason to think that the journalist might destroy or alter important evidence if they receive an advance warning in the form of a subpoena. This exception applies only to documentary materials, not to work-product materials.

The PPA requires that law enforcement authorities must obtain a legal subpoena that may be challenged in court to conduct such a search. The PPA also provides for *a private right of action*. If any member of the news media believes their rights under the PPA have been violated, they may pursue civil action against the relevant law enforcement agency or even against individual government personnel.

Electronic Discovery

Electronic discovery, or *eDiscovery*, is the process of identifying, collecting, and producing electronic records for legal proceedings. Electronic records may be requested to support civil litigation, criminal prosecutions, law enforcement investigations, and other legal matters. Managing the discovery of electronic information requires special procedures to help track down information across disparate systems, extract specialized information from computer systems, and securely transmit and manage the information. When an entity receives a request for eDiscovery, the process is typically managed by the organization's legal counsel. The process may be broken down differently at different organizations, but the steps typically include the following:

Identification   Legal counsel typically determines which types of records may be subject to discovery. The attorneys may identify records associated with a person's name, a set of email accounts, or certain computer servers, or even request identification of records based on certain search terms. IT staff often assist by searching for records across computers and information systems. This process is much more efficient for organizations that maintain a current data inventory, as discussed in Chapter 4, "Information Management."

Preservation   Once records have been identified, the attorneys may request that some or all of the records be preserved under a *legal hold*. Legal holds can be helpful even if the records are never produced. Holds may preserve records that help the organization's case, and organizations may be penalized for destroying records relevant to an ongoing legal dispute or investigation. When a legal hold is placed, the organization's attorneys usually send a notice requiring preservation to anyone who manages the records in question. The attorneys may also ask IT staff for assistance in ensuring the preservation of any data held in enterprise information systems. Some types of records, such as automatic IT system backup files, are often scheduled to autodelete periodically. IT staff may be asked to suspend automatic purging.

Organizations have a duty to preserve evidence whenever they anticipate litigation, and legal holds may be ordered in case of a lawsuit. Sometimes, litigation never materializes. In addition, many lawsuits are settled before records are produced. For these reasons, the eDiscovery process often does not progress beyond the identification and preservation phases.

Collection   If the eDiscovery process continues beyond preservation, then the next steps involve gathering the requested records and sharing them with the organization's legal counsel. As with every step in the eDiscovery process, the collection is triggered when the attorneys request collection for certain records. In most cases, only a subset of preserved records is actually collected. Some companies and law firms use special software or secure file-transfer mechanisms to assist with the secure collection of data.

Processing   Once records have been collected, the information needs to be converted to appropriate formats and cleaned up so that the data can be reviewed. If firms frequently deal with high-volume requests, they often use specialized software. In this case, processing involves formatting records so that they can be ingested and read by the eDiscovery software platform.

Review   Before records are shared beyond an organization and its legal counsel, they must be carefully reviewed. Attorneys manage this step either by manually reviewing records or by using eDiscovery software to assist. In review, attorneys redact or remove any information that is irrelevant, protected by privilege, or protected by some other statute.

Production and Presentation   Finally, if required, the attorneys will produce information as requested and present it as required. eDiscovery information may be requested for a variety of different audiences. For example, the information may be produced for opposing legal counsel, law enforcement, litigants, or others. Sometimes, copies of records are placed in the hands of the recipients. At other times, the recipient may be invited to view the information in a law firm's office under the supervision of the attorneys.

Privacy professionals may be asked to advise on the process and to have established procedures in place to ensure compliance with privacy rules during eDiscovery. Privacy professionals may be asked to contribute subject matter expertise at all stages of the process. For example, attorneys may want information on any applicable privacy regulations that may help them redact information during the review stage or require an understanding of who can access private information at the preservation stage.

Privacy professionals likely have the most impact on eDiscovery *before* eDiscovery happens. An organization's privacy program should ensure that digital and physical information is inventoried and managed securely and that it includes records retention guidelines, appropriate staff training, and access controls. eDiscovery can be very expensive for an organization because of costs associated with staff time, IT systems, and legal fees. A quality privacy program will help an organization reduce costs by enabling efficient and accurate responses to eDiscovery requests.

Summary

The story of federal law enforcement and individual privacy has been shaped by countervailing interests over a history stretching back to the founding principles of the United States. The idea to guarantee individual liberty by limiting the government's ability to interfere in people's private lives is deeply rooted in the U.S. Constitution. So too, however, are principles of law and order and the need to provide for national defense.

The advent of new technologies, beginning with communication by wire, forced the courts and lawmakers to reexamine previously settled areas of law. As third-party providers emerged to manage our communications, the Supreme Court ruled that the Constitution does not protect that information once it leaves a person's possession. This third-party doctrine inspired a bevy of new laws meant to fill a perceived gap in the Fourth Amendment to strengthen individual privacy.

During the latter half of the 20th century, the rise of international terrorism required new tools for national security. Our national security agencies, accustomed to confronting known state actors, suddenly found themselves confronted by unknown attackers operating alone or in small groups. The federal government saw the need to rely heavily on surveillance at the expense of individual privacy rights to combat terrorism.

To further complicate this picture, many states have passed laws that are either more restrictive or more permissive of government requests for private information. Many of these state laws are covered later in this book. The legislative pendulum continues to swing as the government debates the conflicting imperatives of national defense and the liberties it is charged to defend.

Exam Essentials

Explain the Fourth Amendment.   The Fourth Amendment is the foundational law regulating the federal government's right to access an individual's private information. The Fourth Amendment restricts the government's ability to conduct searches without a good reason and appropriate legal authority.

Know the limits of the Fourth Amendment.   The Fourth Amendment protects individuals from warrantless search and seizure. Even electronic records are included. However, in our connected economy, we increasingly share our data with businesses in order to conduct our transactions. In the world of digital information and communication, third-party businesses hold our information more often than not. The *third-party doctrine* holds that information owned by third parties, such as financial records held by banks, is not protected by the Fourth Amendment.

Remember the original purposes behind legislation.   For the exam, it is important to recall the founding principles behind a given law. For example, some legislation was enacted in order to further restrict governmental access to private information, such as the Fair Credit Reporting Act (FCRA). Other laws were implemented to expand the government's access to information, such as the Bank Secrecy Act (BSA).

Follow changes in the law.   It can be confusing to understand how privacy laws interact. For example, the Patriot Act's most controversial provisions were actually changes to the Foreign Intelligence Surveillance Act (FISA). The Patriot Act updated several other privacy laws, such as the FCRA, as well. The USA Freedom Act, in turn, updates the Patriot Act.

Differentiate the levels of privacy protection in different laws.   Each of the statutes described in this chapter sets a somewhat different legal bar the government must meet in order to collect information. For example, the Fourth Amendment allows reasonable searches authorized by a warrant. The Privacy Protection Act of 1980, however, requires a subpoena to compel disclosures from the press.

Know the limits of the government's ability to compel cooperation.   Several laws require cooperation from private sector businesses. For example, the BSA requires banks to take reasonable steps to verify customers' identities, but banks do not have to take extraordinary measures to do so. CALEA compels U.S. companies to make telecommunications technologies accessible to law enforcement but cannot mandate specific technologies or force a company to assist with decrypting information.

Review Questions

1. Which of the following legislative acts was enacted to regulate government surveillance powers after the Watergate scandal?
    A. The USA Patriot Act
    B. EPCA
    C. FISA
    D. CALEA

2. CISA encourages companies to share cyber-threat intelligence with the government by removing disincentives that may have made companies hesitant to share information. All of the following are reasons that corporations may have been reluctant to share information *except*:
    A. Fear of liability for any compliance lapses revealed by sharing information
    B. Fear of making proprietary company information public
    C. Fear of revealing customer PII
    D. Fear of reprisal from cybercriminals

3. Which of the following statements best describes the third-party doctrine?
    A. Information that has been transferred to third parties in the course of doing business is no longer protected by the Fourth Amendment.
    B. The legal obligation of third parties holding customer financial records is to keep records private even when requested by law enforcement.
    C. The Supreme Court precedent holds that information held by third parties, such as financial records, is protected by the Fourth Amendment and may only be disclosed in response to search warrants.
    D. The legal obligation of any third parties holding financial records is to report suspicious financial activities to federal law enforcement.

4. The PPA is enforced by which of the following?
    A. A private right of action
    B. The FBI
    C. State attorneys general
    D. The FCC

5. Which of the following best describes the *primary* legislative purpose for implementing the Right to Financial Privacy Act (RFPA)?
    A. To compel financial institutions to cooperate with government investigations related to national security
    B. To better protect the privacy of financial information held by third parties

    C. To protect banks from liability for financial crimes committed by account holders

    D. To ensure that financial records remain the legal property of account holders and not the bank

6. The Patriot Act amended all of the following laws *except*:

    A. FISA

    B. ECPA

    C. BSA

    D. USA Freedom Act

7. Which of the following are exceptions to the RFPA's customer notification requirements? (Choose all that apply.)

    A. Disclosures made in the course of submitting an SAR

    B. Disclosures made to supervisory agencies that monitor compliance for financial institutions

    C. Disclosures made in response to a judicial subpoena

    D. Disclosures made to the FBI rather than to state or local law enforcement

8. Maya is an FBI agent authorized to begin surveillance on Evile Corp. Her task is to collect all the metadata on incoming and outgoing phone calls made to or from Evile Corp. Maya will most likely use which of the following to accomplish this?

    A. Wiretapping

    B. Pen registers and trap-and-trace devices

    C. Surveillance software installed on Evile Corp.'s computers

    D. Hidden microphones installed in Evile Corp.'s offices

9. Arturo runs the privacy compliance program for AnyBank. He has been asked to develop a program to monitor customer accounts and detect indications that financial crimes may be occurring. This program may be known by which initialism?

    A. CTR

    B. BSA

    C. AML

    D. SAR

10. What event most likely led the legislature to further curtail the government's authority to conduct surveillance in the USA Freedom Act?

    A. Edward Snowden's revelations about the NSA collecting bulk data on Americans

    B. The sudden prominence of WikiLeaks

    C. The death of Osama bin Laden

    D. The cyberattack on Sony Pictures

11. Which of the following provides special privacy protections for journalists?

    A. The First Amendment's provision for a free press

    B. The combination of the First and Fourth Amendments

    C. The Supreme Court decision in *Zurcher v. Stanford Daily*

    D. The Privacy Protection Act (PPA)

12. Jada is an attorney serving as legal counsel for Zbits Co. Zbits is being sued by a customer claiming the company violated their privacy rights. Jada has just sent a notice to company data custodians to place a legal hold on any records related to this customer. She has also asked Zbits' IT staff to avoid automatically deleting any log files related to that customer. Which step of the eDiscovery process has Jada just completed?

    A. Identification

    B. Preservation

    C. Processing

    D. Production

13. Which of the following best illustrates the minimization principle?

    A. Surveillance requests must be kept to a minimum under the USA Freedom Act and only authorized in emergencies where national security is at stake.

    B. Under the ECPA, Internet service providers must destroy all records not deemed essential for conducting business.

    C. Raw intelligence gathered under FISA is reviewed by a third party, which redacts any information not connected to the investigation before transmitting the intelligence to government investigators.

    D. All information gathered through government surveillance is reviewed by federal investigators in case any intelligence that was collected incidentally unrelated to the original investigation may reveal another previously unknown crime.

14. Who usually leads an eDiscovery process within a company?

    A. Chief executive officer

    B. Information technology office

    C. Chief privacy officer

    D. Legal counsel

15. All of the following conditions must be met in order for a federal agency to issue a formal written request for financial records under the RFPA *except*:

    A. The request must be in the scope of the federal agency's statutory authority.

    B. The agency must have reason to believe that the records being requested are relevant to an investigation.

    C. The agency must provide the customer with a copy of the request before the disclosure is made.

    D. The agency must obtain affirmative written consent from the customer before the disclosure is made.

16. National Security Letters are best described as which of the following?

A. Search warrants

B. Administrative subpoenas

C. Judicial subpoenas

D. Gag orders

17. Which of the following is not a requirement under CALEA?

A. Telecommunications companies must design products and services in ways that make them accessible to law enforcement.

B. Telecommunications companies are required to prevent the inadvertent collection of private information that is not related to an investigation.

C. Telecommunications companies are required to implement controls to keep investigations confidential.

D. Telecommunications companies are required to assist law enforcement with decrypting customer data.

18. The USA Freedom Act implemented all of the following to better regulate the government's power to conduct surveillance *except*:

A. Added the option amicus curiae to assist the FISC

B. Required specific selection terms in applications for FISA warrants

C. Implemented National Security Letters

D. Required the U.S. Attorney General to report FISA activity to Congress regularly

19. Which of the following provisions of the Patriot Act have been controversial with respect to privacy and were therefore set to expire unless reauthorized by Congress?

A. The "Lone Wolf" provision, National Security Letters, and the business records provision

B. Roving wiretaps, the FISA Court, and the minimization principle

C. The business records provision, gag orders, and the FISA Court

D. Roving wiretaps, the "Lone Wolf" provision, and the business records provision

20. The foundation of individual privacy rights in the United States stems from which of the following?

A. The Privacy Protection Act

B. Judicial precedents established by the U.S. Supreme Court

C. The Fourth Amendment of the U.S. Constitution

D. Legislation enacted at the state level

Chapter

7

Workplace Privacy

THE CIPP/US EXAM OBJECTIVES COVERED IN THIS CHAPTER INCLUDE:

✓ **Domain IV. Workplace Privacy**

- IV.A. Introduction to Workplace Privacy
  - IV.A.a Workplace Privacy Concepts
  - IV.A.b U.S. Agencies Regulating Workplace Privacy Issues
  - IV.A.c U.S. Anti-discrimination Laws
- IV.B. Privacy Before, During, and After Employment
  - IV.B.a Automated Employment Decision Tools and Potential for Bias
  - IV.B.b Employee Background Screening
  - IV.B.c Employee Monitoring
  - IV.B.d Investigation of Employee Misconduct
  - IV.B.e Termination of the Employment Relationship

This chapter explores the impact of federal privacy regulations on the workplace. Federal workplace privacy laws permit employers to collect and use employee data but also add important safeguards. These include obligations for employers to disclose their practices, use data appropriately, and properly safeguard employee information. Employees also have certain rights to authorize the collection and use of their data in some cases, as well as some rights to access and correct their data.

Introduction to Workplace Privacy

Employers collect and use a great deal of personal information about employees. This information may be collected to help in hiring decisions, performance management, and even the termination of employment. Employers also collect and use personal information to provide benefits and services, such as healthcare, wellness programs, direct deposit, and accommodations for disability.

Workplace Privacy Concepts

Employee privacy rights are derived from a patchwork of sources. Workplace privacy rules stem from a combination of federal and state statutes, tort law, and contract stipulations. Privacy professionals may be called upon to help an organization navigate this regulatory patchwork. Workplace privacy laws aim, in large part, to ensure fair employment practices. Federal statutes that impact workplace privacy, therefore, tend to revolve around eliminating discrimination and ensuring compliance with labor laws.

In most companies, the *human resources (HR)* office is on the front lines when it comes to understanding workplace privacy obligations. HR establishes policies and programs for managing privacy for job applicants, current employees, and employees separating from the business. For example, HR professionals often establish policies to ensure that hiring managers don't ask interview questions about an applicant's protected class status. Questions about marital status, racial identity, and national origin are all generally prohibited. By preventing the collection of this information in the first place, HR policies help ensure that such information cannot be used for discriminatory decision-making.

U.S. Agencies Regulating Workplace Privacy Issues

Because federal rules affecting workplace privacy are scattered throughout multiple statutes, regulatory authority is shared by several federal agencies. Each of the agencies described in this section provides regulatory oversight for workplace privacy laws:

Federal Trade Commission (FTC)   One of the primary ways the FTC regulates workplace privacy is by enforcing requirements of the Fair Credit Reporting Act (FCRA). Although the FCRA is most well known for regulating consumer credit reports, most forms of preemployment background screening are also considered *consumer reports*. The FTC provides regulatory oversight for consumer reporting agencies (CRAs) that most often provide consumer reports to employers. The FCRA even explicitly mentions employee background screening as a defining purpose of a consumer report.

Shared Authority

Federal agencies may share enforcement authority for some laws. For example, the Consumer Financial Protection Bureau (CFPB) shares authority for enforcing the FCRA. The CFPB has regulatory authority for *financial institutions* as defined by the Dodd–Frank Act. The CFPB regularly pursues enforcement actions against providers of employee background checks. In 2019, for example, the CFPB sought a judgment against a large background check company, Sterling Infosystems.

The CFPB alleged that Sterling's work violated the FCRA in ways that harmed job applications. Specifically, the CFPB alleged that Sterling risked providing criminal background data on the wrong person because the company didn't adequately verify identities, provided out-of-date information, failed to provide notification to consumers that their records were being reported, reported information that was too old to be allowed under the FCRA, and failed to verify third-party information. The judgment required Sterling to pay $6 million to victims and a $2.5 million civil penalty.

Department of Labor (DOL)   The U.S. DOL has far-reaching regulatory authority to enforce nearly 200 federal statutes that affect the workplace. The DOL seeks to ensure the rights of the U.S. workforce and good working conditions in its regulatory capacity. Several of the statutes mentioned in this chapter are enforced by the DOL. For example, the DOL enforces the Family and Medical Leave Act (FMLA), the Occupational Safety and Health Act (OSHA), and the Employee Polygraph Protection Act (EPPA).

Equal Employment Opportunity Commission (EEOC)   The EEOC is an independent federal agency with authority to investigate claims of employment discrimination and to bring enforcement action against employers. Laws discussed in this chapter that are enforced by the EEOC include Title VII of the Civil Rights Act, the Age Discrimination in Employment Act (ADEA), Title I of the Americans with Disabilities Act (ADA), and the Genetic Information Nondiscrimination Act (GINA). These are discussed in greater detail later.

National Labor Relations Board (NLRB)   The NLRB was created by Congress in 1935 to help regulate the relationship between organized labor and employers. The NLRB protects the rights of workers to organize unions and to engage in collective bargaining. In this capacity, the NLRB regulates union elections, enforces employer compliance with fair labor practices, and prohibits employer behaviors that are designed to prevent workers from exercising their rights to organize.

Occupational Safety and Health Act (OSHA)   The OSHA establishes standards for workplace safety and is enforced by the Occupational Safety and Health Administration (also referred to as OSHA), a part of the DOL. With respect to workplace privacy, OSHA protects employees' rights to raise complaints and without fear of retaliation. For this reason, employee complaints to OSHA may be kept confidential. OSHA also requires employers to keep records of workplace safety incidents or accidents and to allow access to employee health information relevant to OSHA investigations. For example, OSHA may inspect a workplace to ensure the safe handling of toxic chemicals. Such an inspection may include a review of employee health information to ensure that employees handling the chemicals have not been harmed. OSHA inspections are therefore sometimes listed as permitted disclosures of private employee health information held by employers.

Securities and Exchange Commission (SEC)   The SEC, introduced in Chapter 5, "Private Sector Data Collection," regulates public companies and the U.S. securities markets. As part of its role in enforcing financial regulations to increase corporate transparency, the SEC requires public companies to disclose information about their workforces. In late 2020, the SEC introduced new rules that expanded this disclosure requirement to include any material information about a company's human capital that might be relevant to investors. This could include not only the number of employees at a company but also major investments in the workforce, salary expenses, and metrics the company uses to assess the workforce.

U.S. Antidiscrimination Laws

Discrimination in the workplace is prohibited by a combination of several federal laws. These laws have explicit restrictions on the collection and use of personal information about job seekers and employees that could be used to make discriminatory decisions. Taken together, federal law protects people from discrimination based on race, color, religion, national origin, LGBTQ identity, sex, pregnancy or parental status, age if over 40, disability status, genetic information, and bankruptcy.

As you may expect, it is generally illegal to discriminate by deciding not to hire someone based on one of these characteristics. U.S. law, however, also prohibits discrimination in almost every employment decision that materially affects employees. These decisions include, for example, promotions, compensation, work assignments, transfers, benefits, disciplinary action, and even termination. If employers are not careful in handling information about an employee's status as a member of a protected class (race, sex, national origin, and so on), they may introduce the potential for bias in hiring decisions. Careful practices for managing the privacy of employee personal information in the workplace help mitigate this risk and prevent discrimination before, during, and after employment.

In addition to federal laws, many U.S. states have antidiscrimination laws that offer additional protections for individuals. U.S. contract law also plays a role in regulating workplace discrimination. Many labor union contracts have specific requirements to ensure the fair treatment of union members. Such contracts may also include requirements for collecting and managing the personal information of union members. This section will explore three important federal laws that are most relevant to the CIPP/US exam in more detail.

Civil Rights Act of 1964

The landmark Civil Rights Act of 1964 ended the era of legal racial segregation and outlawed many forms of discrimination. The Civil Rights Act made it illegal to discriminate or segregate people in places of public accommodation (shops, restaurants, hotels, transit, and so forth), public or government facilities, and public education. The Civil Rights Act also expanded protection for voting rights and banned some practices that created discriminatory barriers to voting for people of color.

Title VII of the Civil Rights Act protects job seekers from discrimination based on race, color, religion, national origin, religion, or sex. The act, as subsequently amended, further prohibits discrimination based on pregnancy or childbirth status. The Civil Rights Act was also later aligned with the Age Discrimination in Employment Act (ADEA), which protects anyone over 40 from discrimination based on age.

Americans with Disabilities Act (ADA)

First enacted in 1990, the ADA enacted sweeping reforms to ensure equal opportunity under the law for people with disabilities. The ADA requires that a host of public services be made accessible. For example, public transportation, telephones, public buildings, and many more "public accommodations and services" are included in ADA requirements. The ADA details standards that must be met, such as wheelchair accessibility and elevator availability, for compliance. Employers are also required to make "reasonable accommodations" for people with disabilities to fulfill the functions of their jobs. Reasonable accommodations may include, for example, providing modified workstations or adaptive technology to assist employees.

Key Concepts from the ADA

- *Disability*: The ADA defines disability as "physical or mental impairment that substantially limits one or more life activities." The definition also includes people with a record of such a disability or who are perceived as having such a disability.

- *Accessibility*: This generally refers to the practice of ensuring that physical spaces, digital environments, policies, and practices do not prevent people with disabilities from participating. Such practices may include, for example, adding curb ramps or spacing aisles in a retail store so that wheelchairs can fit. There are multiple standards for accessibility that vary by industry and topic. Such standards may be maintained by federal or state agencies, established in contracts, or implemented as part of self-regulatory frameworks.

- *Reasonable accommodation*: The ADA requires employers to make "reasonable accommodations" to make it possible for a qualified individual to perform the essential functions of a job. According to the ADA, reasonable accommodations may include "making facilities readily accessible and usable" as well as providing modifications to working conditions, including things like equipment, work schedules, or policies that may present barriers to people with disabilities. Examples may include providing a sign language interpreter or a special computer keyboard for an employee.

- *Undue hardship*: Employers are not required to provide accommodations that represent "undue hardships" for the employer. The ADA defines these as accommodations that require "significant difficulty or expense."

With respect to workplace privacy, the ADA makes it illegal to discriminate in employment decisions based on disability status. If an individual is qualified for a job and can perform the essential duties of that job with reasonable accommodations (if needed), then the employer cannot use disability as a reason not to hire someone.

To protect people with disabilities against discrimination, the ADA also prohibits employers from collecting information about disability status for use in hiring decisions. A hiring manager may ask job seekers if they can perform a position's essential duties, but they may not ask about any mental or physical disabilities. If an employer somehow acquires information about a disability through a preemployment health exam or some other mechanism, the information cannot be used to reject qualified individuals who can perform the job's essential duties. Any medical information an employer acquires through preemployment screening or from subsequent voluntary health examinations (such as through a company wellness program) must be maintained in separate confidential files.

Genetic Information Nondiscrimination Act (GINA)

In 2009, Title II of the Genetic Information Nondiscrimination Act (GINA) made it illegal for employers to use genetic information in hiring decisions. GINA defines genetic information to include any information about genetic tests, results, or services, including prenatal health services. Family medical information is also protected in order to prevent discrimination against job seekers who may have increased risk of hereditary medical issues.

GINA forbids genetic discrimination not only in hiring but also in decisions related to compensation, promotion, professional development, assigned work, benefits, termination, and all other aspects of the employment relationship. GINA also protects employees from workplace harassment based on their genetic information. As with many other antidiscrimination laws, GINA makes it illegal to retaliate against employees who allege discrimination under GINA.

GINA further protects employee privacy by prohibiting employers from gathering genetic information in the first place. There are a few exceptions when an employer may encounter genetic information in the course of conducting business. Exceptions include accidentally encountering genetic information, such as when an employee elects to share a personal story, FMLA certifications, employer wellness programs, public information sources (such as the local news), workplace health and safety monitoring programs, or some law enforcement procedures. These exceptions are few in number and narrowly defined. In the event that employers do acquire genetic information, GINA requires that it be stored separately, as with other secure medical information, and kept confidential unless disclosure is legally required.

In general, the law encourages organizations to avoid collecting genetic information altogether to avoid potential compliance concerns. In cases where encountering genetic information about an employee is unavoidable, many organizations use internal processes to ensure the information isn't shared with supervisors or those making employment decisions. For example, an HR specialist may handle FMLA certifications that include a disclosure of genetic information. The supervisor may be informed only that the employee is approved for an FMLA leave and never have access to the private information. This type of practice helps to reduce the risk of introducing genetic discrimination into employment decisions.

Privacy Before, During, and After Employment

Employers collect and use different information from employees in different ways depending on the stage of the employment relationship. Preemployment processes that gather personal information on employees may include criminal background screening, credit checks, job application information, or even interview questions. During employment, organizations gather data by engaging in various forms of employee monitoring. Finally, when an employment relationship comes to an end, employers protect privacy by disabling employee access to information, managing records on ex-employees, and providing appropriate information for reference checks. Along with HR specialists and legal counsel, privacy professionals may be called upon to help an organization establish a privacy program for employee data that includes managing the data lifecycle, training, documentation, and appropriate privacy controls.

Automated Employment Decision Tools

With advances in technology and the availability of big data, employers are increasingly using artificial intelligence (AI) and other automated tools to aid in preemployment screening and decision-making. For example, an employer may ask all applicants for a job to take an online competency test that measures not only relevant knowledge but also candidates' reaction times. Such tests may use video cameras or other sensors to track candidates' eye movements, temperature, or other metrics to evaluate candidates' stress reactions. Other automated screening tools may comb big data sets for information derived about an applicant. Such tools may provide an easy way for employers to automatically verify candidates' credentials or other relevant background information automatically and in bulk.

The use of such automated tools, however, also creates new risks for employers. When automated automation meets big data to analyze large numbers of applicants at scale, it is quite possible for automated tools to collect and reveal protected personal information. Worse still, it is possible that such protected personal information may adversely impact an employment decision in violation of the law. For example, an automated online test that uses retinal tracking to screen applicants may rule out people with vision issues. Such a decision, even if it was made unknowingly by an automated system, may be considered discriminatory under the ADA. Automated analyses of big data may similarly review private information about individuals, even if such tools are not directly searching for personal information. Publicly available data may review all sorts of information about candidates' racial or ethnic backgrounds, language, religion, LGBTQ status, pregnancy status, age, and more. In those cases, the algorithm may unwittingly create a potential for illegal bias to be introduced into employment decision-making.

Several state and local jurisdictions have already started to explore regulations for the use of automated decision-making in hiring. For example, New York City passed a law, effective as of 2023, restricting the use of AI in hiring. The law requires employers to post public disclosures about their usage of such systems, audit AI systems for bias, and provide multiple notifications to job candidates disclosing the use of automated tools in the hiring process. As more such regulations go into effect around the United States, employers must exercise caution when relying on any automation or AI in making employment decisions.

Employee Background Screening

Employers often conduct background screenings as part of hiring processes. Background screenings often consist only of a simple criminal background check but may include other types of data collection as well. Employers may request driving records, credit reports, college transcripts, social media checks, or other personal background data that may bear on a company's hiring decision. Some companies administer tests that collect personal data, such as personality evaluations and drug tests.

Although the United States has not enacted a federal statute dedicated to employee privacy, much of this sort of background screening is regulated under the FCRA. Employers may collect background screening information if they comply with applicable regulations, but they must take care not to use any background information in a way that violates other laws. For example, they may not use information to make discriminatory decisions that violate the Civil Rights Act or the ADA, as described earlier.

Requirements Under FCRA

The Fair Credit Reporting Act regulates many of these types of data collection because background checks usually meet the FCRA definition of a consumer report. As discussed in Chapter 5, these reports include information about a person's creditworthiness. However, a report may be in scope of the FCRA when it contains more amorphous content, such as any information about a person's "character, general reputation, personal characteristics, or mode of living." The FCRA is explicit that if any of this sort of information is disclosed for "employment purposes," that disclosure is considered a *consumer report* and regulated under the FCRA.

FCRA includes important requirements employers must follow in order to conduct background checks on employees. Employers who request background screening information from third parties, such as credit reports or criminal background checks, must meet the following requirements:

- Provide a written notification to potential employees to inform them of the background check process and advise them that the information obtained may have an impact on hiring decisions.

- Obtain written authorization from applicants to perform the background check that specifies whether the background screening is a one-time occurrence or a regular event while employed. The notice mentioned in the first item often includes an authorization form that, when signed by the job seeker, satisfies this requirement.

- If a background screen includes interviews with personal contacts of the applicant to learn more about attributes such as "character" or "mode of living," then it would be considered an *investigative report* under the FCRA. In this case, applicants must be informed of their right to be told about the investigation.

- The employer must provide certification to the furnisher of background reporting information that they are in full compliance with the FCRA and all other applicable federal and state statutes, including laws prohibiting discrimination.

 The FCRA regulates third-party agencies that furnish consumer reporting information to employers. If an employer directly gathers background screening information themselves, then the information would not be considered a consumer report under the FCRA.

Methods

As mentioned earlier, employers may use a wide variety of preemployment screening approaches. Some approaches revolve around gathering existing data on job candidates, such as criminal records and credit reports. Some employers, however, seek to evaluate job candidates on a variety of dimensions during the application process. These evaluations generate new personal information collected by the employer. Privacy professionals may be asked to help design a privacy program for the collection, use, and handling of this information as part of privacy programs for handling employee data in general.

Personality and Psychological Evaluations

Some employers ask job seekers to undergo personality or behavior tests. Such evaluations are increasingly popular in the technology sector, where companies seek employees who drive innovation. These tests seek to provide information that gets at things like an applicant's resilience in the face of change, creativity, and on-demand problem-solving abilities.

Many such tests are permissible under the law, as long as the evaluations are restricted to an applicant's job-related knowledge, skills, and abilities. If, however, such evaluations reveal personal information about an applicant related to a disability or protected class information, then an employer could be in violation of statutes such as the ADA or Civil Rights Act.

Polygraph Testing

In general, private sector employers are not permitted to require polygraph tests as a part of preemployment screening. Private sector employers are also generally prohibited from requiring polygraph tests for existing employees. In 1988, Congress enacted the *Employee Polygraph Protection Act (EPPA)* to protect most employees from polygraph testing.

The EPPA forbids employers from requiring polygraph examinations as part of preemployment screening. The EPPA does not even permit employers to so much as suggest polygraph testing to applicants, lest submission to polygraph testing become such a competitive advantage that it becomes a virtual requirement. Employers may not inquire about the results of third-party polygraph tests or discriminate against applicants who refuse a polygraph.

The EPPA provides for limited exemptions. Government employers are exempt from the EPPA, as are some government contractors engaged in national security work. Prospective employees of private security and pharmaceutical companies in critical roles may also be asked to take polygraph tests. Private employers may administer polygraph tests to existing employees only in very specific cases, such as when they have a reasonable suspicion that an employee is stealing from the company.

Drug and Alcohol Testing

Many employers engage in drug and/or alcohol testing as part of drug-free workplace programs. The national legal landscape surrounding workplace drug and alcohol testing is complex. Several federal laws have implications for drug and alcohol testing, such as the Civil Rights Act, ADA, and FMLA. In addition, several states have laws that impact such programs. These laws are complex in part because legal frameworks seesaw between conflicting aims: protecting employee privacy rights and increasing workplace safety. To further complicate this picture, contract law plays a significant role. Many labor union contracts negotiate specific conditions and protocols around workplace drug and alcohol testing that impact employer programs.

The requirements in the federal laws mentioned here tend to put boundaries around workplace drug-testing programs in favor of protecting employee rights and privacy. Other federal laws, however, encourage employers to crack down on drug use in the workplace. For example, the Drug-Free Workplace Act of 1988 encourages employers to provide antidrug policies and awareness programs and discipline employees who violate drug-free workplace rules. The Drug-Free Workplace Act does not require most employers to have drug-testing programs, but it does illustrate the need for employers to balance laws that protect employee privacy against laws obligating employers to prevent drug use in the workplace.

In general, federal statutes forbid employers from discriminating based on any history of substance use disorders or discriminating against anyone for seeking treatment for substance abuse. Workplace drug- and alcohol-testing programs may not target people from specific identity groups, such as racial, ethnic, or religious groups, or target individuals based on medical conditions, physical abilities, or general behavior. Employers must also take care to avoid inadvertently sanctioning employees taking legally prescribed medication, as required by the ADA.

For a drug- and alcohol-testing program to be permitted under federal law, it must be evenhanded in its application to employees. For example, some programs test all employees on a regular or random schedule, whereas others randomly select employees for testing. Many states, of course, have laws that may add further requirements or restrictions that impact compliance for workplace drug-testing programs.

Finally, some organizations are required to implement programs for workplace drug and alcohol testing to comply with federal, state, and local laws. For example, certain employees of the U.S. Departments of Defense and Transportation and other federal employees involved in national security and law enforcement are required to undergo drug and alcohol testing. In addition, many states and municipalities have laws requiring emergency responders, such as paramedics, firefighters, and law enforcement officers, to be tested for drugs regularly.

Social Media

Social media checks are increasing in popularity as a preemployment screening strategy. Applicants may reveal pertinent information on social media relevant to their skills, qualifications, and dedication to their work. Social media, however, may also reveal personal information. If a hiring manager sees information revealing that an applicant is part of a protected class, then they may be at risk for violating laws such as the Civil Rights Act if the social media check is used in a hiring decision.

In addition, many people use pseudonyms on social media or keep their profiles anonymous altogether. It is critical for employers to ensure they are reviewing social media for the correct individual and viewing only public information or information they have permission to view.

For this reason, many employers use third-party companies to perform social media checks. These third-party providers can obtain proper authorization from job applications to verify they are viewing the correct information. They can also pass along only information that is pertinent to the hiring decision and redact any personal information that may bias the process.

As a note of caution, employers must be cognizant of whether the resulting reports meet the FCRA's definition of consumer reports, discussed earlier. If a social media check takes the form of a report furnished by a third party and contains any information listed in the FCRA definition of consumer report, then the employer would be subject to FCRA requirements, such as obtaining prior consent from the employee.

Employee Monitoring

Employers commonly monitor employee performance. Monitoring may be as simple as a supervisor working alongside subordinates and observing performance. Employee monitoring may also involve sophisticated technology-enabled systems that aggregate data on employee behavior from multiple sources. Companies may want to monitor employee phone conversations with customers, how employees use computers, and employee wellness and even use audio or video systems to record employees at work. In general, such monitoring is legal and employees do not have the right to expect privacy in the workplace.

Technologies

Frequently, companies monitor the ways employees use technology. Companies perform this sort of monitoring for all sorts of reasons. Companies may seek to ensure compliance with company policies, track employee productivity, or monitor systems for cybersecurity reasons. Companies generally provide technology, such as phones and computers, to their employees. Employers almost always assert that the company, not the employee, owns the technology. Because the company owns the equipment, it has the to monitor its use.

When employees use personal technology for work, the privacy issues in play become more complex. Many companies address this in their privacy policies by either banning the use of personal technology for work or requiring employees to agree to monitoring.

Commonly, companies track employee *computer usage*. Monitoring employee web browsing and software usage helps ensure that employees are only using company technology for approved work-related purposes, for example. If a job function is performed entirely on a computer, then monitoring computer usage may help a company measure how quickly employees complete tasks and may play into performance evaluations or disciplinary actions.

Computing technology is increasingly mobile, and many employees perform a lot of their work using smartphones. Because many of these devices have location-tracking or GPS capabilities, it is possible for employers to perform *location-based monitoring*. For example, employers may monitor the location of company vehicles to protect against theft or respond to traffic accidents. It is also possible for companies to track the location of mobile phones and other location-aware technology. This form of tracking has the potential to be much more invasive to employee privacy. Although no federal law currently addresses this form of monitoring, some states have laws limiting this practice and requiring that employers disclose location-based tracking practices. Organizations should consult with legal counsel to determine the jurisdiction and scope of any state laws that may apply.

In recent years, social media activity has emerged as a major concern for employers. This chapter has already discussed the use of social media checks for preemployment screening purposes, but social media information comes into play during employment as well. Companies now commonly engage in *social media tracking* of employees. Social media tracking may be conducted by monitoring the use of computing technology owned by the company or by monitoring social media networks for public posts.

Companies may be concerned about employees for many reasons. Social media can be a distraction at work, and employee posts may damage a company's reputation, constitute harassment of fellow employees, share offensive content, reveal proprietary information, expose the company to hackers, or even create legal risks by revealing confidential information. Federal law does not explicitly prohibit this sort of monitoring, but companies should take care to craft clear policies related to social media to ensure they don't violate any general workplace laws. For example, the NLRB may investigate any social media restrictions that prevent employees from exercising their rights to organize. In addition, social media monitoring may reveal information about employees who belong to a protected class. Employers must be careful to avoid violating antidiscrimination laws when they acquire protected class information.

In some cases, employers may collect and use *biometric* data from employees. Commonly, this involves the use of employee fingerprint scans for use with automatic timekeeping, door access, or computer authentication systems. Recent technological advances have also made it more common for employers to use other biometric data, such as voice prints or facial scans, to identify employees. There is no federal regulation on the collection and use of this data. However, the states of Illinois, Texas, and Washington have enacted state laws regulating biometric data in the workplace. In general, these state laws require employers to notify employees to explain their use of biometric data; obtain consent from employees; create policies for securing, managing, and purging biometric data; and refrain from disclosing or selling biometric data to third parties.

Many companies offer employee *wellness programs*. Such programs may constitute a benefit to employees. Frequently, however, wellness programs are a way for an organization to lower its healthcare costs. Many health insurance plans will offer incentives for employers who provide programs to ensure a healthier workforce that results in a reduction in costly claims. Many wellness programs offer helpful services, such as smoking cessation programs, gym memberships, nutrition coaching, or onsite fitness classes.

Employers must be very careful, however, about information collected about employees through wellness programs. Some wellness programs provide monetary incentives for employees to share health information that, in turn, lowers company healthcare costs. For example, the company might lower insurance costs if it can ensure that some number of employees are nonsmokers. However, some wellness information may reveal information about an employee's protected class. If monetary awards are based on that information, then the practice may be discriminatory and illegal.

Yale University Lawsuit

In 2019, the American Association of Retired Persons (AARP) brought a class-action lawsuit against Yale University for unlawful discrimination in its wellness program. The Yale wellness program required employees to share a great deal of personal health information, including information about existing medical conditions, with the university. The suit alleged that collecting this information violated both the ADA and GINA. Yale also provided a financial incentive for employees who participated in the program. The AARP suit alleged that the wellness program's incentive constituted a penalty to those who opt out and was therefore an example of illegal discrimination. Litigation in this case is ongoing, but the EEOC has since approved rules for wellness programs that limit the practices of using incentives to get employees to share personal information.

Requirements under the ECPA

Several forms of employee monitoring are subject, at least in part, to requirements under the Electronic Communications and Privacy Act (ECPA). These include video and photographic monitoring, as well as monitoring communications by email and telephone. In general, the ECPA and the related Stored Communications Act (SCA) permit these methods of monitoring as long as certain requirements are met:

> **Video and Photographic Monitoring**   Companies may use video or photographic monitoring to ensure workplace safety, prevent theft, monitor employee performance, enhance employee training, or for many other purposes. The ECPA (discussed in Chapter 6, "Government and Court Access to Private Sector Information") is an update to the Wiretap Act, which generally bans the use of systems that eavesdrop on private conversations. Most employers who practice this form of monitoring include a statement of consent in their employee handbooks, which employees are asked to sign.

There are other ways for employers to conduct video and photographic monitoring under the ECPA, but not without complications. First, ECPA contains an exception allowing monitoring for allowed business purposes. However, that exception applies only to monitoring business interactions. The moment a conversation becomes personal, the exception no longer applies. Second, the ECPA requires only one party to consent to eavesdropping, and employers could theoretically rely on getting consent from some employees, but not all. However, such a practice would likely be very damaging to workplace culture, and many states require every party to consent to surveillance.

Email and Telephone Monitoring   As with video and photographic monitoring, companies have similar reasons to monitor employee communications by phone and email. The ECPA's business purpose exception applies here as well, but that exception applies only to work-related communications. This means that employers have to stop surveillance if a conversation seems to be personal. Some employers deal with this through policies banning personal communications using company phones or email. The SCA plays a role here as well. Emails stored on a server are not considered communications by the ECPA and thus not subject to the Wiretap Act. As long as companies notify employees that they do not have an expectation of privacy for information stored on company servers, the SCA permits employers to review information they store.

When it comes to postal mail, organizations are legally allowed to open and read any mail addressed to the organization once delivered, even if a specific employee's name is on the parcel.

Unionized Worker Issues Concerning Monitoring in the U.S. Workplace

In addition to surveillance laws, fair labor standards and labor union contracts may play a significant role in determining a company's employee monitoring practices. For example, the National Labor Relations Board (NLRB) has previously ruled that in union shops, conditions of employment must be negotiated through collective bargaining and detailed in union contracts. If employees must consent to video surveillance as a condition of employment, then the monitoring program must be disclosed and explained in the contract as well. The NLRB also prohibits employers from practices that interfere with employees who are considering unionizing. Employers may not explicitly spy on union activities or even give the impression of doing so, because such tactics might intimidate employees. Even in non-union shops, the NLRB frowns on secret employee-monitoring programs in many cases and generally encourages companies to notify employees of all workplace monitoring programs as a fair labor practice.

The Broad Compliance Picture

This section highlights many areas of federal law that construct large parts of the patchwork of regulations governing workplace monitoring. As mentioned repeatedly, however, many states have laws that add additional requirements that impact workplace monitoring. State laws may aim to increase employee privacy, add protections from discrimination, offer additional rights for labor unions, or regulate surveillance more generally.

Privacy professionals should take note of the many common elements of these requirements to help organizations construct best practices to comply with state and federal regulations as well as any labor contract obligations. These best practices include notifying employees up front about all workplace monitoring practices and obtaining consent for monitoring whenever possible. Once data is collected, companies should ensure that data is kept securely and confidentially, used only for the prescribed purpose, and deleted when no longer needed. Although these practices may lower compliance risks for companies in many jurisdictions, companies must still have a detailed understanding of any specific labor contract or statutory requirements that apply to them.

Investigation of Employee Misconduct

Businesses regularly investigate cases of employee misconduct. Responsible employers have processes in place to examine all sides of a dispute before implementing any sanctions against an employee. Instances of employee misconduct may range from relatively minor infractions, such as tardiness, to serious allegations of illegal behavior such as theft, sexual harassment, or discrimination.

Misconduct investigation procedures must often carefully balance the rights of multiple individuals in one situation. It is critical for organizations to take any allegations of misconduct seriously. For example, if an organization does not properly investigate an allegation of sexist or racist incidents, the business itself may be subject to accusations of discrimination. Ensuring confidentiality in the process also encourages employees to be more forthcoming in sharing relevant information and protects them from possible illegal retaliation.

On the other hand, businesses must be careful to treat employees accused of misconduct fairly and to understand all sides of an issue. Companies usually have carefully documented policies around misconduct investigations to ensure that all investigations are handled consistently. If employers are not evenhanded in their handling of misconduct cases, they may also be vulnerable to charges of inappropriate behavior. Confidentiality is also critical to the fair treatment of employees accused of misconduct. Not all investigations find that misconduct occurred. If an investigation finds no evidence of wrongdoing, it is even more important to prevent the details of the investigation from adversely impacting the employee.

Data Handling in Misconduct Investigations

Human resources professionals typically work with supervisors to lead investigation processes at an organization. Misconduct investigations require that the business gather as much information as it needs to assess how an allegation may be best handled. As a result, businesses often acquire additional personal information about employees that must be managed securely and confidentially. In conducting misconduct investigations, HR professionals are often balancing the rights of victims, witnesses, and bystanders, as well as protecting the organization itself from risk.

Data collected during misconduct investigations may be highly personal to employees. Such information may reveal employee health status, identifiable health and wellness information, financial information, and protected class information. Much of this information may be gathered about employees who are not the targets of the investigation. It is important for organizations to maintain strict confidentiality and to safeguard the information. It is not unlikely that some of the information collected may fall within the scope of one of the many privacy statutes discussed throughout this book. In this case, employers must be mindful of any additional compliance obligations.

All misconduct investigations should be meticulously documented. Organizations should take care to document both the findings and the process of the investigation itself. This practice helps protect the company from any downstream accusations that an investigation may have been conducted improperly. In addition, documenting the process helps ensure accuracy and due diligence and provides an opportunity for the organization to review and improve misconduct-handling processes. Finally, not all misconduct investigations end in termination. Many misconduct processes conclude by recommending additional training or coaching for an employee, especially for first-time violations. If an employee engages in repeated misconduct, however, employers may rely on documentation of previous violations to justify progressively more severe disciplinary actions.

Use of Third Parties in Investigations

Often, businesses choose to use third-party firms to assist in misconduct investigations. The use of third parties may be attractive to businesses because they bring additional resources and expertise, knowledge of applicable laws, and the ability to redact irrelevant private informant before furnishing reports to the business. However, once a third party furnishes information about an individual, it usually meets the definition of a *consumer report* and is regulated under the FCRA.

When the FCRA was first passed, this regulation was problematic for businesses attempting to complete fair misconduct investigations in good faith. The FCRA requires businesses to notify and obtain consent from anyone who is a subject of an investigative report. Such a process makes sense for job applicants, but it is highly problematic for misconduct investigations if employees are allowed to merely withhold consent.

When the Fair and Accurate Credit Transactions Act (FACTA) was passed in 2003, it amended the FCRA by altering the legal definition of *consumer report* to exclude employee misconduct investigations. For a report to qualify for this exception, the business must be able to show that the purpose of the report is indeed to investigate allegations of employee misconduct and does not contain irrelevant information. Employers must also ensure that third-party misconduct reports are disclosed only to the employer and to regulatory authorities as required. If an employer bases a decision on such a report that negatively impacts the employee, then the company must provide the employee with a summary describing the scope of the investigation and the findings.

Termination of the Employment Relationship

Every employment relationship ends at some point. Most often, the employment relationship ends when employees retire or move on to new opportunities. Staff have a chance to congratulate a colleague on obtaining a new position or transitioning into a well-deserved retirement. In these cases, managing the transition to end an employment relationship can be a pleasant process. Unfortunately, the employment relationship is sometimes ended involuntarily through a layoff or termination process. Although there is no federal legislation that regulates the termination of employment absent of layoff, some states have laws that may impact termination practices. Labor union agreements and other employment contracts may affect the process as well. Whether the termination is amicable or adversarial, employers typically follow prescribed practices to protect the privacy of company information and ensure ongoing compliance with privacy regulations when an employment relationship draws to a close. This process is often referred to as *transition management*.

Access Management

As discussed throughout this book, many federal statutes touching on information privacy require that companies implement physical, technological, and administrative controls to ensure that private data is accessible only to authorized employees. When an employment relationship ends, therefore, most companies consult their access management procedures to disable a departing employee's access to private and business information. This includes disabling access to IT systems as well as collecting all keys, access cards, paper files, company property, computers, and other equipment that may store company data. Departing employees may be asked to verify that they are not retaining any company data on their personal devices. Finally, departing employees may be reminded of their ongoing obligations to maintain confidentiality related to any private information they might remember.

In most cases, organizations are able to plan ahead for an employee departure because the employee provides advance notice or because the company has planned an involuntary termination in advance. Advance planning allows the company necessary time to put access control actions into place by verifying an employee's level of access, gathering an inventory of company property an employee may have, and working with IT to modify access to information systems.

If the separation is not amicable, careful planning is important. HR may work with IT staff to disable access to company information systems while the termination meeting is taking place. In some cases, HR may also plan to have security personnel or other staff on hand in order to monitor the return of company property and even to escort the employee off the premises after the meeting. These practices ensure that private information is immediately protected from potentially disgruntled ex-employees.

Records Retention

After an employee departs, organizations still possess records relating to that person's employment relationship. These may include common elements of a personnel file, such as performance evaluations, commendations, or records of disciplinary actions. Other records may include information gathered from company wellness programs, workplace accident records, requests for disability accommodations, and more. Private companies usually have records-retention policies that detail how long each type of record should be maintained and when records should be destroyed. Records-retention policies are important tools for reducing company risks related to eDiscovery requests. If, for example, a company becomes a defendant in a civil action brought by a former employee, following a records-retention policy will reduce the risk that the company may be accused of mismanaging or hiding important evidence.

References

There is no federal law requiring companies to furnish reference information upon request, but most companies provide references for ex-employees. Some states also have laws, known as *service letter acts*, requiring employers to furnish employees with verification of basic employment information. There are some risks, however, presented when companies provide reference information. Some states have laws that restrict a company from sharing private information that might adversely affect an ex-employee. In some cases, ex-employees may attempt to bring civil actions against companies if they believe the company made inappropriate, inaccurate, or illegal disclosures. These risks vary widely depending on the jurisdiction, the employment relationship, and the nature of the information.

Many companies mitigate these risks by creating written procedures for reference checks that govern what sort of information may be shared and who in the organization can respond to reference requests. For example, some reference check policies may allow only HR to provide reference checks and limit the disclosure to a simple verification of dates of employment and job title.

Summary

Workplace privacy is not regulated by any single governing U.S. law. Neither is workplace privacy overseen by a single regulatory agency. Workplace privacy practices are the result of provisions embedded in a variety of federal statutes, state law, tort law, and labor contracts.

At the federal level, employee privacy in and of itself is not a primary driver of regulations that affect workplace privacy. Instead, employee privacy is an important strategy for protecting other rights. First, everyone should have the right to be free from discrimination and enjoy equal opportunities for employment. Second, employees have the right to engage in collective bargaining and organize into labor unions. Key federal statutes prohibiting discrimination and upholding labor rights include the Civil Rights Act, ADA, and GINA.

Federal laws that impact workplace privacy are enforced by a variety of government agencies, including the FTC, CFPB, DOL, OSHA, NLRB, EEOC, and SEC. Each of these agencies has regulatory authority for different laws and industries. For example, some of these agencies help promote fair labor standards, others enforce antidiscrimination laws, and some do both.

State laws and union contracts create additional obligations for employers to protect employee privacy in certain circumstances. Some states have more stringent requirements for notice and consent for employee monitoring or background screening, for example. Privacy professionals may be called up to create best-practice frameworks for companies for compliance with the federal legal landscape, state law, contract obligations, and the nature of employee data companies collect.

In most cases, HR departments manage the employment lifecycle, from application to retirement. HR often implements the procedures necessary to manage private data collected on employees in ways that protect employee rights, allow organizations to conduct their business, and limit organizational risk.

HR usually takes the lead, but privacy professionals may be asked to help develop and maintain privacy programs for employee data. General best practices for workplace privacy help companies minimize compliance risk. These include minimizing the collection of personal information, maintaining strict confidentiality, employing information safeguards, establishing writing policies to manage practices such as workplace monitoring, and providing notice and obtaining consent for collecting and using private information.

Exam Essentials

Recognize the limits of workplace privacy. In the United States, employees do not enjoy a general expectation of privacy in the workplace. Although some regulations discussed in this chapter impose limited requirements on employers for managing privacy, employers are largely permitted to gather information about employees and to monitor most employee activities in the workplace.

Identify the diverse sources of workplace privacy regulations. Because the United States lacks any central governing statute on workplace privacy, regulations come from a patchwork of sources. These include provisions of some federal laws, state laws, tort law, and labor union contracts. For the exam, aspiring privacy professionals should study the specific federal laws and regulatory agencies discussed in this chapter and be aware of the other possible sources of regulation.

Know the drivers of federal legislation on workplace privacy. To the degree that federal statutes protect workplace privacy, it is only to help protect other employee rights. These include the rights to be free from discrimination and to participate in collective bargaining as part of a labor union. Privacy protections help ensure that employees aren't unfairly targeted for belonging to a protected class or for union participation.

Recognize the distinct phases of the employment relationship.   Organizations collect information during three distinct phases of employment: preemployment, during employment, and at the end of employment. Each of these phases usually includes different processes that impact workplace privacy. Preemployment processes often involve collecting data on employees and preventing discrimination. During employment, privacy practices often involve employee monitoring and complying with labor laws. At the end of employment, processes revolve around protecting company data and risk management.

Identify common methods for screening and monitoring.   Privacy professionals should be able to identify the common technologies and techniques organizations use for preemployment background screening as well as for employee monitoring during employment. These include techniques such as social media tracking, drug testing, and personality tests, as well as technologies, such as location-based tracking, biometrics, and computer usage tracking.

Review Questions

1. Which of the following is *not* an exception under the EPPA?

   A. Government agencies

   B. Private security companies

   C. Law firms

   D. Pharmaceutical companies

2. Which of the following does *not* constitute a protected class in federal antidiscrimination legislation?

   A. Religion

   B. National origin

   C. Political affiliation

   D. Age

3. Under which conditions are employers prohibited from denying employment based on disability?

   A. Employers are never permitted to deny employment based on disability even if the job seeker is unable to perform the essential functions of the position with reasonable accommodations.

   B. Employers are prohibited from denying employment based on physical disabilities but not mental disabilities.

   C. Employers are prohibited from denying employment when the business is designated as a place of public accommodation under the ADA.

   D. Employers are prohibited from denying employment when the job seeker meets the qualifications for a position and can perform the essential functions with or without reasonable accommodations.

4. Which of the following departments in a given business is *most* likely to have primary responsibility for implementing company policies that govern workplace privacy?

   A. Information privacy office

   B. Human resources

   C. Legal counsel

   D. Office of the CEO

5. Which of the following statements is not accurate with respect to workplace drug and alcohol testing?

   A. The Drug-Free Workplace Act of 1988 required many employers to implement mandatory drug-testing programs.

   B. Employers should use an evenhanded testing protocol that does not single out individuals for drug and alcohol testing.

C. Many labor union contracts include procedures for drug and alcohol testing of employees.

D. Employers must be careful to avoid collecting private medical information, such as the legal use of prescription medications.

6. Age discrimination is prohibited by which of the following?

A. State laws banning employment discrimination based on age

B. The Age Discrimination in Employment Act

C. The Fair Labor Standards Act

D. Tort law arising from court decisions in civil litigation

7. Which of the following is *not* commonly a reason why employers implement employee-monitoring programs?

A. To monitor employee performance

B. To ensure compliance with company policies

C. To prevent cybersecurity incidents

D. To prevent unionizing activity

8. What is the main reason that employee background screening is regulated by the federal government?

A. Background screening is regulated by the NLRB to prohibit employers from using background screening to discriminate against members of labor unions.

B. Employee background screening is monitored by the Department of Justice to ensure that information is not gathered in a way that violates the Fourth Amendment.

C. The gathering of background information is regulated by the EEOC because the process may reveal information about an applicant's protected class status.

D. Background screening reports furnished by third parties constitute consumer reports as defined by the FCRA.

9. When an employer hires an outside investigator to furnish an investigative report as part of an employee misconduct investigation, which of the following requirements apply?

A. The employer must notify the employee of the investigation in advance.

B. The employer must obtain written consent from the employee prior to the investigation.

C. The employer must furnish the employee with a complete copy of the investigative report.

D. If the report leads to an adverse decision for the employee, then the employer must give the employee a summary of the nature of the investigation.

10. Which of the following processes takes place during the transition management phase of ending an employment relationship?

A. Employees are informed of the results of a misconduct investigation.

B. The company revokes a departing employee's access to information systems.

C. The company purges records pertaining to an ex-employee from personnel files.

D. The company provides reference check information about an ex-employee to another prospective employer.

11. Which of the following best describes the primary source of workplace privacy regulations in the United States?

   A. The U.S. Constitution

   B. A combination of federal requirements, state laws, tort law, and contracts

   C. The Privacy Act of 1974

   D. Industry self-regulation programs

12. Todd works in the risk management office at MagicFactory, Inc. Todd is aware that some employees have begun to meet on Tuesday nights to talk about whether to unionize. Todd also learns that just after these meetings began, MagicFactory's management team started holding mandatory trainings at the same time, which prevents many staff from attending the meetings about unionizing. Todd suspects the company may be at some risk of investigation for interfering with employee efforts to unionize. Which agency would most likely initiate such an investigation?

   A. EEOC

   B. OSHA

   C. NLRB

   D. DOL

13. Which of the following statements is incorrect when it comes to records retention of personnel files?

   A. Companies should have written records-retention policies.

   B. Records-retention policies may reduce legal risks if a company faces eDiscovery requests.

   C. Records-retention policies should ensure that important personnel information is never misplaced or destroyed.

   D. Records-retention policies should include instructions on how long different types of records should be kept.

14. Which of the following statements is not true of employee misconduct investigations?

   A. All misconduct investigations should be carefully documented.

   B. Companies should have a written policy for handling misconduct investigations.

   C. The primary goal of misconduct investigations is to protect the rights of any victims.

   D. Human resources departments typically coordinate misconduct investigation processes.

15. Why does OSHA's oversight impact workplace privacy?

   A. OSHA protects the right of employees to file confidential complaints about workplace safety without fear of retaliation.

   B. OSHA may authorize covert monitoring of workplace safety programs.

   C. If employees file false complaints to harm a company, OSHA may disclose the complaint to that company.

   D. OSHA may inadvertently collect personal information from employees in the course of performing workplace inspections.

16. Which interview practices may HR recommend to reduce the risk of discrimination in hiring?

  A. Refrain from asking any questions that may reveal a job seeker's status as a member of a protected class.

  B. Conduct separate confidential interviews with HR to allow job seekers to disclose information about their protected class status.

  C. Invite job seekers to sign legal waivers to allow more candid conversations in job interviews.

  D. Only inquire about protected class status, such as a disability, if the hiring manager thinks it might impact the job seeker's ability to do the job.

17. Which of the following federal agencies has primary responsibility for enforcing workplace privacy legislation?

  A. DOL

  B. EEOC

  C. FTC

  D. No single agency has primary responsibility.

18. Which exceptions to the ECPA allow employers to conduct video monitoring in the workplace?

  A. The business purpose exception and the exception for workplace safety

  B. Obtaining consent and the business purpose exception

  C. Obtaining consent and eDiscovery requirements

  D. Obtaining consent and an exception for data loss prevention (DLP) programs

19. Which of the following does *not* meet the definition of genetic information employers are prohibited from collecting?

  A. Results of genetic tests

  B. Genetic information collected on hereditary conditions

  C. Information from prenatal healthcare services

  D. Information shared in the process of certifying an FMLA request

20. Which of the following reasons might lead an employer to exercise caution in monitoring employee social media activity?

  A. Social media posts may reveal information about an employee's membership in a protected class.

  B. It is difficult to verify a person's identity on social media and easy to collect information from the wrong person.

  C. Once a company has knowledge of employee misconduct via social media, it is obligated to investigate.

  D. Both A and B

Chapter

8

State Privacy Laws

THE CIPP/US EXAM OBJECTIVES COVERED IN THIS CHAPTER INCLUDE:

✓ **Domain V. State Privacy Laws**

- ▪ V.A. Federal Versus State Authority

  - ▪ V.A.a State Attorneys General

  - ▪ V.A.b California Privacy Protection Agency (CPPA)

- ▪ V.B. Data Privacy and Security Laws

  - ▪ V.B.a Applicability

  - ▪ V.B.b Data Subject Rights

  - ▪ V.B.c Privacy Notice Requirements

  - ▪ V.B.d Data Security Requirements

  - ▪ V.B.e Data Protection Agreements

  - ▪ V.B.f Data Protection Assessments

  - ▪ V.B.g Health Data Rules

  - ▪ V.B.h Data Retention and Destruction

  - ▪ V.B.i Selling and Sharing of Personal Information (PI)

  - ▪ V.B.j Enforcement

  - ▪ V.B.k Cookie and Online Tracking Requirements

  - ▪ V.B.l Facial Recognition Use Restrictions

  - ▪ V.B.m Biometric Information Privacy Regulations

  - ▪ V.B.n AI Bias Laws

  - ▪ V.B.o Important Comprehensive Data Privacy Laws

- ▪ V.C. Data Breach Notification Laws

  - ▪ V.C.a Elements of State Data Breach Notification Laws

  - ▪ V.C.b Key Differences Among States Today

  - ▪ V.C.c Significant Developments

As mentioned throughout this book, the United States does not have a European Union (EU)-style comprehensive privacy regulation. The lack of a comprehensive federal privacy statute leaves ample room for states to create their own privacy laws.

There is a lot of variation in how U.S. state laws regulate privacy. Many states have crafted laws that address narrow areas of privacy law, such as biometrics or health information. Other states, like California, have enacted more comprehensive privacy statutes that mimic the EU's General Data Protection Regulation (GDPR).

This chapter begins with a broad explanation of state authority for enacting and enforcing privacy regulations. Then, we move on to explain the common components of many state privacy laws. Finally, this chapter covers examples of comprehensive state privacy laws and state laws that address specific privacy topics.

Federal Versus State Authority

Federal laws generally preempt similar state laws, unless otherwise specified. However, since federal privacy regulation isn't comprehensive, there are many unregulated areas of privacy practice that states may freely regulate. For example, the United States does not have a national law requiring corporations to notify consumers when their personal information is compromised in a data breach. As a result, every state has enacted laws requiring some form of data breach notification. These laws are explored later in this chapter.

States create and enforce privacy regulations in much the same way as the federal government. Laws are passed by state legislatures and signed into law by governors. Typically, state attorneys general and/or state agencies are granted authority for rulemaking and enforcement. Attorneys general may attempt to seek remedies for violations against their state residents even if the offending organization is based in another state.

The state of California provides an example of a state that uses an agency to oversee privacy regulations. The California Privacy Rights Act (CPRA) established an agency called the California Privacy Protection Agency (CPPA) to enact and enforce privacy regulations in the state. The CPPA is governed by a five-member board. The California Attorney General still has a role because the attorney general appoints one of the five board members. The others are appointed by the governor, state senate rules committee, and speaker of the state assembly.

Elements of State Privacy Laws

Many U.S. state privacy regulations share a common anatomy of structures that compose a given law. For the exam, it will be helpful to develop an understanding of these elements and how they show up in various state laws.

Applicability

State laws only come into play in when the laws apply to a specific privacy situation. In determining whether a state law applies in a given case, consider factors in the law that may act as triggers. For example, some state privacy laws apply to commercial businesses but not to nonprofit or state entities.

> The concepts of *jurisdiction* and *applicability* are not quite the same thing. As you learned earlier in this book, jurisdiction refers to the ability of a legal authority to enforce a law and render judgements. Applicability describes which situations are covered by a given law.

Thresholds

Some laws apply only when certain *thresholds* are met. For example, certain requirements of some state breach notification laws are only triggered if a breach affects some number of residents in that state. In other cases, laws are designed so they don't apply to small businesses. This makes sense because difficult or expensive compliance requirements may be nearly impossible for small businesses to implement, and the privacy risks posed by small businesses may be small. Some laws, therefore, may only apply to businesses with more than some number of customers or that earn more than some amount of revenue in a given state.

Thresholds for applicability describe a condition that triggers the application of a given law. A threshold is often an amount, such as a number of customers or amount of revenue as described in the examples above.

Available Exemptions

Some state laws include *exemptions* to applicability. Like thresholds, exemptions help determine when a given law does or does not apply. Exemptions are circumstances described within a law that explain where the law does not apply, in part or whole. For example, some state privacy laws exempt nonprofit entities from their requirements.

Most state data breach notification laws require that organizations notify consumers when they experience an event that meets the definition of a data breach and, sometimes, meets a certain threshold number of impacted people. However, many states provide an exemption to this requirement in cases where data has been adequately encrypted.

Exemptions can be tricky because they describe situations when a privacy provision doesn't apply as it normally would. It's worth paying special attention to the exemptions mentioned in this chapter (and throughout the book) for the exam.

Data Subject Rights

Many state privacy regulations include a list of *data subject rights*. The *data subject* is the individual about whom the information is collected. Even if a company has data about you, such as your birthday or purchasing history, you may not actually own that information. However, many state laws grant rights to individuals when organizations have data about them. Many laws refer to people about whom data is collected as "data subjects," but laws may also refer to consumers, residents, citizens, persons, etc. While these rights vary depending on the law, they often include rights such as:

- **Access.** Data subjects may request access to data about them. A right to access may specify how quickly an organization must respond to requests for access as well requirements for which information they have to disclose.

- **Deletion/correction.** Data subjects may request that an organization delete or correct information about them. Some laws require that information be deleted or corrected within some time frame. Other laws only allow data subjects to request deletions and corrections without compelling organizations to accede to such requests.

- **Portability.** This grants data subjects a right to obtain a copy of their data that they may use personally or transfer to another entity. Portability rights usually require organizations to provide a copy of the data in a non-proprietary readable format that that can be read and used elsewhere.

- **Opt out.** Many state laws provide data subjects with the opportunity to opt out of various processes that impact their privacy. For example, data subjects may be able to opt out of having their data collected, shared, sold, or processed under certain conditions. Some laws may require that data subjects should be given the chance to opt out in advance and/or require businesses to comply with opt-out requests in some timeframe.

- **Opt in.** Some laws require that that organizations must obtain the permission of a data subject to collect, share, or process their information. This is a more stringent standard than an opt out requirement and provides more control to data subjects.

- **Selling and sharing of private information.** Many laws provide a data subject rights related to sharing or selling of their private information. These rights vary. They may take the form of a right to opt in or opt out, merely provide the right to know if private information is shared or sold, or even prohibit sharing and selling of private information entirely.

- **Automated decision-making and artificial intelligence (AI).** As with the rights around sharing and selling of private information described above, rights relating to automated decision-making or AI may take many forms. Automated decision-making often shows up when software programs use machine learning or AI to make decisions that might negatively affect a person. For example, a system that uses AI to select resumes for hiring managers to review may negatively affect those whose resumes aren't selected.

State laws may merely give data subjects the right to know if this is happening, regulate the use of automation, or prohibit it.

Privacy Notice Requirements

Many state privacy laws require organizations to disclose their privacy practices via a written *privacy notice*. Privacy notices are described in more detail in Chapter 1. Some state laws may require privacy notices to be posted publicly online, shared with customers directly, and/or updated periodically.

Privacy notices provide people with a clear and transparent picture of how an organization protects their data. This helps consumers make informed choices and manage personal risk. Privacy notices also help with legal enforcement, because they enable authorities make sure that an organization's privacy practices comply with applicable laws. Many federal laws, cybersecurity frameworks, and industry standards also mandate privacy notices. Sometimes organizations are subject to state laws, federal laws, and other rules that all require privacy notices. In these cases, most organizations craft a single privacy notice that satisfies the requirements all applicable rules.

 The California Online Privacy Protection Act (COPPA), discussed later in this chapter, provides an excellent example of a privacy notice requirement.

Data Protection

Most state privacy laws have various requirements for protecting private information. This include requirements for keeping data secure, managing data that is shared with third parties, and for data retention and destruction.

Data Security Requirements

Many state laws require organizations to implement data security controls to protect personal information. These controls vary from state-to-state and law-to-law, but they often follow the same blueprints as some of the federal laws discussed earlier in this book.

As you learn the nuances of state privacy laws, it is important to recognize these requirements and understand how they may vary by state. While data security controls may be categorized in many different ways, the following categories may help you identify the security controls you are likely to encounter when reviewing state privacy laws:

- **Managerial or administrative** controls include polices for things like role-based access, responsibility for data security programs, training, and risk assessments.
- **Technical** controls include things like encrypting data or implementing multifactor authentication to keep information secure.

- **Operational** controls include practices like logging and monitoring of systems to detect irregularities.
- **Physical** controls include thinks like locks on doors, security gates, and security cameras.

 Different information security frameworks categorize data security controls in different ways. The ISO standards (discussed in Chapter 1) and the NIST standards (discussed in Chapter 4) are frameworks that include lists of security controls that are categorized in different ways. Many organizations choose to adopt standards such as those from NIST or ISO because their rigorous control frameworks are likely to satisfy most legal data security requirements.

Data Protection Agreements

State laws often require that organizations implement procedures for protecting data that is shared with third parties. When an organization is considering sharing private data with a third party, they often review the third-party's data protection policies, controls, and historic track record on privacy. But what happens down the road? It is all too easy for a third party to alter their privacy programs after a data sharing agreement is already in place.

It is easy to imagine a scenario where Company A decides to use Company B to process private information on their behalf. Before agreeing to share data, Company A reviews Company B's privacy practices and is satisfied that their new partner has excellent privacy practices. The risk is that, five years later, Company B's privacy program flounders, privacy practices are watered down, and data protection is no longer adequate to satisfy Company A.

Data protection agreements are helpful in this case because they obligate both parties to maintain an agreed-upon standard for data protection over time. Data protection agreements are particularly helpful when it comes to meeting state law requirements. In the prior example, the two companies may do business in different states. A data protection agreement could specify that Company B (the third party) agrees to conform to the laws of Company A's state. Some state laws require this sort of language to be explicit in data protection agreements to ensure that state laws are followed, even by companies from outside the state.

Data Protection Assessments

Data protection assessments are important tools that enable organizations to determine privacy risks across their operations. Organizations may use data protection assessments to review internal privacy risks and/or privacy risks in vendor operations. The privacy assessment process, described in Chapter 1, provides an example of this sort of assessment.

Data protection assessments may show up in state privacy laws in a couple of ways. First, state laws may require organizations to periodically conduct data protection assessments. Some state laws even require organizations to submit these assessments to a state agency annually. Second, state laws may require organizations to include data protection assessments in any data sharing agreements with third parties.

Data Retention and Destruction

Data retention and destruction practices have been discussed throughout this book. Data retention is discussed in Chapter 1 as part of the Generally Accepted Privacy Principles (GAPP). Many of the privacy regulations discussed throughout this book include provisions requiring policies and procedures for data retention and destruction. State laws contain similar provisions as well.

As always, it is important to keep in mind the principle that state laws do not preempt federal laws. This means that a state law cannot let organizations off the hook from federal laws that have more stringent data retention requirements. However, state law is usually able to add additional requirements that are stricter than the federal law.

Enforcement

Most state laws include provisions that explain how the law may be implemented and enforced. Enforcement provisions may contain several key features, including which part of the state government enforces the law, how complaints are investigated, the penalties for violations, and how appeals are handled.

Cure Periods

When an enforcement authority receives a complaint about a potential privacy violation, they typically begin by investigating the complaint. If the state finds that a violation has taken place, some state laws give the offending organizations a short period of time to rectify the problem before they are penalized. This is known as a *cure period*.

This is a period during which an organization has a chance to "cure" the privacy problem. Cures could mean correcting insufficient policies, implementing better controls, improving training, or complying with requests to exercise data subject rights. If an organization is not able to cure the privacy violation in the specified time period, the enforcement action usually proceeds to the penalty phase.

Penalties

Most privacy laws, including state privacy laws, specify penalties for violations. Penalties may include specified fines and/or the potential for enforcement agencies to seek civil damages. Penalties may also be nonmonetary. For example, an organization may be barred from doing business in the state or required to alter their business practices. Some penalties include a private right of action as well, which allows individuals (not just the state) to sue for damages.

State laws may also include critical details for assessing monetary penalties. For example, penalties may be levied per violation or per incident. Penalties may also be capped at some upper limit. Laws may also include harsher penalties for repeat offenders and so forth.

Exam Tip

It's worth taking a bit of extra time to learn about the potential penalties for violating different state laws. Pay special attention to whether or not each state law discussed provides for a private right of action.

Data Breach Notification

When an organization suffers any sort of breach or unauthorized disclosure of private information, they must manage the problem at several levels. They must respond defensively to stop the breach and recover lost and damaged systems and data. They must also manage any interruption to their business processes or company operations. Organizations must also meet all of their legal and ethical obligations to their customers and regulatory authorities when a breach occurs. Privacy professionals and legal counsel are most often called on to help manage these compliance requirements.

State breach notification laws are an important pillar of data privacy protection in the United States. State breach notification laws help ensure that individuals can protect themselves if their information is compromised. Without such laws, individuals may be at risk for identity theft and never know it. Perhaps just as important, however, is the role state breach notification laws play in holding the U.S. private sector accountable. These laws serve as a powerful incentive for industry to protect personal information contained in physical or digital information systems from unauthorized access. Responding to the various requirements in all these laws is costly. These laws also increase corporate transparency and encourage organizations to protect their reputations by using personal information responsibly.

Elements of State Data Breach Notification Laws

Most state data breach notification laws share a similar DNA but vary in the specifics. It is important to spend time learning these differences. A company may have an incident that is considered a "breach" in some states but not in others. In the event of a breach, organizations may be subject to different time frames, formats, and content requirements for making breach notifications. Different states also have different requirements for what organizations must offer to support victims and/or pay for damages that result from a breach.

Definitions

Most state laws contain a section called "definitions." These definitions often expose critical differences among state laws. Here are two examples of important definitions in data breach notification laws:

Breach   This is a legal term that means different things in different states. Security professionals should be careful to use the term correctly because incidents that meet the definition of a data breach in a state trigger breach notification requirements. Most states consider a breach to have occurred when an organization discovers that a third party has obtained unauthorized access to personal information. In some states, however, a theft of data that has been properly encrypted is not considered a security breach. Some states, such as Alaska and Kentucky, trigger breach notification requirements when an organization has a reasonable belief that unauthorized access took place, even if they aren't completely certain.

Personal Information   Most states trigger breach notification rules if a breach includes personal information on state residents. The definitions of personal information have broad similarities across most state laws. Typically, personal information must include a person's full name, or first initial and last name, linked with another piece of identifying information.

Common pieces of identifying information defined in state breach notification laws include Social Security numbers, driver's license numbers, financial account or credit card numbers, and other identification numbers, such as state identification card numbers or passport numbers. In addition to these common identifiers, some states include various forms of biometric data and healthcare information, such as health insurance numbers or medical record information.

Conditions for Notification

If an organization determines that a breach that involves personal information has occurred, as defined in a given state, they must comply with the state's breach notification rules. These rules may contain several key parameters that vary by state. States have rules that specify whom to notify, when an organization must deliver those notifications, and how those notifications must be transmitted. In many states, these rules vary depending on the scale of the breach (how many people are affected) and the level of risk posed to those affected.

- *Whom to notify:* States may require notification to individuals affected, state regulatory bodies, or even local media outlets. Most states also require organizations to notify the major national credit reporting agencies of breaches as well.

- *When to notify:* Most state laws give an organization a deadline for delivering breach notifications. The clock typically starts when an organization is made aware of a breach, but states vary in how much time an organization has to provide notification. All states prefer speedy notification, but some specify a 30-, 45-, or 60-day deadline, and some merely require notification "without unreasonable delay."

- *How to notify:* Some states have specific requirements that detail how notifications must be composed and/or transmitted. Some states require a notification to be sent by postal mail, whereas others allow electronic notifications.

Subject Rights

Data breach notification laws often require a company to comply with specific rights granted to individuals impacted by a data breach. These may include, for example, a requirement for an organization to pay for credit monitoring services for some period following a data breach. Individuals may also have a private right of action to sue organizations for harms caused by a data breach. Many notification laws include a requirement for organizations to inform people of their rights in the data breach notification itself, as discussed above.

Key Differences Among States

When contending with so many different legal requirements in the midst of a breach, it may be tempting for organizations to simply pick the strictest set of legal requirements and notify all constituents accordingly. Such a strategy, however, carries risks of its own. Providing notifications beyond the legal requirement in a given jurisdiction may unnecessarily alarm individuals, expose the organization to increased legal risk, and damage the organization's reputation. Typically, organizations take care to tailor breach notifications to the laws of each state. This means that organizations must have access to a detailed knowledge of state laws as well as a detailed understanding of the information affected by the breach.

One compelling argument in favor of an overarching federal breach notification law is that a single unified federal law may greatly simplify the compliance picture for businesses.

Most state data breach notification laws include the elements just described, but the details vary by state. For example, states typically define personal information as a person's full name in combination with another bit of identifying information. This second bit of information often varies by state. Arkansas includes "biometric data" as a secondary piece of information and Connecticut does not. A breach of names and linked fingerprints, therefore, may require notification in Arkansas but not in Connecticut. Other variations may occur in each of the areas outlined above. In addition to variations in the definition of personal information, watch for differences among states in each common element of breach notification laws:

- **Breach definition.** If stolen information is encrypted, many states do not consider it to be breached. Some states require that encryption keys be stored separately or certain types of encryptions to consider encrypted data exempt from the definition of a breach.

- **Whom to notify.** Most states require notification to consumers, but some require notification to state agencies or consumer reporting agencies.
- **When to notify.** Some states set strict deadlines for states to provide required notifications, and others merely state that notifications should be made as soon as possible.
- **How to notify.** Some states require notification in some specific medium, like physical mail. Others allow for a variety of notification methods. Some states specify what the notifications must include. Others do not.
- **Subject rights.** Some laws specify remedies that may be provided to victims of data breaches. For example, some laws may require businesses to pay for identity monitoring services for some period.

Significant Developments

While all 50 U.S. states have data breach notification laws on the books, those laws continue to evolve. Following are examples of some notable recent developments in state breach notification laws.

Utah SB 127

Utah's recently enacted SB 127 amended Utah's data breach notification law, the Utah Protection of Personal Information Act. Notably, SB 127 created a new governmental agency called the Utah Cyber Center. The Utah Cyber Center is charged to collaborate with other state and federal agencies to enact a statewide strategic plan for cybersecurity, coordinate incident response processes for any security breaches involving Utah governmental entities, and improve cybersecurity for the state overall. Finally, private sector security breaches of personal information must be centrally reported to the Utah Cyber Center if a breach impacts 500 or more Utah residents.

Utah Data Breach Notification Law Summary

Definitions

Personal Information. First name or initial and last name combined with any of the following: Social Security number, financial account or credit number and access code or password, driver's license or other state identification number.

Breach Notification Requirement. All potential breaches of system security that may compromise personal information require the system owner to investigate. If misuse of data for fraud or identity theft is likely, then notification requirements are triggered. Encrypted data is not considered breached.

Notification Requirements

Whom to Notify.   Any breach requires notification to each affected resident of Utah. Breaches that affect 500 or more residents require further notification to the Utah Attorney General and the Utah Cyber Center. If the breach affects 1,000 residents or more, consumer reporting agencies must also be notified.

When to Notify.   As quickly as possible, while allowing for delays related to system restoration and time for law enforcement activities.

How to Notify.   Notifications to affected residents may be provided by mail, electronic means, phone call, or, if necessary, via publication in a newspaper. Notification to state agencies must include the date the breach occurred and when it was discovered, the number of Utah residents as well as total people impacted, the categories of personal information involved, and a brief description of the incident.

Data Subject Rights

This breach notification law does not include provisions requiring businesses to offer any specific remedies to those affected by data breaches, other than the notifications mentioned above.

Pennsylvania SB 696

In 2022, Pennsylvania amended its existing data breach notification law principally to expand the definition of "personal information." The amendment added medical and health insurance information not otherwise protected HIPAA to its definition of personal information protected by the law. In addition, the definition of personal information was also updated to include information that, when combined, could give an attacker access to a person's online accounts. For example, a username and/or email address combined with a password now constitute personal information.

Pennsylvania Data Breach Notification Law Summary

Definitions

Personal Information.   First name or initial and last name combined with any of the following: Social Security number, financial account or credit card number and access code or password, driver's license or other state identification number, medical information, health insurance information, or a username or email address combined with a password or security code that would grant access to an online account.

Breach Notification Requirement.   Unauthorized access and acquisition of personal information that is likely to cause loss or harm to state residents. The loss of encrypted data is not considered a breach if the encryption key was not compromised and there is a low probability that data may be read.

Notification Requirements

Whom to Notify.   Affected state residents must be notified. Consumer reporting agencies must be notified if the breach affects over 1,000 people.

When to Notify.   Without unreasonable delay.

How to Notify.   Notification by mail, phone, and email are allowed, as is electronic notice prompting users to change usernames or passwords if accounts have been compromised. If the cost of notification is greater than $100,000 or if more than 175,000 people need to be notified, then alternative notifications may be made via a combination of email, posting on the web, and to statewide media.

Data Subject Rights

This breach notification law does not include provisions requiring businesses to offer any specific remedies to those affected by data breaches other than the notifications mentioned above.

Arkansas

Arkansas amended its data breach notification law to include biometric data in the definition of "personal information" that triggers notification requirements when breached. In the Arkansas law, biometric data includes anything that automatically measures someone's biological characteristics, including fingerprints, faceprints, retinal and eye scans, handprints, voiceprints, DNA, or any other biological characteristic that may be captured and used to identify somebody.

Arkansas Data Breach Notification Law Summary

Definitions

Personal Information.   First name or initial and last name combined with any of the following: Social Security number, financial account or credit number and access code or password, driver's license or other state identification number, medical information, or biometric data.

Breach Notification Requirement.   Unauthorized acquisition of unencrypted data that compromises the security, confidentiality, or integrity of personal information.

Notification Requirements

Whom to Notify.   Affected state residents must be notified of breaches. If a third-party has a breach of personal information that belongs to another entity, they must notify the owner immediately. If a breach affects over 1,000 people, the attorney general must be notified.

When to Notify.   Without unreasonable delay. When required, the attorney general must be notified at the same time as affected residents or within 45 days, whichever is sooner.

How to Notify.   Notifications may be made by mail or email. Alternative notification methods may be used if notification costs exceed $250,000, notifications must be made to more than 500,000 people, or if contact information for affected individuals is not available.

Data Subject Rights

This breach notification law does not include provisions requiring businesses to offer any specific remedies to those affected by data breaches other than the notifications mentioned above.

State privacy laws are evolving as states enact new statutes and amend existing laws. It wasn't until 2018, when Alabama enacted SB 318, that all 50 states had enacted breach notification regulations. At the same time, state breach notification laws change frequently because of changes in technology and the landscape of cybersecurity threats. Privacy professionals should collaborate with information security professionals as well as legal counsel in ensuring that an organization's breach notification procedures support compliance across all relevant jurisdictions. As a helpful resource, the National Conference of State Legislatures (NCSL) maintains a reference guide for state breach notification laws:

`[www.ncsl.org/research/telecommunications-and-information-technology/security-breach-notification-laws.aspx]`

Other Recent Updates to State Breach Notification Laws

As states update their regulations and develop new ones, a couple of key trends become apparent. First, not all encryption is created equal. Some state laws have treated encryption as if it were impervious to disclosure and exempted all disclosures of encrypted information from notification requirements. Recently, however, states have recognized that encryption standards vary widely and offer different levels of protection. Additionally, encryption doesn't help one bit if an attacker also gets their hands on the encryption keys.

Recent changes in many states, therefore, take a more nuanced view of encryption and no longer automatically consider all encrypted information to be safe from disclosure. Second, states have begun to expand their definitions of personal information to include important identifiers emerging from our online world. These include information such as IP addresses, email addresses, and biometric information.

Tennessee SB 2005

In 2016, SB 2005 updated Tennessee's breach notification rules to include even encrypted data in the definition of a breach of personal information. Subsequent revisions to Tennessee's breach notification statute have updated this, however. Tennessee's current regulations implement a higher bar for encrypted data to be exempt from breach notification rules. In order to avoid breach notification requirements, organizations must show that data was encrypted according to a specific federal standard and that the encryption keys have not been compromised.

Illinois HB 1260

In 2017, Illinois expanded its definition of personal information for the purposes of breach notification. Under HB 1260, usernames or email addresses count as personal information if they are disclosed in combination with any information, like a password, that would allow an unauthorized party to get access to someone's account. Before HB 1260, it may have been possible for a company doing business in Illinois to discover a breach of usernames and passwords without any requirement to notify affected individuals.

California AB 2828

In 2016, California passed a law, similar to Tennessee, to tighten up data breach notification requirements related to encrypted data. Under AB 2828, organizations are required to trigger breach notifications for disclosures of encrypted data if they have reason to believe encryption keys may have been compromised along with the data.

New Mexico HB 15

In 2017, New Mexico became one of the last states to enact a comprehensive data breach notification law. Perhaps as a consequence, New Mexico's HB 15 includes many of the updated provisions that have appeared in other states as amendments to existing statutes. Like California and Tennessee, HB 15 requires notifications for breaches of encrypted information when encryption keys are compromised. New Mexico HB 15 also includes biometric information in the definition of personal information.

Massachusetts HB 4806

Massachusetts passed a significant update to its data breach notification laws in 2019. Under HB 4806, the commonwealth added requirements for organizations to provide more information in their notifications to state regulators, included instructions for affected individuals on how to place a free security freeze on their credit reports, and tightened up requirements for timely notifications. Most notably, HB 4806 requires companies to contract with third parties to offer free credit monitoring services for affected individuals.

Comprehensive State Privacy Laws

Several states have enacted comprehensive data privacy laws. Most of these laws are modeled, at least in part, after Europe's GDPR. This section will cover applicability, data subject rights, requirements, and enforcement for each comprehensive state law discussed. There is also a summary of the relevant state data breach notification law following each comprehensive privacy law. Studying the features of these state breach notification laws should help you further prepare for the exam.

California Consumer Privacy Act (2018) and California Privacy Rights Act (2020)

The United States has no sweeping federal regulation, nor does the U.S. Constitution comprehensively protect consumer privacy at the federal level. To address the lack of federal privacy protection in the United States, California enacted the California Consumer Privacy Act (CCPA). In general, federal statutes in the United States offer a mixed perspective on who owns and controls personal information held by third parties. Federal law generally allows businesses to control and use personal data while providing consumers with limited rights to know and control information collected about them. CCPA tips this balance squarely in favor of giving consumers more rights to control their personal information.

> The CCPA shares many features common to progressive privacy regulations that give individuals greater control over their data. Such laws often include a more expansive definition of personal information and confer individual rights to ensure that people know what information is collected, get copies of their information, restrict the use of their information, or request that their information be deleted. These features may appear in newer state laws, industry privacy frameworks, international safe harbor programs, or international laws such as the GDPR (discussed in Chapter 9, "International Privacy Regulation").

California Privacy Rights Act

In 2020, California passed the California Privacy Rights Act (CPRA). The CPRA went into effect in 2023 and amends the CCPA. Interestingly, the CPRA was passed by California voters directly as a proposition on the ballot, which makes it difficult to repeal without employing a similar ballot measure. As with any state law, it is important to remember that the CPRA's provisions may still be the subject of federal court decisions, future ballot measures, or preemption by federal statutes.

The CPRA expands the scope of the CCPA to cover more businesses and adds a new category of protected information called "sensitive personal information." The CPRA strengthened the four main consumer rights in the original CCPA and added new privacy rights. The CPRA establishes a state-level regulatory agency, called the California Consumer Privacy Protection Agency (CPPA), to make rules and enforce the law.

Applicability

The CCPA includes thresholds that determine whether an organization is subject to the law. First, only for-profit businesses are subject to the CCPA. In addition, the business must gross over $25 million in annual revenue, broker the data over 100,000+ California residents, or make at least half of their annual revenue from selling Californians' information. The CCPA does not apply to nonprofit or government entities.

Data Subject Rights

The CCPA provides Californians with a set of consumer rights, including these:

- *Right to know:* Businesses are required to notify customers about what information they collect and how that information is used "at the point of collection" and may not collect or use information in any other ways.

- *Right to access:* Upon request by a consumer, businesses must disclose what categories of information they've collected about them. If requested, businesses must provide consumers with a copy of their personal information in a "portable" format. Consumers may not be charged a fee for these disclosures.

- *Right to delete:* Upon request, businesses must delete any personal information that has been collected about a consumer. There are exceptions that include, for example, the information needed to complete transactions, detect cyberattacks or fraud, comply with legal requirements, and a handful of other limited circumstances.

- *Right to opt out:* Consumers have the right to restrict businesses from selling their personal information to third parties. If businesses intend to sell personal information, they must notify consumers and inform them of their right to opt out.

- *Nondiscrimination:* Businesses may not treat anyone differently because they exercise their consumer rights under the CCPA. Businesses must charge the same prices and provide the same quality of products and services.

The CPRA added two additional rights to the CCPA:

- *Right to correct:* Companies must correct inaccurate information they have about consumers upon request.

- *Right to limit:* Consumers can limit business from using and disclosing their personal information.

Requirements

The CCPA's provisions require businesses to perform regular risk-assessment audits and specifically regulate the use of personal information for targeted behavioral advertising. The law also adopts several principles that feature in the EU's GDPR. These include requirements for businesses to minimize the collection and use of personal information, to restrict the collection and use of personal information to the stated purpose, and to disclose records retention policies for all personal information collected.

Enforcement

The CPRA established a state-level regulatory agency, the CPPA, to make rules and enforce the law. The CPRA specifies fines of up to $2,500 per violation, or $7,500 per violation if the violations were intentional and/or involved information about someone under 16 years old. The CPRA does not include an automatic cure period before administrative fines are imposed. However, the CCPA may choose to grant businesses time to cure violations on a case-by-case basis.

Notably, the CCPA is enforced, in part, by providing a limited *private right of action* that permits California citizens to pursue civil penalties directly for violations. The law does allow for a 30-day cure period before a consumer can sue under the CCPA. To begin the process, a consumer must notify the business of their complaint. The business then has 30 days to successfully cure the problem and respond to the consumer. If the business does not comply, then the consumer may proceed with a civil action.

To pursue a private civil action, the consumer must claim that their "unencrypted or nonredacted personal information" has been disclosed in a way not authorized by the law. Such unauthorized disclosures could occur as the result of a security breach, accidental disclosure, or even by a company that shares data with advertisers in violation of the CCPA. In addition, the unauthorized disclosure must include a combination of a person's name and some other indicator of identity, such as a Social Security number or a driver's license number. Consumers may pursue damages that range from $100 up to $750 per incident. Consumers may also pursue actual damages if they are greater.

California Data Breach Notification Law Summary

Definitions

Personal Information.　First name or initial and last name combined with any of the following: Social Security number, financial account or credit number and access code or password, driver's license, passport, tax ID, or other unique identification number, medical information, health insurance information, biometric data, genetic data, license plate recognition system data, and usernames or email addresses combined with passwords or security codes that grant access to online accounts. The CCPA adds IP addresses, email addresses, biometric information, web browsing history, geolocation data, retail transaction records and "inferences drawn from any of the information..." to the definition.

Breach Notification Requirement. Unauthorized acquisition of unencrypted data that compromises the security, confidentiality, or integrity of personal information. The loss of encrypted data is not considered a breach if the encryption key was not compromised and there is a low probability that data may be read.

Notification Requirements

Whom to Notify. Affected state residents. If the breach affects more than 500 California residents, then a copy of the notification must also be supplied to the state attorney general.

When to Notify. Without unreasonable delay.

How to Notify. Notifications may be sent in writing by mail or by email. Alternative notification methods may be used if notification costs exceed $250,000, notifications must be made to more than 500,000 people, or if contact information for affected individuals is not available. California has detailed requirements for the content of notifications and provides a template for notification. The law specifies the title of the notification, headings for each required sections, a minimum font size (10 pt), and the specific content to be included.

Data Subject Rights

If the notification is coming from the source of the breach, then consumers must be offered at least 12 months of identity theft protection services free of charge if their personal information was compromised.

Virginia Consumer Data Protection Act

The Virginia Consumer Data Protection Act (VCDPA) was passed in March 2021 and went into effect on January 1, 2023. The VCDPA is another example of state-level comprehensive consumer privacy protection statutes. While not identical, the VCDPA shares many features with the CCPA.

Applicability

The VCDPA's protections apply to the personal data of all Virginia residents who are "acting only in an individual or household context." The law explicitly excludes data generated in a business context from its provisions. The VCDPA offers a simple definition of personal data as "any information that is linked or reasonably linkable to an identified or identifiable natural person." Public and deidentified data are excluded from this definition and not covered by the provisions of the VCDPA. The VCDPA imposes requirements on anyone doing business in Virginia as well as anyone with "products or services that are targeted" at Virginia consumers if they meet one of two criteria:

- They control or process the personal data of 100,000 or more Virginia consumers in a calendar year.

▪ They control or process the personal data of 25,000 or more Virginia consumers and they earn 50% or more of their gross revenue by selling this personal data.

The law exempts several types of organizations, including nonprofits, colleges and universities, government agencies, and any organizations or data governed by other federal statutes, such as organizations regulated under GLBA or HIPAA.

Data Subject Rights

Like California's CCPA, the VCDPA also confers certain data privacy rights on Virginia consumers. These include:

▪ *Right to confirm:* Consumers have the right to find out if their personal data is being collected and to access that data.

▪ *Right to correct:* Consumers may request the correction of inaccurate information contained in their personal data.

▪ *Right to delete:* Consumers require data controllers to delete their personal data.

▪ *Right to obtain:* Consumers have the right to get a copy of their personal data in a "readily usable" format.

▪ *Right to opt out:* Consumers may opt out of allowing their personal data to be processed for targeted advertising, the sale of their personal data, the use of data in "profiling" the consumer in ways that might influence decisions that have "significant effects" on the consumer.

Requirements

The VCDPA imposes several requirements on anyone doing business and acting as a data controller under the scope of the law. First, data controllers must ensure compliance with all the data subject rights listed. Data controllers must respond to any consumer requests to exercise their rights within 45 days. Data controllers have an option to extend the response period by another 45 days if needed to comply with any especially complicated or difficult requests. If a data controller decides they are not required to comply with a consumer's request, they must inform the consumer and provide the justification. If a consumer requests information, such as a copy of their personal data, then the data controller must provide it free of charge up to two times per year. Finally, data controllers must provide an appeals process for consumers who believe their requests have been unfairly denied.

In addition to complying with the exercise of consumer rights, data controllers are also required to limit data collection and processing to only the intended purposes that have been disclosed to consumers. Data controllers must obtain consent from consumers in order to expand the collection or processing of personal data beyond the original disclosed scope. Data controllers also have to implement information security safeguards and provide detailed privacy notices that include information about how they collect and use personal data as well as the exercise of consumer rights under the VCDPA. Data controllers are required to conduct annual *data protection assessments* to ensure compliance and review their data processing activities. Records of these assessments must be maintained because the VCDPA enables the Virginia Attorney General to compel data controllers to disclose their annual assessments while conducting investigations.

Enforcement

Unlike the CCPA, the VCDPA does not provide a private right of action and is enforceable only by the Virginia Attorney General. Violators may be subject to injunctions and/or civil penalties of up to $7,500 per violation. Interestingly, the VCDPA allows for a grace period for any data controller or processor to remedy a potential violation before penalties are imposed. When a complaint is received, the attorney general will notify the data controller or processor about the alleged violation. If the issue is remedied within 30 days, then no penalties are imposed.

Virginia Data Breach Notification Law Summary

Definitions

Personal Information.   First name or initial and last name combined with any of the following unencrypted and unredacted data: Social Security number, financial account or credit number and access code or password, driver's license, passport, or military identification number, or other state identification number. Note that the law requires at least five digits of a social security number and the last four digits of a license or account number to be deleted for those elements to be considered redacted.

Breach notification Requirement.   Unauthorized access and acquisition of personal information and is likely to cause loss or harm to state residents. The loss of encrypted data is not considered a breach if the encryption key was not compromised and there is a low probability that data may be read.

Notification Requirements

Whom to Notify.   Affected state residents and the state attorney general. Consumer reporting agencies must be notified for breaches affecting over 1,000 people.

When to Notify.   Without unreasonable delay.

How to Notify.   Notifications may be made by mail, phone, or email. Substitute notification methods may be used if notification costs exceed $50,000, notifications must be made to more than 100,000 state residents, or if contact information for affected individuals is not available. Substitute notifications include email notices, online posting, and notice to statewide media. Notifications must include a description of the incident, the types of personal information involved, actions taking to protect the data from further compromise, a phone number to call for assistance if there is one, and advice on checking credit and account reports for signs of fraud.

Data Subject Rights

This breach notification law does not include provisions requiring businesses to offer any specific remedies to those affected by data breaches other than the notifications mentioned.

Colorado Privacy Act

In 2021, Colorado passed the Colorado Privacy Act (CPA), which introduces new requirements for the handling of personal information belonging to Colorado residents. This law is quite similar to the provisions of the California Consumer Privacy Act and the California Privacy Rights Act. It went into effect in 2023.

Applicability

The CPA covers Colorado residents' personal data, defined as any private information that might be linked to an individual consumer. The law also recognizes that some personal data requires additional protections. This category of personal data is called *sensitive data*. Sensitive data includes any personal information on a child under 13 years old; biometric data that identifies individuals; and information that reveals a person's race, ethnicity, religion, sexual orientation, health status, or citizenship. The law applies to any organization that conducts business in Colorado or produces or delivers products or services that are intentionally targeted at residents of Colorado if that business either:

- Controls or processes the personal information of 100,000 or more Colorado residents, or
- Controls or processes the personal information of 25,000 residents and the business either earns revenue or receives discounts from selling personal information.

One of the important distinctions for this law is that the Colorado law does apply to the handling of information by nonprofit organizations even though those organizations are exempted from similar laws in California and Virginia. There is, however, an exception in the law for businesses handling information about their own employees or other businesses.

Data Subject Rights

The CPA creates a series of consumer privacy rights, including:

- *Right to opt out:* Colorado consumers may restrict organizations from selling their data and from using their data for targeted advertising.

- *Right to know:* Organizations must inform consumers if they collect personal information.

- *Right to access:* Consumers may request access to any personal data that has been collected.

- *Right to correct:* Consumers may request corrections to any errors in data that has been collected about them.

- *Right to delete:* Consumers have the right to have their personal data deleted upon request.

- *Right to download and remove:* This right falls into the portability category described earlier in this chapter. Consumers have the right to get a copy of their data in a format that can be ported into a new platform.

Requirements

The Colorado Privacy Act requires data controllers under the scope of the law to comply with all data subject rights. The Act gives data controllers up to 45 days to respond to consumer requests to exercise their rights, and a business may extend that timeline for another 45 days if they provide the consumer with notice and a reason for the delay.

Businesses under this law are required to notify consumers about the data they collect, store, and share, and they must also disclose the purposes for which they use the data. Businesses must also practice data minimization, so they only collect data to fulfill the purposes they've disclosed and avoid allowing data to be used for secondary purposes. Businesses also adopt "reasonable security practices" to ensure data security.

Before sharing or selling any personal data or doing any sort of processing with sensitive data, businesses must conduct a data protection assessment to guard data subjects against the financial harm, injury, privacy violations, and other unfair or deceptive practices. When it comes to sensitive data, businesses must also get prior consent from consumers before processing, sharing, or selling the data.

Enforcement

The Colorado law does not provide a private right of action and is enforceable only by government authorities, such as the Colorado Attorney General. The CPA does not confer a private right of action. When enacted, the CPA included a provision to allow businesses a 60-day cure period if the attorney general believes the problem can be fixed. Importantly, however, the provision that created the cure period included an end date of January 1, 2025. After that data, the law no longer allows for a cure period. By offering a cure period during the first couple of years after the law was enacted, the state of Colorado is giving businesses some time to improve their privacy practices to comply with the law.

Violations of the CPA are considered deceptive trade practices under Colorado law. The state attorney general may pursue legal action against businesses to impose penalties.

The penalty for deceptive trade practices is defined by a different Colorado law: the Colorado Consumer Protection Act. Under the Colorado Consumer Protection Act, each violation may carry a penalty of up to $20,000.

As you study the structure of state and federal laws, you'll notice that many laws reference other laws. In the example of Colorado, the CPA doesn't explicitly set a penalty for violations. Instead, the CPA defines violations as "deceptive trade practices," and that term is already defined, along with penalties, in another law. For another example, notice that many state privacy laws discussed here don't include data breach notification provisions. That's because many of these states have a separate data breach notification law (discussed later in this chapter) that they can reference. This practice helps states avoid defining the same concepts repeatedly in separate laws. This practice also helps states keep common definitions and legal procedures consistent across many laws to reduce confusion.

Colorado Data Breach Notification Law Summary

Definitions

Personal Information. First name or initial and last name combined with any of the following unencrypted and unredacted data: Social Security number, financial account or credit number and access code or password, driver's license, student, passport, or military identification number, or other state identification number, medical information, insurance identification number, biometric data, or usernames, passwords, or account numbers combined with passwords or security codes that grant access to online accounts.

Breach Notification Requirement. Unauthorized acquisition of unencrypted personal information that comprises the security, confidentiality, or integrity of the information.

Notification Requirements

Whom to Notify. Affected state residents. Consumer reporting agencies must be notified for breaches affecting over 1,000 people.

When to Notify. Within 30 days after determining a breach has occurred.

How to Notify. Notifications may be made by mail, phone, or email. Substitute notification methods may be used if notification costs exceed $250,000, notifications must be made to more than 250,000 state residents, or if contact information for affected individuals is not available. Substitute notifications include email notices, online posting, and notice to statewide media. Notifications must include the date of the breach, a description of the personal data involved, contact information, toll-free phone numbers, addresses, and websites for consumer reporting agencies, and information on getting information from the FTC on fraud alerts and credit freezes.

Data Subject Rights

This breach notification law does not include provisions requiring businesses to offer any specific remedies to those affected by data breaches other than the notifications mentioned.

Connecticut Data Privacy Act

The Connecticut Data Privacy Act (CTDPA) is a comprehensive consumer data privacy law that went into effect on July 1, 2023. The Act provides Connecticut residents with rights regarding the collection, sale, and disclosure of their personal data by businesses operating in the state.

Applicability

The CTDPA applies to businesses that control or process data of 100,000 or more Connecticut residents annually or derive over 25% of their gross revenue from selling personal data and control or process the data of at least 25,000 Connecticut residents. It does not apply to certain entities such as state and local governments, nonprofits, higher educational institutions, financial institutions under the GLBA, entities under the HIPAA, and data covered by the FCRA.

Data Subject Rights

The rights under CTDPA granted to Connecticut residents include access, correction, deletion, data portability, and opt out of certain data processing. The Act also allows residents to appeal denials of requests by controllers and designates another person as an authorized agent to exercise the right to opt out on their behalf.

Requirements

The CTDPA imposes various obligations on data controllers and processors. Controllers must provide transparency, limit data collection, avoid secondary use, ensure security, handle sensitive data with care, avoid discrimination, and conduct data protection assessments. Processors must adhere to controller instructions, assist in responding to consumer rights requests, and ensure data security. Controllers and processors are also required to have a contractual relationship that lays out the data protection responsibilities of each party.

Enforcement

There is no private right of action under the CTDPA. Instead, the Connecticut Attorney General has exclusive authority to enforce the law, with violations considered as unfair trade practices under the Connecticut Unfair Trade Practices Act (CUTPA). Civil penalties under CUTPA are set at up to $5,000 for each violation.

Like the Colorado privacy law, the CTDPA provided for a cure period for a window of time after the law was enacted. The CTDPA's cure period provision extends only to December 31, 2024. Before this date, the CTDPA allows for a cure period only in cases where the attorney general believes it is possible for the data controller to remedy the issue. If the attorney general determines that the issue isn't fixable, then no cure period is provided.

If a cure period is granted, the attorney general must notify controllers of violations. Controllers are then granted 60 days to remedy the problem. If the problem is not fixed within 60 days, the attorney general may file a lawsuit seeking penalties.

Connecticut Data Breach Notification Law Summary

Definitions

Personal Information. First name or initial and last name combined with any of the following unencrypted and unredacted data: Social Security number, credit card number, financial account and access code or password, driver's license, passport, or military identification number, or other state identification number, medical information, insurance identification number, biometric data, or usernames, passwords, or account numbers combined with passwords or security codes that grant access to online accounts.

Breach Notification Requirement.   Unauthorized access to unencrypted personal information.

Notification Requirements

Whom to Notify.   Affected state residents and the state attorney general. Consumer reporting agencies must be notified for breaches affecting over 1,000 people.

When to Notify.   Within 60 days after discovering a breach has occurred.

How to Notify.   Notifications may be made by mail, phone, or email. Substitute notification methods may be used if notification costs exceed $250,000, notifications must be made to more than 500,000 people, or if contact information for affected individuals is not available. Substitute notifications include email notices, online posting, and notice to statewide media. Notifications must include information on how to enroll in free identity theft protection services.

Subject Rights

Affected individuals are entitled to be offered free identity theft protection and, if necessary, mitigation services for at least 24 months.

Utah

The Utah Consumer Privacy Act (UCPA) was enacted in 2023. The UCPA is another example of a comprehensive state privacy law.

Applicability

The Utah privacy law applies to companies doing business in Utah or those who market to Utah consumers. There are additional thresholds for applicability. First, the law only applies to businesses with $25,000 or more in annual revenue. In addition, businesses must either manage personal data of 100,000+ people in a year or manage the personal data of only 25,000+ people but earn more than half of their gross revenue from selling that data.

The UCPA includes several exemptions to applicability. The Act does not apply to governmental organizations and organizations carrying out government contracts. Higher education institutions, tribes, nonprofits, and covered entities and business associates under HIPAA are also exempt. The Act does not apply to personal information that is regulated under federal laws that include HIPAA, GLBA, FERPA, the Driver's Privacy Protection Act, and the Farm Credit Act. Certain personal data related to employees is also exempt.

Data Subject Rights

The UCPA grants several data subject rights. These include the right to know if a business is processing their personal information and to access that information. Consumers also have the right to delete any data they provided to a data controller. The UCPA grants a right to get a copy of any personal data they provided in a portable and readable format that can be reused. Finally, consumers may opt out of targeted advertising or the sale of their personal data.

Requirements

Businesses must comply with all data subject rights listed above. Data controllers have 45 days to act on any requests from consumers to exercise their data subject rights. Controllers have the option for a one-time extension of another 45 days so long as they notify the consumer about the extension and the reason for it. Controllers are also prohibited from charging fees for fulfilling consumer requests except for small fees to cover costs in the case of particularly difficult requests.

Before contracting with third parties performing data processing activities, controllers are required to put data protection provisions in place as part of their contracts. These contracts must include provisions that define the data processing activities, assure confidentiality, and obligate data processors to follow the same requirements as the data controller.

Data controllers must demonstrate transparency and provide clearly written privacy notices. Controllers are required to implement reasonable data privacy and security controls. Consumers must be given reasonable time to opt out before a business starts processing their data. Controllers are prohibited from discriminating against consumers for exercising their data subject rights under the UCPA, but controllers are allowed to charge different rates if a consumer opts out of targeted advertising or chooses to participate in a loyalty program.

Enforcement

The Utah Attorney General has the sole authority to enforce the UCPA. There is no private right of action. This law does provide for a cure period. The attorney general must notify data controllers of violations and allow for a 30-day cure period before initiating enforcement. If the data controller does not notify the attorney general that the violation has been successfully cured in that time frame, then the attorney general may pursue penalties. Penalties may be as high as $7,500 per violation as well as any actual damages.

 Utah's state breach notification laws are summarized in the section on significant developments in state data breach notification laws.

Florida

In 2023, Florida passed SB 262, which is known as the Florida Digital Bill of Rights (FDBR). This law is perhaps less comprehensive than other laws discussed in this section. As you'll see below, Florida's law only applies when a very high revenue threshold is met.

Applicability

The FDBR has a series of thresholds used to determine applicability. If all of these conditions are met, a business meets the definition of a "controller" and the FDBR applies. First, the FDBR applies to for-profit entities that do business in Florida. The business must also collect personal consumer information and control the means and reasons for processing personal information. Businesses also have to earn more than $1 billion in gross annual revenue. Finally, a business must either earn more than half of their revenue from targeting advertising and selling personal data or operating a smart speaker and voice command system.

Certain types of data are exempted from the scope of the FDBR. These include personal information used for processing short-term payments, deidentified information, information collected for legal compliance purposes, data collected on employees related to their employment, PHI covered by HIPAA and other personal information covered by other federal laws such as GLBA and the FCRA.

Data Subject Rights

The FDBR grants consumers the right to know what personal information a controller collects and/or shares about them, including the specific information collected, the sources of that data, and the identities of any third parties with whom their information has been shared. This information must be provided to consumers within 45 days of receiving a request.

Consumers have the right to request that controllers correct or delete personal information about them. Upon receipt of such a request, controllers have 90 days to comply unless the information is required to complete the transaction with the consumer, fulfill legal obligations, for cybersecurity purposes, academic research, or reasonable internal business purposes.

Consumers have the right to opt out of allowing their personal information to be sold or shared. Controllers are required to maintain an obvious form allowing consumers to opt out of the sharing and sale of their personal information and must respect a request to opt out for at least a full year before they can ask the consumer for permission to sell or share their information again.

Requirements

The FDBR requires controllers to comply with all data subject rights as describes above. Controllers are also prohibited from denying consumers access to products and services because they exercise their data subject rights. However, controllers may charge different prices and/or offer a different quality of product or service if a consumer exercises their rights.

As with other state laws, the FDBR requires controllers to implement data security and privacy controls, including records retention. Controllers are required to maintain a privacy policy and share a privacy notice that includes information about consumer data subject rights. Finally, any contracts that allow data to be shared with third parties must include data protection language that obligates the third party to the same requirements as the controller.

Enforcement

Violations of the FDBR are considered unfair and deceptive trade practices under existing Florida law. The FDBR is solely enforced by the Florida Department of Legal Affairs. Violations may carry hefty fines of up to $50,000 per violation. Penalties may be increased beyond this amount for repeat offenses or for violations involving minors.

The law does allow for a 45-day cure period, but that cure period is not guaranteed. The Florida Department of Legal Affairs is empowered to grant a cure period—or not—at its discretion. When considering whether to grant a cure period, several factors are taken into consideration, including the severity, number, and frequency of violations, as well as any safety concerns. The FDBR does not include a private right of action.

Florida Data Breach Notification Law Summary

Definitions

Personal Information.   First name or initial and last name combined with any of the following unencrypted and unredacted data: Social Security number, credit card or financial account and access code or password, driver's license, passport, or military identification number, or other state identification number, medical information, insurance identification number, biometric data, geolocation, or usernames, passwords, or account numbers combined with passwords or security codes that grant access to online accounts.

Breach Notification Requirement.   Unauthorized access to personal information.

Notification Requirements

Whom to Notify.   Affected state residents. If the breach affects more than 500 state residents, then the Florida Department of Legal Affairs must also be notified. Consumer reporting agencies must be notified for breaches affecting over 1,000 people.

When to Notify.   Within 30 days after determining a breach has occurred.

How to Notify.   Notifications may be made by mail or email. Substitute notification methods may be used if notification costs exceed $250,000, notifications must be made to more than 500,000 people or if contact information for affected individuals is not available. Substitute notifications include an online posting and notice to statewide media. Notifications must include the data of the breach, a description of the personal information involved, and contact information for questions.

Subject Rights

This breach notification law does not include provisions requiring businesses to offer any specific remedies to those affected by data breaches other than the notifications mentioned.

Oregon

The Oregon Consumer Privacy Act (OCPA) went into effect on July, 1, 2024. For nonprofits, however, the OCPA is in effect as of July 1, 2025. The OCPA protects information defined as personal data and provides additional protections for category of personal data that is defined as "sensitive data." Personal data is any data that can be linked to a person or their household devices. Sensitive data includes data that reveals a person's protected identities (race, ethnicity, national origin, religion, sexual orientation, citizenship, immigration status), health status, LGBTQ status, crime victim status, identifiable genetic or biometric data, data on children under 13, or specific location information.

Applicability

The OCPA applies to any entity or person that is considered a "controller" under the law. Controllers are defined as any entity or person who does business in Oregon and meets one of two criteria. For the OCPA to apply, an entity must process or control the personal data of at least 100,000 people or process or control the data of only 25,000 people but earn at least 25% of gross yearly revenue by selling personal information.

Note that controllers do not need to be based in Oregon or specifically target Oregon residents for the OCPA to apply. If an entity provides services or products to Oregon residents and meets one of the data collection thresholds described above, then they are a controller under the law.

The OCPA exempts some types of entities and some types of information. Unlike some other state privacy laws, however, the OCPA does not provide a blanket exemption for nonprofit organizations. As noted, the law did allow an extra year before going into effect for nonprofits.

The OCPA does not apply to public corporations. The law specifically mentions that the Oregon Health and Science University and the Oregon State Bar are both exempt, as are other public entities as defined in existing Oregon law. Government agencies, some insurance-related entities, and financial institutions are also exempt.

The OCPA also exempts certain categories of information. The Act does not apply to data used only for completing payment transactions. PHI covered by HIPAA and personal information that is mingled with PHI is exempt. Other exemptions include scientific research, information collected solely for employment purposes, and credit reporting information already covered by other financial privacy laws, such as the FCRA. Finally, the OCPA exempts data covered by other notable federal laws such as GLBA, FERPA, and the Driver's Protection Act. Information used for noncommercial purposes by publishers, news media, radio stations, television networks, and other media programming operations is also exempt.

Data Subject Rights

The OCPA confers several data subject rights on Oregon residents. These include the rights to access personal information collected about them, know with whom their data has been shared, correct their data, delete their data, get a copy of their data, and opt out of targeted advertising and profiling based on their personal information.

Requirements

Controllers must comply with data subject rights within 45 days of receiving a request. As of January 1, 2026, controllers will be required to respect universal opt outs, such as opt-out mechanisms in web browsers. Data controllers are required to provide a privacy notice that discloses what data they collect and process and the purposes for which the data is used. Controllers must also inform consumers about their rights under the OCPA and how to make requests to exercise those rights. Controllers must put data minimization practices in place to ensure that data collection and processing limited to only what is necessary. Controllers must obtain consent before collecting or processing data for any other purposes.

Similar to the GDPR regulation, the OCPA requires controllers to conduct *data protection assessments* before beginning data processing activities that may be high risk. Controllers are also required to have data security and privacy safeguards in place to protect personal and sensitive information. Controllers have additional obligations when it comes to sensitive data. They must obtain consent prior to collecting or processing sensitive data.

Enforcement

The OCPA is enforced by the Oregon Attorney General. There is no private right of action. The Act provides an option for a cure period but only until January 1, 2026. After that, cure periods are no longer allowed. Until January 1, 2026, however, the attorney general may grant a 30-day cure period if they determine that the controller can remedy the issue. The attorney general may seek civil penalties of up to $7,500 per violation.

Oregon Data Breach Notification Law Summary

Definitions

Personal Information.   First name or initial and last name combined with any of the following unencrypted and unredacted data: Social Security number, credit card or financial account and access code or password, driver's license, passport, or military identification number, or other state identification number, medical information, insurance identification number, biometric data, or usernames, passwords, or account numbers combined with passwords or security codes that grant access to online accounts. This law also includes a catch-all provision that personal information includes any combination of information that would enable identity theft.

Breach Notification Requirement.   Unauthorized acquisition to personal information that compromises security, confidentiality, or integrity.

Notification Requirements

Whom to Notify.   Affected state residents. If the breach affects more than 250 consumers, then the state attorney General must also be notified. Consumer reporting agencies must be notified for breaches affecting over 1,000 people.

When to Notify.   Within 45 days after discovering a breach has occurred.

How to Notify.   Notifications may be made by mail, phone, or email. Substitute notification methods may be used if notification costs exceed $250,000, notifications must be made to more than 350,000 consumers, or if contact information for affected individuals is not available. Substitute notifications include an online posting and notice to statewide media. Notifications must include the data of the breach, a description of the personal information involved, and contact information for the entity that experienced the breach, contact information for consumer reporting agencies, and advice on how to report identity theft.

Subject Rights

This breach notification law does not include provisions requiring businesses to offer any specific remedies to those affected by data breaches, other than the notifications mentioned above.

Texas

The Texas Data Privacy and Security Act was enacted in July 2024. The Act applies to businesses that operate or sell products or services in Texas. The act applies to Texas businesses that collect, process, or share personal information.

Applicability

Generally, the Act exempts any small businesses as defined by the U.S. federal government's Small Business Administration (SBA). Other exempt entities include higher education institutions, state government agencies, electrical and other power utilities, nonprofits, and entities covered by HIPAA or GLBA. Information that is governed by other federal laws, needed for legal compliance, scientific research, and for employment is also exempt.

The Act also defines a category of personal information called sensitive data. Sensitive data includes any personal information on children under 13 years old and any specific location data. While small businesses are largely exempt from this law, they must obtain prior consent from consumers before selling sensitive data.

The U.S. Small Business Administration's definition of a small business varies by industry and considers both revenue and number of employees. The SBA publishes these definitions at https://www.sba.gov/document/support-table-size-standards

Data Subject Rights

The Texas privacy law provides several consumer rights. Consumers have a right to know what data is being collected and to get a copy of their information in a portable format. Data subjects have the right to request corrections to their information and to have their information deleted. Consumers also have the right to opt out of targeted advertising or the sale of their personal information. Interestingly, the Act also allows consumers the right to opt out of allowing their personal data to be used for profiling in cases where profiling could inform decisions about financial services, housing, insurance, health care, education enrollment, criminal justice, or access to basic needs.

Finally, businesses are prohibited from retaliating or discriminating against consumers for exercising these rights. Many state laws prohibit retaliation. In the Texas law, however, this prohibition against retaliation and discrimination is expressed as a data subject right.

Requirements

Controllers subject to the Texas Data Privacy and Security Act are obligated to comply with data subject rights within 45 days. Controllers my extend this period by another 45 days if they notify the consumer and provide a reason for the delay. Controllers may generally only charge a fee for complying with data subject requests if a consumer makes more than two requests in a year. Controllers may also charge a fee if the request is particularly onerous or unfounded.

The Act requires controllers to post privacy notices that disclose what types of information they collect and why, what types of information they share with third parties, what type of third parties they share with, and information for consumers on how to exercise their data subject rights. The Act also specifies exact language that must be included in the privacy notice if the controller sells any sensitive or biometric data. Controllers must collect and use data only as necessary to fulfill the purposes disclosed in their privacy notices.

Enforcement

The Texas Data Privacy and Security Act is solely enforced by the Texas Attorney General. There is no private right of action. The Act includes a 30-day cure period to allow controllers an opportunity to remedy any violations. If violations cannot be cured within 30 days, then the attorney general may pursue civil penalties of up to $7,500 per violation. The attorney general may also seek legal fees, court costs, and court orders (injunctions) that create compliance requirements for controllers.

Texas Data Breach Notification Law Summary

Definitions

Personal Identifying Information. First name or initial and last name combined with any of the following unencrypted and unredacted data: Social Security number, date of birth, mother's maiden name, electronic identification number, address, or routing code, credit card or financial account and access code or password, driver's license or other government identification number, medical information, or biometric data.

Breach Notification Requirement. Unauthorized acquisition of unencrypted personal information that compromises security, confidentiality, or integrity. Note that data are considered breached encryption keys have been compromised.

Notification Requirements

Whom to Notify. Affected state residents. If the breach affects more than 250 state residents, then the state attorney general must also be notified. Consumer reporting agencies must be notified for breaches affecting over 10,000 people.

When to Notify. Within 60 days after discovering a breach has occurred.

How to Notify. Notifications may be made by mail or email. Substitute notification methods may be used if notification costs exceed $250,000, notifications must be made to more than 500,000 people, or if contact information for affected individuals is not available. Substitute notifications include email, an online posting, and notice to statewide media. The law does not specify what content must be included in notifications to individuals. Notices to the attorney general must be made via an online form and include a description of the breach, the types of personal identifiable information involved, the number of affected state residents and the number of those who have been notified, and actions taken so far in response to the breach as well as actions planned for the future, and finally, information on whether law enforcement is involved.

Subject Rights

This breach notification law does not include provisions requiring businesses to offer any specific remedies to those affected by data breaches other than the notifications mentioned.

Montana

In 2023, the Montana legislature passed the Montana Consumer Data Privacy Act (MTCDPA). This law protects personal data, defined as any data that can be reasonably linked to a person. The law also creates a category of personal data, called "sensitive data," defined as personal data that reveals a person's race, ethnicity, religion, health status, sexual activities, sexual orientation, citizenship, immigration status, genetic data, biometric data, location data, or any personal data on a child under 13 years old.

Applicability

The MTCDPA applies to any business operating in Montana or businesses that target Montana residents that meet one of two criteria. For the MTCDPA to apply, a business must control or process the data of 50,000 or more people or the data of only 25,000 people but earn more than 25% of their annual revenue from selling personal information.

Several categories of organization are exempt from the MTCDPA. These include governmental bodies, nonprofits, higher education institutions, organizations regulated under the Securities Exchange Act, and organizations or data covered by GLBA, HIPAA, FCRA, the Driver's Privacy Protection Act, FERPA, COPPA, the Farm Credit Act, human subjects in scientific research, and information related solely to employment.

Data Subject Rights

The MTCDPA confers many familiar data subject rights. These include the right to know if their data is being processed and to access their personal data, correct their data, delete their data, get a copy of their data in a readable and portable format, and to opt out of targeted advertising, sale of their data, and profiling activities that may be used for decisions that have real impact on the consumer.

Requirements

The MTCDPA requires controllers to comply with any requests from data subjects to exercise their rights within 45 days. This period may be extended one time by another 45 days if the controller notifies the consumer with the reason. In general, consumers are entitled to have their requests fulfilled at no charge at least once every 12 months. If consumer requests are repeated or excessive, controllers are allowed to charge reasonable administrative fees.

Controllers are required to provide a clear privacy notice that discloses what types of data they process, the purposes of the data processing, what types data may be shared with third parties, and what types of third parties with whom they may share data. The privacy notices must inform consumers of their rights under the act and provide a way for consumers to easily contact the controller to exercise their rights.

Controllers must conduct data protection assessments before conducting any high-risk processing activities. Any contracts that allow third parties to process personal information must include data protection provisions to assure confidentiality, data minimization, and to generally obligate any third parties to the same requirements as the controller. Finally, controllers must have reasonable controls in place to protect information security and privacy.

Enforcement

The MTCDPA is enforced by the Montana Attorney General and does not include a private right of action. The law allows for a 60-day cure period before the attorney general may seek penalties. However, the provision allowing a cure period ends April 1, 2026. After that date, no cure period is provided. Interestingly, this law does not specify a monetary cap on penalties for violations. The law says only that the "Attorney General may bring an action" against controllers who violate the law.

Montana Data Breach Notification Law Summary

Definitions

Personal Identifying Information.   First name or initial and last name combined with any of the following unencrypted and unredacted data: Social Security number, credit card or financial account and access code or password, driver's license, taxpayer ID, or other government identification number, medical information, or identity protection identification number.

Breach Notification Requirement.   Unauthorized acquisition of unencrypted personal information that compromises security, confidentiality, or integrity and is likely to cause harm to state residents.

Notification Requirements

Whom to Notify.   Affected state residents and the state attorney general's consumer protection office.

When to Notify.   Without unreasonable delay.

How to Notify.   Notifications may be made by mail, phone, or email. Substitute notification methods may be used if notification costs exceed $250,000, notifications must be made to more than 500,000 people, or if contact information for affected individuals is not available. Substitute notifications include email, an online posting and notice to statewide media.

Subject Rights

This breach notification law does not include provisions requiring businesses to offer any specific remedies to those affected by data breaches other than the notifications mentioned.

Subject-Specific State Privacy Laws

Many states have enacted privacy laws to safeguard specific categories of data. These include laws to protect the privacy of health and genetic information, improve online privacy, protect biometric data, and financial information. As you study this section, it is important to keep in mind that many of the comprehensive privacy laws discussed also protect these types of information.

Health and Genetic Information

Several states have laws on the books that specifically govern the privacy of health-related information, including privacy protections for genetic data.

Washington My Health My Data Act

The Washington My Health My Data Act is intended to protect consumer health information that is not otherwise protected by HIPAA. HIPAA covers only certain types of entities and transactions, so there is potentially a lot of health information that doesn't have privacy protections.

This Washington law provides privacy protections for information it defines as "consumer health data." According to the law, consumer health data includes any information that can be linked to an identifiable person that discloses their "physical or mental health status." Consumer health data also includes data that entities may infer about a person's physical or mental health status. Organizations and information already covered by HIPAA or other federal laws are exempt. This law covers all "regulated entities," which it defines as any organization that does business in Washington or targets Washington consumers that collects, controls, or processes consumer health data.

A regulated entity may only collect consumer health data with the consumer's consent or only as needed to provide services or products to a customer. Regulated entities are also prohibited from sharing any consumer health data without prior consent, or unless necessary to deliver services or products to customers.

This law gives consumers the right to know if their consumer health data is being collected, to withdraw any previous consent, and to have their data deleted by regulated entities and any third parties.

Regulated entities are required to maintain data security and privacy controls to safeguard consumer health data, provide a privacy policy and notice that informs consumers of data collection and processing practices and consumer rights, and to minimize access to consumer health data. This act makes it illegal to sell consumer health data without prior authorization from the consumer. Consumer authorizations must include specifics such as the data in question, all the parties involved, the purpose, how the data will be used, and when the authorization expires.

This Act also makes it illegal to set up a geofence within 2,000 feet of any facility that provides healthcare services if that geofence is intended to track individuals seeking healthcare, collect consumer health data, or engage in targeted advertising based on consumer health information.

 Laws that restrict geofencing to protect healthcare information are relatively new and worth studying for the exam. A geofence is defined in this Washington State law as any technology used to "establish a virtual boundary" around a physical location that can be used to determine the precise geolocation of an individual.

Violations to this law are considered "unfair business practices" under the Washington Consumer Protection Act. Under Washington law, the Act may be enforced by the attorney general and via a private right of action. The Washington Consumer Protection Act allows violators to be sued for actual damages, court costs, or other penalties. The court may even increase damages awarded beyond actual costs—up to three times more, not to exceed $25,000—in egregious cases.

Illinois Genetic Information Privacy Act

The Illinois Genetic Information Privacy Act (GIPA) is aimed at prohibiting discrimination based on genetic information. GIPA focuses on prohibiting discrimination in employment as well as in health insurance and accident insurance. GIPA also classifies genetic information as confidential, thus obligating companies that collect and process genetic information to safeguard the data.

GIPA not only prohibits employers from using genetic information to discriminate in decision-making, it also prohibits them from soliciting, seeking, or requiring genetic data on individuals.

Notably, GIPA is enforced by a private right of action, and several high-profile lawsuits have already been filed under GIPA. Under GIPA, individuals can sue for $2,500 per violation and/or actual damages if actual damages are higher. If the violation was intentional or especially reckless, then damages may increase to $15,000 per violation.

There have been several class action lawsuits resulting from breaches to the confidentiality of genetic information. For example, the popular genetic testing company 23andMe disclosed a serious data breach in 2023 in which the data of nearly 7 million consumers was compromised. Multiple class action lawsuits have been filed against 23andMe under GIPA as well California's CPRA.

In addition, several class action lawsuits have been filed against employers for alleged GIPA violations. For example, some employers require employees to have regular medical exams that may include questions about family medical history. These sorts of questions may constitute genetic information and thus risk a violation of GIPA. Many of these lawsuits remain in litigation and are yet to be settled.

Nevada Consumer Health Data Privacy Law

The Nevada Consumer Health Data Privacy Law has several features in common with Washington's My Health My Data Act. The law intends to add privacy protections for consumer health data that isn't already protected by HIPAA. The law applies to "regulated entities" that do business in Nevada or target Nevada consumers and control, process, or sell consumer health data. This law may also be referred to as Nevada SB 370.

Consumer health data includes any data that might be reasonable linked to an identifiable individual that reveals mental or physical health conditions, medical procedures, medications, reproductive care, gender-affirming care, genetic and biometric information, or location where related services are received. This law does not apply to organizations or information already covered by HIPAA or other federal laws, such as GLBA.

The law grants consumers several rights. First, consumers have the right to opt in. Regulated entities must seek prior authorization before collecting or sharing any consumer health information. Consumers also have the right to know with whom their data have been shared, as well as to request that their data be deleted. Consumers may also opt out of data collection and sharing.

This law requires that regulated entities implement information security and privacy safeguards and limit access to consumer health data. Regulated entities must also post privacy notices that disclose what data they collect, how the data is used, and with whom it is shared. Privacy notices must also include information on how consumers may exercise their rights under the law. This regulation also prohibits anyone from setting up a geofence around any facility where a person may receive health care services if that geofence is intended to identify individuals seeking healthcare, harvest their consumer health data, or engage in related targeted advertising. Violations to this law are considered deceptive trade practices under Nevada law.

Online Privacy

Online privacy is a broad category that includes state privacy laws related to website operators, online cookies and tracking, as well as special provisions to protect the privacy on children online.

Cookies and Online Tracking

In today's digital world, consumer behavior online is increasingly tracked. Individual online activities are often tracked through the use of cookies. At a technical level, a cookie is a small computer file. When a person visits a website, the site collects and stores a bit of identifying information, such as user name or a computer's Internet Protocol (IP) address. Storing cookies allows websites to offer convenience for users, such as remembering an individual user's preferences. Cookies, however, may also be used to track individual online activity by associating everything a given user does on a website with a specific person or device. In many cases, users and their online activities are easily identifiable by anyone with access to the tracking data.

The California Consumer Privacy Act (CCPA) already includes cookies in its definition of personal information. Businesses subject to the CCPA must disclose their collection and use of data through cookies and must allow consumers to opt out of cookies. The Virginia Consumer Data Protection Act (VCDPA) also has implications for regulating cookie privacy because it defines personal data as any data that is "reasonably linkable" to a person's identity.

As the use of cookies and other techniques for tracking individual activities online continues to grow, many more states are considering updating their privacy laws to include cookies and other online tracking information in their definitions of personal information. Such definitions could help bring personally identifiable data on consumers' online behavior under the scope of state-level data privacy regulations. In many cases, data generated by cookies may also be subject to state breach notification laws.

Delaware Online Privacy and Protection Act (2016)

The Delaware Online Privacy and Protection Act (DOPPA) obligates website operators to additional privacy requirements. DOPPA's requirements fall into three main areas: privacy policies, protections for children, and protections for the privacy of users' reading habits. DOPPA applies to operators of any website, app, or online service that is accessible to Delawareans.

 DOPPA's definition of website operators explicitly excludes web hosting services that have nothing to do with operating the actual site. Amazon Web Services, therefore, would not be liable under DOPPA for websites it hosts but doesn't run.

DOPPA requires all website operators to make their privacy policies "conspicuously available" on their web pages. Privacy policies must detail what PII is collected, a process for users to review and request changes to their personal information, a process for notifying users about changes to the privacy policy, how the site handles "do not track" settings or requests from user web browsers, effective date of the policy, and information about any third parties collecting PII in connection with the website.

DOPPA also builds on the Children's Online Privacy Protection Act (COPPA) discussed in Chapter 5 by prohibiting certain forms of marketing to children. Unlike COPPA, DOPPA defines children as anyone under 18 years old. Website operators are prohibited from knowingly advertising certain adult products and services to children. These include, for example, alcohol, tobacco, firearms, tanning beds, lottery tickets, pornography, and even "tongue splitting."

Finally, DOPPA prohibits any "book service provider" from voluntarily sharing information about users' reading habits with any government entities. Book services information includes any user personal information and any information about books accessed by a user. Almost every U.S. state has laws that protect the confidentiality of library patron records, but DOPPA is broader in that it applies to all book service providers. There are some exceptions. For example, book services information may be shared in response to appropriate court orders or in emergencies that threaten serious injury. DOPPA is enforced by the Delaware Department of Justice. The Delaware Attorney General may pursue civil action and fines for violations.

Nevada NRS Chapter 603a

Nevada's privacy regulations appear in Nevada's state law, or Nevada Revised Statutes (NRS) as "Chapter 603a—Security and Privacy of Personal Information." This law has been amended a few times, including SB 538 in 2017 and SB 220 in 2019. In 2021, Nevada amended these existing laws further with the passage of SB 260. SB 260 is notable in that it expands privacy regulation to "data brokers" and applies similar requirements to data brokers. SB 260 defines a data broker as "a person whose primary business is purchasing covered information about consumers with whom the person does not have a direct relationship and who reside in this State from operators or other data brokers and making sales of such covered information."

Nevada's existing privacy laws require website operators to disclose clear privacy policies. Nevada's requirements for website privacy policies are similar to those of DOPPA, described earlier. Nevada law requires website operators to disclose what PII is collected, how it is used, the process for users to review and correct their information, the effective date of the privacy policy, and any third-party data sharing. Nevada consumers may also submit written requests to opt out of allowing website operators to sell their personal information.

Unlike DOPPA, however, Nevada's law is intended primarily to regulate commercial websites with significant operations in Nevada. It exempts noncommercial websites and those with fewer than 20,000 visitors per year. Nevada law also excludes web hosting services from liability for violations. If a website operator is found to be in violation, the law grants the operator 30 days to bring the site into compliance. After that, the Nevada Attorney General may pursue civil penalties of up to $5,000 per violation.

California Age-Appropriate Design Code

In 2022, California passed the California Age-Appropriate Design Code Act (CAADCA) to implement new data protection requirements for websites likely to be used by children. The provisions of this law are scheduled to go into effect on July 1, 2024. CAADCA applies to websites that are subject to CCPA and also meet any of the following criteria:

- It is directed to children as defined by COPPA.

- It is routinely accessed by a significant number of children, based on competent and reliable evidence regarding audience composition.

- It is substantially similar to an online service, product, or feature that is routinely accessed by children.

- It has advertisements marketed to children.

- It has design elements that are known to be of interest to children, including, but not limited to, games, cartoons, music, and celebrities who appeal to children.

- A significant amount of the audience of the online service, product, or feature is determined, based on internal company research, to be children.

Websites that are subject to CAADCA must meet the following requirements:

- Conduct a Data Protection Impact Assessment (DPIA) at least every two years and each time they add new products or services.

- Document any risks to children discovered by the DPIA and develop a timed plan to mitigate or eliminate those risks before the service is used by children.

- Comply with requests from the California Attorney General for copies of DPIAs.

- Estimate the age of child visitors to the site.

- Use default settings that protect the privacy of children.

- Create privacy notices that are clearly written and may be understood by children.

- Notify children that they may be tracked.

- Provide tools and information that children and parents may use to enforce their privacy rights.

Violations of the CAADCA may result in fines of up to $2,500 per child for negligent violations and up to $7,500 per child for intentional violations. Notably, there is no private right of action under CAADCA.

California Electronic Communications and Privacy Act (2015)

The California Electronic Communications and Privacy Act, known as *CalECPA*, requires state law enforcement officials to obtain warrants in order to search most electronic data generated by Californians. CalECPA protects "electronic communication information" from warrantless searches, as well as devices and services used to transmit or store that information. This includes information such as email, web browsing history, text messages, communications metadata, and anything else transmitted electronically by a Californian.

Since this data may be transactional in nature and is typically held by third parties, it is not generally protected by the Fourth Amendment of the U.S. Constitution (Chapter 6, "Government and Court Access to Private Sector Information," covers the *third-party doctrine* in more detail). CalECPA adds to the privacy protections outlined in the federal ECPA and provides protections on par with those of the Fourth Amendment. Without a warrant, CalECPA only allows government to access personal electronic information with the owner's permission in limited ways to recover stolen property or in case of an emergency that threatens human safety.

Any information obtained by law enforcement in violation of CalECPA may not be admissible in court. In addition, the California Attorney General may pursue civil action to compel compliance from state law enforcement agencies. Individuals who believe their information has been obtained in violation of CalECPA may also petition California courts to modify any warrants and destroy any information that was obtained illegally. CalECPA builds on the federal ECPA, discussed in Chapter 6, by offering additional protections for Californians and imposing additional requirements of California's law enforcement agencies. CalECPA does not diminish any of the protections offered by the federal ECPA, nor does it impose requirements of federal law enforcement agencies.

Biometric Information Privacy Regulations

Many states have implemented privacy regulations to better protect biometric information. Some states have implemented laws to specifically safeguard biometric data. Others have added protection for biometric data to their definitions of personal information in existing privacy regulations and/or data breach notification laws.

Washington Biometric Privacy Law (HB 1493) (2017)

As mentioned in Chapter 7, biometric tracking is becoming more common, particularly in the workplace. Biometric identifiers may include fingerprints, facial recognition, or even voiceprints. Biometric data may be used to verify identity for employee timekeeping, access to secure facilities, computer access, and more. Biometric data, however, is deeply personal. A person cannot easily change their face or fingerprints if their biometric data is compromised. Biometric data, such as facial recognition technology, also has big implications for privacy in general. Facial recognition data can be captured from video cameras in any location without the consent, or even the knowledge of, the subject. Such tracking technology could be used for many purposes, such as invasive advertising and surveillance by employers or by law enforcement.

Washington's Biometric Privacy Law regulates the collection, use, and disclosure of *biometric identifiers* of Washington residents. Such identifiers are defined by the law to include any data collected based on a person's "biological characteristics" that may be used to uniquely identify an individual. These include any "automatic measurements" of features such as a "fingerprint, voiceprint, eye retinas, irises," and other unique features. However, the definition excludes photographs, videos, and audio recordings from the definition of biometric identifier. This means that businesses do not have to follow the requirements of this law when collecting and using, for example, video footage of a retail store.

If biometric indicators are collected, the Washington law requires, in general, that organizations must provide notice to individuals and obtain consent before the data can be "enrolled" in a database for commercial purposes. The law also requires businesses to provide a way for consumers to prevent the future use of their biometric identifiers. There are some exceptions to the requirement to obtain prior consent. In some specific cases, the law allows organizations to disclose the data merely by providing customers with notification and the chance to opt out. These examples include the need to use biometric identifiers to complete a transaction or deliver products and services to a customer; to comply with legal obligations; or, if the data is shared with a third party under a contractual obligation, to follow the requirements of this law.

The law generally prohibits organizations from selling or disclosing biometric data and adds requirements for data security controls. The law does not provide citizens with a private right of action and is enforceable only by the Washington Attorney General.

Illinois Biometric Information Privacy Act (BIPA)

The Illinois Biometric Information Privacy Act (BIPA) is like the Washington law in that it requires that companies get consent before collecting and using biometric data. Unlike the Washington law, however, BIPA includes a private right of action, allowing Illinoisans to pursue civil action in response to violations. In 2021, Facebook agreed to pay $650 million to settle a class-action lawsuit brought by Illinois residents for violations of BIPA. Facebook was accused of using facial recognition data to suggest photos of people to "tag" without first obtaining consent.

Texas

In Texas, the Capture or Use of Biometric Identifier (CUBI) Act regulates biometric privacy. CUBI broadly requires consent before an individual's biometric data may be collected. CUBI applies to any individual or entity capturing biometric indicators for commercial use.

In addition to requiring prior consent, the law also prohibits the sale and sharing of biometric data unless it is required by a legal warrant, to complete a transaction, or in case of an emergency. Biometric data must also be safeguarded and destroyed within a year after the purpose for which it was collected has been fulfilled.

The Attorney General enforces CUBI. Penalties may reach as high as $25,000 per violation. There is no private right of action.

New York City

New York City has enacted regulations to protect biometric privacy in several ways. City code requires that any commercial establishment that collects, stores, or shares biometric data must conspicuously disclose these practices to consumers on signs located at entrances to the business. The act also prohibits the selling or sharing of biometric data for profit.

Financial institutions and government agencies are exempt from this regulation. Data collected in photographs and video recordings is also exempt so long as computer software isn't used to analyze those materials to identify individuals and the materials aren't sold to third-parties.

This regulation is enforced by a private right of action. Anyone who believes their biometric data has been illegally collected or shared may sue for specified damages and legal fees. Damages begin at $500 per violation but may reach as high as $5,000 per violation if the violation was "intentional or reckless."

New York City's Tenant Data Privacy Act also includes provisions that regulate the way landlords may use biometric information. Landlords often use biometric identifiers to provide tenants with keyless access to buildings. The Tenant Data Privacy Act requires landlords to provide a privacy policy that includes data retention policies and a schedule for the anonymization and/or destruction of the data. Landlords must also get consent from tenants to use or share their biometric information.

As with the administrative code on biometric information described above, these provisions of the Tenant Data Privacy Act are enforced by a private right of action.

Arkansas amended its breach notification law to include a biometric data in the definition of personal information. This is covered in more detail in the section on significant developments in state data breach notification laws.

AI and Automated Decision-Making

Artificial intelligence systems are increasingly used to make assessments about consumers and to make, or at least help to make, important decisions about people. AI systems can help make decisions about whether a person should get a job, get a loan, or be accepted to an educational program. While these tools may be incredibly powerful, there is a risk that these tools may make decisions that unfairly discriminate against people. Some jurisdictions have begun to enact laws to guard against the risk of such discrimination by regulating the use of AI systems in decision-making.

Colorado SB 24-205

Colorado's SB 24–205 was approved in 2024, and the requirements are effective as of February 1, 2026. This law provides protections for consumers related to AI. SB 24–205 applies to AI systems that are defined as "high risk" to consumers, defined as an AI system that helps to make "consequential" decisions that impact consumers.

This Act requires that developers of such systems exercise care to mitigate against the risk that consumers could experience discrimination at the hands of AI system. Those who deploy such systems are expected to:

- Share key information about the system with system deployers.
- Provide deployers with the information they need to conduct an informed impact assessment.
- Publicly disclose all high-risk systems the developer has built, along with information on how they manage possible risks.
- Inform the attorney general of any incidents of discrimination caused by an AI system within 90 days.

Deployers of these systems are also required to implement risk management programs, complete impact assessments, and complete annual reviews of each system to guard against the risk of discrimination. The act requires that consumers must be notified when AI systems will take part in making any consequential decisions about them. Consumers are also entitled to correct any inaccurate data that about them that may be in use by a high-risk system. Violations of this Act are considered deceptive trade practices under the Colorado Consumer Protection Act. Under the Colorado Consumer Protection Act, each violation may carry a penalty of up to $20,000.

New York City

New York City's local law 144 regulates the use of automated systems that are used to make employment decisions. Local law 144 applies to systems known as "Automated Employment Decision Tools" (AEDT). The law applies to employers hiring for jobs located in New York City or, if the job is remote, for which the home office is in New York City.

This law requires employers to conduct an independent bias audit prior to using any AEDT for employment decisions. Bias audits are intended to assess the decision-making tool to ensure that it does not produce biases against anyone based on sex, race, ethnicity, or other protected identity categories. Employers are also required to publish the results of the most current bias audits.

If these requirements have not been fulfilled, then employers are prohibited from using AEDTs. Interestingly, the law does not require employers to stop using a tool if an audit reveals a problem with bias. However, the law does note that employers are already bound by other state and federal antidiscrimination laws. Local law 144 is enforced by New York City's Commission on Human Rights.

Data Brokers

Laws regulating data brokers have begun to gain momentum at the state level. Perhaps the most prominent example of a law specifically targeting data brokers is the California Delete Act.

California Delete Act

The Delete Act amends existing California laws, including the CPRA, to further regulate data brokers. Existing California law already requires data brokers to register with the state. California maintains a public website that discloses the list of registered data brokers. Most of the Delete Act's provisions go into effect on January 1, 2026.

The Delete Act transfers enforcement of the data broker registry over to the California Consumer Protection Agency (CCPA), which also enforces the CPRA. The Delete Act is intended to make it easier for consumers to delete personal information held by data brokers. The Act mandates the creation of a single centralized service that consumers use to request the deletion of their personal data.

Data brokers are required to check the services every 45 days at a minimum and comply with any requests for deletion that consumers have filed. Once a data broker has processed a request for deletion, they are also prohibited from selling or sharing that data in the future. The Delete Act also requires data brokers to conduct a third-party compliance audit every three years.

Financial Privacy

Financial information is tightly regulated by the federal government under statutes such as the Fair Credit Reporting Act (FCRA) and the Gramm–Leach–Bliley Act (GLBA). In a few areas, however, states have added regulations to protect personal financial information. Several states have laws regulating the use of credit reports in employment decisions. In addition, California has led the way in state-level protections for financial information in general.

Consumer credit reports are broadly regulated under the FCRA and the Fair and Accurate Credit Transactions Act (FACTA), as discussed in Chapter 5, "Private Sector Data Collection," and Chapter 7, "Workplace Privacy." Although the use of credit history information is allowed for several purposes under federal law, it is particularly controversial when used in employment decision-making. Critics argue that the use of credit histories in employment decisions bears not on the skills and abilities of a job seeker but rather on the circumstances of a job seeker's birth. Using credit histories in employment decisions, therefore, may unfairly disadvantage people from nonaffluent backgrounds and may even reinforce systemic and institutional racism.

At least 11 states and the District of Columbia have passed laws that restrict the use of credit reports in employment decisions. In addition, some local jurisdictions have similar rules. For example, New York City largely banned employment discrimination based on credit history in 2015. Although no similar federal legislation has yet been signed into law, federal legislation to this effect has been introduced and is in consideration by Congress. This is an important area of privacy law for employers to track, as more states consider adopting similar restrictions.

As a reminder from Chapters 5 and 7, FCRA and FACTA require employers to obtain authorization prior to conducting a background check. However, if an employee declines to authorize a credit report, nothing in the FCRA prohibits an employer from removing that job seeker from employment consideration.

California Financial Information Privacy Act

The California Financial Information Privacy Act (CFIPA) builds on the GLBA by adding additional requirements for financial institutions that operate in California. Most notably, CFIPA further restricts financial institutions from sharing personal financial information with third parties. Under GLBA, financial institutions must notify customers of any data shared with third parties and allow customers to request restrictions on such sharing.

Exam Tip

When CFIPA was first passed in 2004, it was known commonly as California's Senate Bill 1, or *SB-1*. It is a good idea to be familiar with both names for this act.

Under CFIPA, however, financial institutions must offer consumers more choices. To share private consumer data with an affiliated third party, a financial institution is required to provide notifications to consumers in advance and allow time for consumers to opt out of such sharing in advance. To share with unaffiliated third parties, financial institutions must obtain express written permission from consumers in advance. The law also prohibits financial institutions from discriminating against consumers who do not allow their data to be shared.

CFIPA applies to financial institutions doing business in California even if those companies are not based in California. There are limited exceptions that allow financial institutions to share private consumer information. These include an exception for sharing necessary to conduct business and complete transactions and limited exception for joint marketing efforts. Any joint marketing effort must relate to a product or service of the financial institution itself, and consumers must have the ability to opt out of sharing for joint marketing purposes. Violations of CFIPA may incur civil penalties of up to $2,500 per violation, with a maximum of $500,000 for a given incident. If, however, the financial institutions knowingly committed the violations, there is no cap on the total penalty for an incident.

In general, state law cannot limit the application of any federal laws. For this reason, CFIPA adds requirements to GLBA but does not supplant the GLBA. Other examples of federal preemption include the FCRA and the HIPAA. Information sharing under the FCRA or HIPAA is not restricted by CFIPA.

NYDFS Cybersecurity Regulation (2017)

The New York Department of Financial Services (NYDFS) Cybersecurity Regulation requires financial institutions operating in New York to implement cybersecurity controls in addition to those required by federal statues such as the GLBA. The law applies to any organizations defined as banking, insurance, or financial service providers under New York State law. This regulation requires financial institutions to implement information security programs that conform to the U.S. Commerce Department's National Institute of Standards and Technology (NIST) cybersecurity framework.

The NIST framework includes detailed controls for managing cybersecurity risk divided into five "functions." According to NIST, these include functions to *identify* threats, *protect* against threats, *detect* incidents, *respond* to incidents, and *recover from incidents*. The NYDFS Cybersecurity regulation explicitly references these functions as part of its requirements for financial institutions' cybersecurity programs.

Read more about the NIST cybersecurity framework online here:
[www.nist.gov/cyberframework]

In alignment with the NIST framework, this regulation requires financial institutions to fulfill obligations such as appointing a chief information security officer. They must also provide annual reports on cybersecurity programs, perform risk assessments, and implement specific cybersecurity controls and practices. These include, for example, requirements to encrypt all confidential data, perform penetration testing, provide an annual certification of compliance, securely dispose of data according to a data retention policy, use multifactor authentication, and report cybersecurity incidents to the designated state officials or agencies.

Recent Developments

Many states have additional laws with implications for individual privacy. For example, Massachusetts's 201 CMR 17.00 requires all companies that store PII on residents of Massachusetts to have a written information security plan such as described at the beginning of this chapter. Washington state enacted HB 1149 in 2010, which makes businesses that manage electronic payment transactions liable to help cover the costs involved with issuing new bank cards if their negligence causes a breach. This rule helps incentivize every business to protect the security of electronic payment information, not just the bank that issues a payment card.

There are many more examples of state laws that include privacy regulations. As discussed, state privacy regulations continue to expand. Several state legislatures are debating proposals similar to California's sweeping CCPA, and more are likely to follow.

New Jersey Personal Information and Privacy Protection Act (2017)

Retailers routinely collect information on their customers' identities. Often, retailers collect scans or copy information from customer identity cards in the process. There are valid reasons for retailers to scan customer ID information. For example, a retailer may want to verify customer identities to approve returns or for retail credit card applications and transactions. Such information may be collected too often and stored even after it is no longer needed. These practices also create cybersecurity and privacy risks for both businesses and consumers. Additionally, retailers could sell customer identity information, perhaps linked with transactional information, to online advertisers.

In 2017, New Jersey passed the Personal Information and Privacy Protection Act to regulate retail businesses that scan customer ID cards. Under the law, retailers may only retain limited information from customer IDs. In addition, the law requires secure storage of the data, adds data retention and destruction rules, and prohibits disclosure of customer identity information for any other purposes.

The law allows retailers to collect information from customer ID cards for only eight specific purposes:

- Validate customer identities for refunds
- Verify customer age if necessary
- Prevent fraud in product returns
- Prevent identity fraud in retail credit accounts
- Creating and continuing customer contracts
- Comply with laws that compel collection or disclosure
- Disclose records to financial regulation in compliance with laws such as the GLBA or FCRA
- Comply with HIPAA

If the retailer is scanning ID information for refund or age verification, they may not store the information after it is needed. Violations may be subject to civil penalties of $2,500 for first offenses and up to $5,000 per subsequent violation.

Marketing Laws

As discussed in Chapters 1 and 5, marketing privacy in the private sector is enforced through a patchwork of federal, state, and tort law, as well as industry self-regulatory regimes. At the federal level, consumer privacy related to marketing is usually regulated by the FTC as part of its mission to prevent unfair or deceptive acts or practices (UDAP).

Beginning in the 1970s and 1980s, U.S. states began to adopt laws to combat UDAP on their own. These days, every state has a law or laws regulating UDAP. Although these laws vary widely by state, most share a few common features:

- State UDAP laws build on the federal framework and definitions established in Section V of the FTC Act.

- Since the FTC Act preempts state law, state-level laws are crafted to add requirements and consumer protections above and beyond those in the FTC Act.

- Most state UDAP laws empower state attorneys general to initiate enforcement actions. Some also provide a private right of action.

 State attorneys general are sometimes granted enforcement authority by federal statutes as well. For example, the Controlling the Assault of Non-solicited Pornography and Marketing (CAN-SPAM) Act, discussed in Chapter 5, allows state attorneys general to sue violators under the law.

Most U.S. states have laws that further regulate telemarketing. In addition to the rules outlined by the Telephone Consumer Protection Act (TCPA), discussed in Chapter 5, state telemarketing rules often include "curfews" that restrict what time of day telemarketers may call, mandate disclosures about the nature of telemarketing calls, include regulations on recording calls, or provide consumers with opt-out procedures. Most states have some sort of rule requiring telemarketers to register to do business in the state and, often, to obtain an appropriate state license or bond.

It is important to keep in mind that many other state laws covered in this chapter may impact marketing privacy. Beyond UDAP and telemarketing laws, marketing privacy may be regulated by general state privacy laws, biometric privacy laws, and breach notification laws. For example, the CCPA is a general consumer privacy regulation with rules that apply to the use of personal data for marketing purposes.

Summary

Since there is no comprehensive national privacy regulation in the United States, states play a very important role in rounding out the patchwork that is the U.S. privacy landscape. States are able to pass laws regulating areas of privacy that are not addressed by federal regulation without running afoul of preemption issues.

States enact privacy laws for many reasons. Some add requirements that are industry specific. Common examples include state laws that enhance consumer protections enumerated by the FTC Act with state UDAP laws. Other examples include additional state regulations for financial privacy that enhance GLBA or electronic communications privacy that enhance the ECPA. In most of these cases, state laws empower their attorneys general to pursue enforcement actions independently.

State laws reinforce and expand many basic privacy protection practices that appear in federal statutes. These include requirements for organizations to implement data security and privacy programs that protect the confidentiality, integrity, and availability of personal information. Most states also require policies for securely storing customer identity information, such as Social Security numbers, and deleting them when no longer needed. Although these requirements are familiar features of federal privacy laws, it is important to recall that federal privacy laws are often narrow in scope. State laws help to greatly expand these requirements to additional geographic and subject matter jurisdictions.

Some states, such as California, have passed comprehensive privacy regulations. California has several progressive privacy statutes on the books, the most sweeping of which is the California Consumer Protection Act (CCPA), which provides GDPR-like rights for Californians. The CCPA may also be enforced under some circumstances via *a private right of action*, which gives the CCPA more legal teeth than many other state privacy laws.

Finally, states fill in important gaps in federal privacy regulation through breach notification laws. Breach notification laws ensure that consumers are told when their personal information is at risk. These laws also help to define what counts, legally speaking, as personal information so that businesses know what to protect. Breach notification laws also contain powerful incentives for organizations to prevent breaches in the first place.

Exam Essentials

Understand how state privacy laws mesh with federal laws. Because there is no comprehensive federal privacy law, states are able to make laws to cover areas of privacy where no federal law exists. States are also able to make laws that add or enhance existing privacy requirements, as long as they don't conflict with federal requirements. States are an important pillar to fill gaps in privacy regulation left unregulated by the federal government.

Know the California privacy laws. California often leads the nation in establishing progressive privacy regulations. California privacy laws often serve as a model that predicts regulatory trends across other states and at the federal level. In particular, it is important to be familiar with CFIPA, CalECPA, and the CCPA.

Explain the components of state breach notification laws. Even though breach notification laws are a bit different in every state, they all contain the same basic components. They define what constitutes personal information and what constitutes a breach. They lay out notification requirements, including who must be notified, timelines for notifications, and how notifications are to be composed and transmitted. Finally, these laws also contain provisions for enforcement and penalties for noncompliance.

Identify the ways in which state breach notification laws may differ. Although most state breach notification laws share the same anatomy, the individual components often vary. For example, the definitions of personal information and breach may be more broadly or narrowly construed, depending on the state. Different states have different notification requirements. Some require notifications to regulators and/or credit reporting agencies in addition to consumers. State rules also impose different timelines for notification and different penalties for noncompliance.

Review Questions

1. Which of the following best describes the notice and choice rules implemented by CFIPA?

   A. Consumers must be notified annually of any personal data shared with affiliated or unaffiliated third parties and given the option to opt out of data sharing.

   B. Financial institutions must obtain prior written consent from consumers before sharing personal data with affiliated or unaffiliated third parties.

   C. Consumers must be notified of any personal data shared with affiliated third parties and given the option to opt out. Financial institutions must obtain prior written consent to share with unaffiliated third parties.

   D. Financial institutions are prohibited from sharing personal data with any third parties except as required to provide products and services.

2. Which of the following is *not* a common feature of state data security requirements?

   A. Policy to destroy personal information when it is no longer needed

   B. Written information security policy

   C. Requirement for third-party cybersecurity insurance

   D. Data security controls to protect personal information

3. Jorge runs a smartphone app that allows users to take pictures of their faces and alter them to see how they might look as they age. The app collects scans of facial geometry and stores those scans as data. Jorge earns revenue by selling the user data to third parties. What is the best way for Jorge to avoid violating Washington State law?

   A. Notify users about the use of their data and obtain written consent before storing their facial recognition data.

   B. Provide users with clear notification about the practice of collecting and selling facial recognition data.

   C. Notify users about the use of their data and provide a clear opportunity for users to opt out.

   D. Provide an annual report to the Washington Attorney General detailing information privacy and security safeguards and reporting any breaches.

4. The CCPA may be enforced by which of the following?

   A. The state attorney general, CPPA, and a limited private right of action

   B. The state attorney general and the Office of Civil Rights

   C. The appropriate self-regulatory framework, depending on the industry

   D. Only through a private right of action

5. NYDFS requires financial organizations to implement a program of data security controls aligned with which of the following?

   A. GLBA requirements

   B. The NIST framework

    C. APEC safe harbor agreements

    D. FASB accounting rules

6. Which privilege does the CAN-SPAM Act grant to states?

    A. The option for state attorneys general to exempt certain industries from regulation under CAN-SPAM

    B. The option for state legislatures to pass less stringent regulations that may preempt CAN-SPAM

    C. The ability for state regulators to customize the definitions for which communications are in scope under CAN-SPAM for their states

    D. The ability for states attorneys general to sue violators

7. What is the main reason why each of the 50 states has its own breach notification laws?

    A. Each state has different circumstances that lead to differing breach notification requirements.

    B. The federal government has mandated that states must develop breach notification regulations.

    C. The U.S. Attorney General has referred breach notification authority to the states.

    D. There is no comprehensive federal breach notification law.

8. State breach notification laws may require organizations to notify which of the following parties?

    A. Consumers impacted by the breach

    B. State regulatory authorities

    C. National credit reporting agencies

    D. All of the above

9. Tennessee's SB 2005 changed the state's breach notification laws in which respect?

    A. Encrypted data was no longer automatically exempted from the state's definition of a breach.

    B. The state's notification timeline was reduced to 30 days.

    C. SB 2005 added a private right of action for violations of the Tennessee breach notification law.

    D. SB 2005 expanded the definition of personal information to include biometric data.

10. What is the primary reason that states are able to pass sweeping privacy regulations?

    A. Federal statutes require states to develop state-level privacy regulations.

    B. Previous Supreme Court rulings have established the right of states to enact privacy legislation.

    C. There is a lack of an overarching federal privacy regulation.

    D. States have principal authority for privacy legislation as part of the U.S. system of checks and balances on federal authority.

11. Washington's definition of biometric data protected by law specifically excludes which of the following?

    A. Fingerprints collected by law enforcement

    B. Facial geometry

    C. Photographic, video, and audio recordings

    D. Iris scans

12. Which of the following is a reason many states have restricted the use of credit reports in employment decisions?

    A. Credit reports from national credit reporting agencies do not contain state-specific information.

    B. State attorneys general have insufficient authority to regulate credit reports since they are regulated under the federal FCRA.

    C. The practice may bias employers against job seekers from disadvantaged backgrounds.

    D. The use of credit reports in employment decisions has been ruled in violation of the Fair Labor Standards Act in various circuit court decisions.

13. AllData, Inc. has just experienced a data breach resulting from a cyberattack by unknown attackers. Despite some weaknesses in their cybersecurity defenses, AllData wasn't grossly negligent. Which of the following is *not* a potential consequence that AllData may face under state laws following a breach?

    A. An obligation to provide free credit monitoring to affected consumers

    B. Enforcement actions, including penalties, from state attorneys general

    C. Civil actions brought by consumers under a private right of action

    D. Criminal prosecution of company employees who allowed the breach to occur

14. Which of the following states does *not* have a specific timeline requirement for breach notifications to consumers?

    A. Indiana

    B. Alabama

    C. Washington

    D. Colorado

15. All of the following are reasons states may enact privacy regulations, except:

    A. States enact privacy laws to address privacy concerns that are not regulated under federal law.

    B. States enact privacy laws so state businesses can avoid complying with more stringent obligations in federal regulations.

    C. States enact privacy regulations to allow states to participate in privacy enforcement actions.

    D. States enact privacy regulations to impose requirements in addition to those in federal laws.

16. Which of the following was the 50th state to enact a comprehensive breach notification law?

A. New Mexico

B. Alabama

C. Arkansas

D. Idaho

17. Which of the following must an organization consider in determining whether they must notify consumers of a breach in a given state?

A. The nature of the breach and level of risk for consumers

B. The state in which the organization is headquartered

C. The state definitions for personal information and breach

D. The penalties for noncompliance in a given state

18. The New Jersey Personal Information and Privacy Protection Act addresses privacy for which of the following?

A. Survey information collected by retailers about customer purchasing preferences

B. Information that retailers scan or collect from customer ID cards

C. Customer credit card information collected by retailers

D. Retail customer transaction histories

19. Which of the following laws includes regulations to protect the privacy of consumer reading habits?

A. Nevada SB 538

B. DOPPA

C. The New Jersey Personal Information and Privacy Protection Act

D. CCPA

20. CalECPA provides additional privacy protections for which of the following?

A. The education sector

B. Electronic health information

C. Online communications and activities

D. Electronic payment transactions

Chapter

9

International Privacy Regulation

THE CIPP/US EXAM OBJECTIVES COVERED IN THIS CHAPTER INCLUDE:

✓ **Domain I. Introduction to the U.S. Privacy Environment**

- I.B. Enforcement of U.S. Privacy and Security Laws

  - I.B.g Cross-Border Enforcement Issues (Global Privacy Enforcement Network (GPEN))

- I.C. Information Management from a U.S. Perspective

  - I.C.k International Data Transfers

  - I.C.l Other Key Considerations for U.S.-Based Global Multinational Companies

  - I.C.m Resolving Multinational Compliance Conflicts

Many of the largest U.S. corporations have business operations established in countries all over the world. These companies must manage internal logistics, shipping, taxes, information security, product development, sales, and virtually every critical business function across international boundaries. For example, it simply does not make business sense to have separate web servers in every single country hosting the same website. Companies must and do transfer data all around the world in order to deliver products and services and to run their internal operations.

International Data Transfers

When it comes to privacy, there are important implications for international data transfer. If the laws of one nation confer more data privacy rights to individuals, yet the personal data of its citizens is flowing to nations with lesser privacy rights, then those strict rights may be essentially meaningless. On the other hand, if a country with strict privacy laws were to prohibit all international data transfer, it would make it nearly impossible for multinational corporations to do business in that country. Potentially grave economic consequences could follow.

Even though each U.S. state presents a patchwork of differing laws, companies do not face such challenges when transferring data across state lines inside the United States. This is because U.S. law clearly defines *preemption,* and companies are able to know which legal standard applies. When the privacy laws of two nations conflict, however, there is no concept of preemption. If one country requires a specific disclosure of data and another country prohibits that same disclosure, then it is impossible for a company to comply with both laws at the same time.

This chapter examines key international privacy standards that affect the U.S.-based multinational corporations. The European Union's (EU) *General Data Protection Regulation (GDPR)* of 2018 provides a prominent example of progressive international privacy legislation that impacts U.S. companies. Several strategies have been developed to facilitate international data transfer, especially given the EU's strict standards for data privacy. In general, these strategies are designed to ensure that countries agree on common standards to allow the transfer of international data that best aligns with the laws of each nation. These strategies include *safe harbor* programs, *binding corporate rules, standard contractual clauses*, and other programs to encourage greater international cooperation and alignment on privacy issues.

European Union General Data Protection Regulation

The General Data Protection Regulation (GDPR) took legal effect in May 2018 and set a new standard for privacy protection. Even though the GDPR is promulgated by the EU, the law has sweeping implications for any U.S.-based corporations with operations in Europe or that transfer personal information to or from Europe. The GDPR is celebrated as a win by privacy advocates and a model for progressive privacy legislation in the United States.

Compared with existing U.S. law, the GDPR grants individuals far more rights to access and control how and by whom their data are accessed and used. In general, ensuring more rights for individuals means more restrictions for businesses that rely on customer data. For this reason, the GDPR may present challenges for some non-EU businesses. At a minimum, businesses may have to implement costly compliance programs and manage increased legal risks. GDPR may affect some U.S.-based corporations more. For example, some businesses in the United States, such as data brokers of large datasets for digital advertising, may generate revenue through the relatively unfettered use and disclosure of customer data from the EU.

GDPR Scope

The scope of GDPR is notable for its breadth. The GDPR aims to protect all personal data for everyone in the EU by regulating any entity that handles the data. The GDPR defines several key concepts critical to understanding the full scope of the law:

Personal Data   Personal data includes any information that identifies an individual. Examples include name, geolocation information, as well as any characteristics of a person that might be used individually or in combination to identify someone. The GDPR refers to individuals protected by the law as *natural persons* or *data subjects*. Importantly, the GDPR does not restrict its scope only to citizens of EU member states. GDPR rights and protections apply to anyone physically located within the EU at the time they are sharing their personal information.

 U.S.-based privacy professionals should note that U.S. corporations may collect data that is not protected by U.S. law as personal information but that is considered personal information in the EU.

Data Controllers and Processors   The GDPR applies to both *controllers* and *processors* of data. A data controller is usually the entity that is ultimately in charge of data. The GDPR says that a controller "determines the purposes and means of the processing of personal data." A data processor is any other entity that handles personal data for the controller. For example, a retailer may hire a digital marketing firm to help it increase online sales with better website analytics. In this case, the retailer would be the controller and the marketing firm would be the processor. Under the GDPR, both controllers and processors have obligations and liabilities. With this framework, the GDPR aims to protect data even as it changes hands.

Territorial Jurisdiction   As mentioned earlier, the GDPR confers rights on anyone in the EU, whether or not they are citizens of the EU. However, there is less certainty about whether non-EU organizations must comply with GDPR requirements. According to the text of the GDPR, it applies to all organizations established in the EU as well as any organizations that control or process data on EU data subjects for "the offering of goods or services" or for "the monitoring of their [EU data subjects'] behavior" within EU territory. This may be interpreted to mean that GDPR regulates any e-commerce website that a person in the EU happens to click on.

Boundaries of GDPR

A body of case law is slowly taking shape to further define the GDPR's applicability beyond the geographic boundaries of the EU. Many of these issues are considered by the Court of Justice of the European Union (CJEU). The issue is difficult for the CJEU because their authority exists only within the EU, whereas data on the Internet isn't constrained by geographic borders. In a series of prominent cases, EU data subjects have attempted to enforce GDPR provisions such as the right to be forgotten (discussed later) against Google's search engine.

An Internet search engine does not explicitly host web pages that contain personal information, but search results may make reference to websites that do. For this reason, EU data subjects have asked the CJEU to order Google to remove references to certain websites from search results. This process, called *dereferencing*, only meaningfully protects privacy if Google dereferences websites globally, not only in the EU.

The CJEU, however, has ruled that it can only order Google to dereference search results for EU versions of its web pages and to discourage anyone in the EU from finding the dereferenced results. Without further restrictions, it remains relatively simple for a person in the EU to navigate to a U.S.-based Google website and search for any dereferenced information.

This area of law is by no means settled. Because the GDPR claims to apply to any monitoring of EU data subjects' behavior, it is difficult to enforce unless it applies to every website in the world. However, the CJEU does not claim extraterritorial jurisdiction over non-EU countries.

Despite the ongoing controversy, many U.S. companies consider it to be in their best interest to move toward compliance with the GDPR. Many large U.S. companies have substantial operations in the EU and have an interest in compliance with EU law. For many companies, it may be far simpler and more cost effective to apply GDPR-style compliance across all of their operations rather than to create and maintain separate compliance programs for EU and non-EU operations. In addition, U.S. states are beginning to consider and adopt GDPR style regulations, as discussed in Chapter 8, "State Privacy Laws."

Even though the GDPR may not be directly enforceable across the globe in every case, the law limits how personal data can be shared outside the EU. GDPR prohibits the transfer of data to non-EU countries unless the recipient offers the same privacy protections as the EU. The GDPR offers a few avenues for approving data transfers outside the EU. For example, EU authorities decide in advance that a non-EU country has adequate data privacy protections in place and allow data transfers to take place. This is known as an *adequacy decision*. Mechanisms to facilitate data transfer between the United States and the EU are in flux, but they include binding corporate rules and standard contractual clauses. Until 2020, the U.S.–EU Privacy Shield Program also facilitated data transfers with the EU, but the Privacy Program was struck by the EU. These are discussed later.

Data Subject Rights

The GDPR provides comprehensive rights to data subjects. Not unlike many U.S. laws, the GDPR requires that all data processors and controllers provide transparent notice to customers explaining what data are collected, how data are used, and information about any third parties with whom data may be shared.

The GDPR imposes specific requirements that companies must satisfy in order to process personal data. Companies may collect personal data as needed to fulfill contracts with data subjects, to comply with legal obligations, to protect a data subject's "vital interests," to complete a task "in the public interest," and where the processing is necessary to the interests of the business. Businesses must obtain consent from data subjects before collecting personal data in almost all other circumstances.

Consent must be meaningful, and controllers must be able to show that they have obtained consent. The GDPR requires that written consent must be "clearly distinguishable from other matters," easy to understand, and accessible. This means that a consent clause may not be buried in some long and obtuse end-user agreement. Data subjects may also retract their consent whenever they like. Most U.S. privacy laws, in contrast, require (at most) that data subjects be given the chance to opt out of data collection and use, whereas the GDPR generally requires an opt-in by default.

The GDPR provides a notable list of additional *data subject rights*. These are contained in Articles 15–22 of the GDPR and include the well-known *right to erasure*, also known as the *right to be forgotten*. The right to be forgotten means, quite simply, that EU data subjects have the right to ask data controllers to erase all of their personal data. A request for erasure may be made in a number of circumstances, including when a data subject withdraws consent. In such cases, controllers are required to erase the personal data in question "without undue delay." After receiving a request to be forgotten, a data controller or processor may only retain personal data as required to meet other legal compliance obligations. Other data subject rights include the following:

- *Right of access*: Data subjects have the right to know what data are collected and why, to know how their data will be processed and with whom their data may be shared, and to obtain a copy of their personal data as well as information about how to request erasure under GDPR.

- *Right to rectification*: Data subjects have the right to request corrections to the information collected about them.

- *Right to restriction of processing*: Data subjects have the right to request that controllers halt processing activities, without requesting full erasure, in some circumstances.

- *Notification obligations*: Controllers have to notify data subjects when they fulfill requests for erasure, rectification, or restriction of processing.

- *Right to data portability*: Data subjects have the right to get a copy of their data in "machine readable format" so that it can be ingested by other information systems. This right, for example, helps prevent companies from locking customers into their products by keeping their data in a proprietary format that can't be moved to a competitor.

- *Right to object*: Data subjects have the right to object to any processing of their personal data they believe to be out of compliance with GDPR or to opt out of certain processing activities, such as direct marketing. The burden is on the data controller to demonstrate that data processing activities are authorized under GDPR in order to resume.

- *Automated individual decision-making, including profiling*: This right means that AI, or any "automated processing" alone, can't make any decisions that have a significant or legal impact on a person.

Penalties for violating the GDPR can be steep. Depending on which provision of the GDPR is violated and whether the violation was intentional or negligent, administrative penalties for infringements may reach up to €20,000,000, or 4% of a company's annual revenue, whichever is greater. Data subjects may also pursue damages for any harm caused by a violation of the GDPR.

Adequacy Decisions

Probably the smoothest and simplest mechanism to allow international data transfers to and from the EU is via an *adequacy decision*. An adequacy decision occurs when the EU reviews the privacy laws of another nation and decides those laws are adequate to protect EU data subjects' privacy at a level commensurate with the provisions of the GDPR.

The European Commission is empowered to make adequacy decisions under the GDPR. Once such a decision is made, international data transfers may occur to and from the EU and that country without the need of any further legal approval. An adequacy decision allows the EU to treat a company from another country virtually just like a European country. There is a long history of dispute surrounding the treatment of the United States under the adequacy decision program.

U.S.–EU Agreements

Before the EU made a general adequacy decision under GDPR in favor of the United States, there were efforts to provide a safe harbor program to enable data transfers with approved U.S. companies. Safe harbor programs establish a common set of privacy regulations, and member nations commit to enforcing those privacy standards.

Such arrangements allow companies established in nations with strict privacy regulations to transfer data to and from countries with less strict laws. Typically, safe harbor frameworks are aligned with the strictest domestic laws of all members in order to function. Once a nation becomes a member of a safe harbor program, individual companies may join by seeking third-party certification to verify that their privacy practices meet the safe harbor standards.

Designed by the U.S. Department of Commerce in conjunction with EU authorities in 2016, the Privacy Shield program was created to provide a framework to allow U.S. companies to transfer data to and from the EU without running afoul of the GDPR. The Privacy Shield program attempted to accomplish this by creating a privacy framework with provisions that matched the requirements of the GDPR. U.S. companies could earn Privacy Shield status by demonstrating compliance with the framework and be free to transact data to and from the EU. With the Privacy Shield program in place, the EU was able to make an adequate decision to authorize data transfers with U.S. companies in the program. However, as a result of privacy-related lawsuits in the EU, the U.S.–EU safe harbor program was struck down in 2020 and is no longer an approved mechanism for data transfer between the EU and U.S. companies.

Schrems Decisions

Max Schrems, an Austrian privacy advocate, brought a series of legal challenges to the U.S.–EU safe harbor program. In light of Edward Snowden's revelations (discussed in Chapters 4 and 6) about the U.S. government's mass surveillance programs, Schrems and other privacy advocates were concerned that U.S. regulations could not ensure adequate privacy projections for EU data subjects. In 2013, Schrems filed his initial privacy complaint against Facebook in Ireland. This case became known as Schrems I. While the complaint was initially rejected in Ireland, Schrems continued to appeal his case for years. By 2015, the outcome was still inconclusive.

After GDPR was implemented in 2018, Schrems filed a new complaint and pressed his case all the way to the Court of Justice of the European Union (CJEU). This was the second privacy case brought by Schrems, and the resulting decision became known as Schrems II. In July 2020, the CJEU struck down the Privacy Shield program and reversed the earlier adequacy decision. Although the Privacy Shield program imposed GDPR-like privacy regulations on U.S. companies, the program could not impose such regulations on the U.S. government itself. The CJEU ruling arose from concern that the U.S. government's far-reaching legal authority to conduct surveillance, particularly after Edward Snowden's revelations, could violate the rights of Europeans, and nothing in the Privacy Shield program provided adequate protection from data collection by the U.S. government.

In the Schrems II ruling, the CJEU left two other avenues in place for U.S. companies to engage in data transfer with the EU. These include binding corporate rules (BCRs) and standard contractual clauses (SCCs). Both of these are discussed in more detail later. The Schrems II decision, however, did suggest that the use of both BCRs and SCCs may be more limited than previously thought. For example, BCRs and SCCs must address concerns about

U.S. government surveillance by putting safeguards in place, and EU authorities may abruptly order data processing by U.S. companies to cease if concerns arise.

EU–U.S. Data Privacy Framework

In July 2023, the European Commission issued an adequacy decision for the EU–U.S. Data Privacy Framework (DPF), a new transatlantic data transfer framework designed to replace Privacy Shield. The DPF aims to reconcile the distinct privacy regimes on either side of the Atlantic while ensuring robust protection for European data subjects from potential excessive surveillance by U.S. authorities. This involves establishing robust safeguards, clear transparency requirements, and effective redress mechanisms. The goal is to develop a reliable privacy-respecting system that supports data transfers essential to their intertwined economies. The International Trade Administration (ITA) of the U.S. Department of Commerce administers the DPF for the United States.

DPF Certification and Enforcement

Organizations wishing to participate in the DPF do so by visiting the ITA website at `https://www.dataprivacyframework.gov/` and completing a self-certification. This self-certification is a voluntary process, but organizations that choose to self-certify must then comply with the DPF requirements. That commitment to comply with the DPF then becomes enforceable under U.S. law. Specifically, the Federal Trade Commission (FTC) considers the failure of a participating company to comply with DPF to be an unfair or deceptive trade practice that may be sanctioned under Section 5 of the FTC Act.

DPF Requirements

The ITA provides the following summary of DPF requirements for companies that choose to participate in the framework:

1. Informing individuals about data processing

    ▪ A participating organization must include in its privacy policy a declaration of the participating organization's commitment to comply with the DPF Principles so that the commitment becomes enforceable under U.S. law.

    ▪ A participating organization's privacy policy must include a link to the U.S. Department of Commerce's DPF program website and a link to or the web address for the relevant website or complaint submission form of the independent recourse mechanisms available to investigate individual complaints brought under the DPF Principles.

    ▪ A participating organization must inform individuals of their rights to access their personal data, the requirement to disclose personal information in response to lawful request by public authorities, which enforcement authority has jurisdiction over the participating organization's compliance with the DPF Principles, and the participating organization's liability in cases of onward transfer of data to third parties.

2. Providing free and accessible dispute resolution

- Individuals may bring a complaint directly to a participating organization, and the participant must respond to the individual within 45 days.

- Participating organizations must provide, at no cost to the individual, an independent recourse mechanism by which each individual's complaints and disputes can be investigated and expeditiously resolved.

- If an individual submits a complaint to a data protection authority (DPA) in the European Union / European Economic Area, the United Kingdom (and/or, as applicable, Gibraltar), or Switzerland, the U.S. Department of Commerce's ITA has committed to receive, review, and undertake best efforts to facilitate resolution of the complaint and to respond to the DPA within 90 days.

- Participating organizations must also commit to binding arbitration at the request of the individual to address any complaint that has not been resolved by other recourse and enforcement mechanisms.

3. Cooperating with the U.S. Department of Commerce

- Participating organizations must respond promptly to inquiries and requests by the ITA for information relating to the EU–U.S. DPF and, as applicable, the UK Extension to the EU–U.S. DPF and/or the Swiss–U.S. DPF.

4. Maintaining data integrity and purpose limitation

- Participating organizations must limit personal information to the information relevant for the purposes of processing.

- Participating organizations must comply with the data retention provision.

5. Ensuring accountability for data transferred to third parties

To transfer personal information to a third party acting as a controller, a participating organization must:

- Comply with the Notice and Choice Principles; and

- Enter into a contract with the third-party controller that provides that such data may only be processed for limited and specified purposes consistent with the consent provided by the individual and that the recipient will provide the same level of protection as the DPF Principles and will notify the organization if it makes a determination that it can no longer meet this obligation. The contract shall provide that when such a determination is made, the third-party controller ceases processing or takes other reasonable and appropriate steps to remediate.

To transfer personal data to a third party acting as an agent, a participating organization must:

- Transfer such data only for limited and specified purposes;

- Ascertain that the agent is obligated to provide at least the same level of privacy protection as is required by the DPF Principles;

- Take reasonable and appropriate steps to ensure that the agent effectively processes the personal information transferred in a manner consistent with the organization's obligations under the DPF Principles;

- Require the agent to notify the organization if it makes a determination that it can no longer meet its obligation to provide the same level of protection as is required by the DPF Principles;

- Upon notice, take reasonable and appropriate steps to stop and remediate unauthorized processing; and

- Provide a summary or a representative copy of the relevant privacy provisions of its contract with that agent to the U.S. Department of Commerce upon request.

6. Transparency related to enforcement actions

- Participating organizations must make public any relevant DPF-related sections of any compliance or assessment report submitted to the FTC or the U.S. Department of Transportation if the organization becomes subject to an FTC or court order based on noncompliance.

7. Ensuring commitments are kept as long as data is held

- If an organization leaves the relevant part(s) of the DPF program, it must annually affirm to the ITA its commitment to apply the DPF Principles to information received under the relevant part(s) of the DPF program if it chooses to keep such data; otherwise, it must provide "adequate" protection for the information by another authorized means.

Binding Corporate Rules

The GDPR allows data transfer outside the EU to take place when all parties in a given corporate group agree to adopt specific rules for data privacy and security. BCRs are complex agreements wherein each party agrees to adhere to GDPR standards for data protection. The agreements must be legally binding in all jurisdictions concerned. In addition, an EU organization that acts as either a controller or processor must assume liability for any damages caused as a result of violations by non-EU partners unless they can prove they weren't at fault.

BCRs require approval by an EU member state supervisory authority and undergo rigorous review. Once established, however, BCRs provide a common framework for privacy compliance to which many organizations may agree. Despite the complexity of the arrangement, BCRs may be a good way to facilitate ongoing data transfer arrangements among multiple large multinational corporations.

In some cases, BCRs may obligate an organization to follow GDPR rules that conflict with laws in a non-EU country. For example, the U.S. government may require disclosure of personal data that would be prohibited by the GDPR. In such cases, BCRs generally require that the organizations must notify the appropriate EU authority. This is one of the areas of controversy surrounding BCRs that arose from the Schrems II case. It remains unclear how organizations that enter into a BCR arrangement can provide adequate safeguards to reconcile conflicting laws.

Standard Contractual Clauses

For smaller companies or more limited business relationships, setting up a full BCR framework may be overkill. In these cases, two parties entering into a contract may opt instead to include contract language that obligates the non-EU company to follow GDPR practices. The European Commission issues prescribed and standardized contractual clauses that must be used for such arrangements.

To use SCCs, the company in the EU that plans to share data is designated as the *data exporter*. The non-EU company planning to receive the data is designated as a *data importer*. The European Commission's approved contractual clauses specify the contractual obligations for each party. The European Commission provides a couple of sets of SCCs that vary depending on whether the parties involved are controllers or processors and the level of legal liability assumed by each party. The SCCs must be used exactly as provided by the European Commission and may not be altered for specific contracts.

Other Approved Transfer Mechanisms

The GDPR allows for a limited number of circumstances in which data may be transferred to non-EU entities. These are known as *derogations* and describe specific and limited exemptions when an isolated data transfer may take place. Derogations that permit the transfer of personal data outside the EU, without the protections of an adequacy decision, BCRs, or SCCs, may occur only in these circumstances:

- With the informed consent of the data subject
- To fulfill contractual obligations with the data subject
- For "important reasons of the public interest"
- To fulfill legal obligations
- To safeguard the "vital interests" of the data subject, and only if the data subject is unable to provide consent
- If the information is open to the public already

The only other exemptions permitted outside of these very limited derogations apply to one-time transfers that affect only a small number of data subjects when the data controller has a "compelling legitimate interest" in making the transfer that doesn't conflict with any rights of the data subject. In this case, a data controller has to notify its local EU supervisory authority of the transfer, and the supervisory authority will inform the affected data subjects. Under the GDPR, exercising such an exemption likely represents elevated legal risk to an organization and should be used only sparingly in cases of dire need.

APEC Privacy Framework

The Asia-Pacific Economic Cooperation (APEC) was founded in 1989 to help accelerate economic growth among member nations. As of 2021, APEC has 21 member nations, including the United States, Australia, Canada, Indonesia, Japan, South Korea, Mexico, and Russia, among others. APEC aims to promote international trade by reducing barriers and streamlining international cooperation. APEC develops frameworks to help reconcile differing regulatory requirements among member nations so that conflict regulations do not unintentionally restrict trade.

It may be surprising to note that India is not a current member of APEC, despite the fact that India shares a geographic affinity with many APEC members and was the world's fifth-largest economy by GDP in 2020.

Among its many initiatives, APEC manages a privacy framework to allow for data transfer among member nations. The privacy framework was adopted by APEC in 2005 to facilitate collaboration among member nations for digital trade. The framework is not a specific regulation, nor is it a binding agreement of any sort. The framework provides an agreed starting point for bilateral or multilateral trade agreements among APEC members. The APEC privacy framework details nine core principles:

- *Preventing Harm*: The framework puts individuals, not businesses or member nations, at the center of this principle. Privacy protections should be "designed to prevent harms" to individuals that arise from the mishandling of personal information.

- *Notice*: Individuals should be informed when their information is collected and why, the type of personal information collected, how it is collected, by whom, of any disclosures to third parties, and how their data is safeguarded.

- *Collection Limitation*: Personal information should be collected only to the degree it is needed for the stated purpose and nothing more.

- *Uses of Personal Information*: Once collected, personal information should only be used for the stated purposes unless a limited exception, such as a legal requirement for disclosure, applies.

- *Choice*: Individuals should be able to choose whether and how their information is collected, used, and shared "where appropriate."

- *Integrity of Personal Information*: Individuals should expect that personal data maintained by controllers is correct, complete, and current.

- *Security safeguards*: Data controllers should employ adequate safeguards to reduce the risk of unauthorized access to personal data.

- *Access and Correction*: Upon request, data controllers must be able to inform individuals about any personal data collected, provide copies of that data to the individual, and provide a process for individuals to request corrections to any inaccurate data.
- *Accountability*: Data controllers should be accountable for ensuring these principles are followed in managing personal data, and if disclosed to a third party, controllers should get permission and "take reasonable steps" to confirm that these principles will be followed by the third party as well.

The APEC privacy framework shares some features with the GDPR. It offers a minimum standard for data privacy protection among its members, defines personal information in a similarly broad fashion, and provides for some similar individual rights, such as the right to expect that personal data will be held securely and to be notified of data collection, usage, and disclosures. But keep in mind that GDPR is a legal statute across all EU member states and enforceable within EU jurisdiction. The APEC privacy framework is not a law, and even when members or companies choose to use the framework, the APEC privacy framework does not overrule domestic legislation in member nations.

To implement the APEC privacy framework consistently and with regulatory oversight, APEC also created a safe harbor program based on the framework. The APEC program is known as the Cross-Border Privacy Rules (CBPR) system. Joining the CBPR system is also voluntary for APEC member nations. Member nations must identify a government agency to provide regulatory oversight and enforcement. Member nations must also designate at least one third-party organization to provide verification of compliance for participating businesses.

In the United States, the FTC provides regulatory oversight and TrustArc provides third party verification of compliance with CBPR. Once a U.S. company earns certification through TrustArc and is approved to participate in the CBPR system, the company is free to conduct digital trade, including transfers of personal data, following the standards outlined by the APEC privacy framework.

The CBPR should at least match the strictest data protection standards of member nations. Nations with stricter privacy standards may choose not to join safe harbor programs that would force them to adopt lower standards. However, nothing in the CBPR explicitly prohibits disclosures of personal data as required by domestic laws in member nations. For example, the CBPR system does not provide legal grounds for a U.S. company to refuse to comply with a duly authorized government order for disclosure.

For nations with strict data privacy laws, safe harbor programs may present potential weaknesses. First, the safe harbor program may hold participants to a lower privacy standard. Second, stricter privacy standards may not be enforceable in all member nations, no matter what the safe harbor program requires. Concerns of this sort played into the EU's decision to strike down the U.S.–EU Privacy Shield program.

Cross-Border Enforcement Issues

As discussed throughout this chapter, it can be tricky to ensure that privacy regulations are enforced across national boundaries. Residents of countries with strict privacy laws have an expectation that their personal data will be protected according to their countries' laws. However, their personal data may be exported to countries with looser privacy regulations and somehow compromised. Even when nations or businesses have entered into safe harbor arrangements, domestic laws, such as those permitting government surveillance, may preempt any safe harbor privacy assurances.

Global Privacy Enforcement Network

In 2007, the *Organisation for Economic Co-operation and Development (OECD)* developed the *Global Privacy Enforcement Network (GPEN)* and a GPEN Action Plan to improve international cooperation in enforcing privacy regulations in member nations. The United States belongs to both OECD and GPEN.

GPEN helps domestic government regulatory agencies in member nations collaborate on cross-border privacy enforcement issues. GPEN is not a privacy framework and does not, in itself, outline specific privacy practices or requirements. GPEN has a five-point mission centered on facilitating the sharing of information and best practices, training, promoting communication, and developing methods for international cooperation among members. Although GPEN does not offer a privacy framework, its mission does include support for existing internationally recognized privacy standards.

Resolving Multinational Compliance Conflicts

As you've seen, difficulties may often arise when a company wishes to transfer data between nations with conflicting privacy laws. As discussed earlier, for example, the EU's GDPR offers more protection for personal information than does U.S. law. A U.S. company managing the personal information of EU data subjects may be compelled to disclose information to the U.S. government. Such a disclosure may be legally required in the United States and illegal in the EU.

Frameworks such as the APEC Cross-Border Privacy Rules system and other safe harbor programs discussed in this chapter attempt to solve these cross-border contradictions, but domestic laws may still override safe harbor agreements. GPEN doesn't apply a set of privacy rules, but it does try to coordinate enforcement efforts and help regulators in member nations better understand the multinational privacy landscape.

There is no easy answer or legal framework that solves the problem of international compliance conflicts. U.S. companies must implement strong data management programs to ensure that they are able to track all international data transfers and seek legal advice when dealing with contradictory compliance obligations.

Summary

Considerations for most U.S.-based multinational companies include the need to understand and comply with data standards required to do business in international jurisdictions with more progressive privacy laws. In today's digital world, the click of a button in Rome, Italy, may transfer personal information to the custody of a firm located in Rome, New York. Once such data is effectively exported to a U.S.-based company, it might be difficult for another country to ensure that transferred data is protected according to its standards.

The European Union (EU) offers perhaps the most progressive model in the world for comprehensive personal privacy protection. Whereas U.S. law usually seeks to balance individual privacy with the needs of business, the EU's GDPR clearly puts individual rights first. The GDPR applies across all sectors for all EU member states and offers a sweeping definition of personal information.

Under the GDPR, personal information is primarily controlled by the individual, and companies may only use personal data with permission or within specified parameters. The GDPR also confers a series of *data subject rights*. Among these is the well-known *right of erasure*, or right to be forgotten, that enables an EU data subject to order any controller or processor to delete all of their personal information. The GDPR is also notable because it is enforceable and violations bring steep penalties.

In order to protect data subject rights, the EU does not allow data transfer to companies based in other nations unless the EU believes personal data will be adequately protected. Thus far, the EU has not made a data privacy *adequacy decision* in favor of the United States. U.S.-based multinational corporations must therefore find other ways to qualify for doing business with the EU. These include the use of standard contractual clauses (SCCs) and binding corporate rules (BCRs). Until 2020, the U.S.–EU Privacy Shield program was also available, but this was struck down by the Court of Justice of the European Union over concerns that the program could not protect EU data subjects' personal information from U.S. government surveillance.

Beyond the EU, the United States belongs to other multinational organizations that offer cooperation to facilitate international data transfers and international coordination for privacy law enforcement. The United States is a member of the Asia-Pacific Economic Cooperation (APEC) that maintains both an international privacy framework and a safe harbor program called the Cross-Border Privacy Rules (CBPR) system. In addition, the United States belongs to the Organisation for Economic Co-operation and Development (OECD), which has created the Global Privacy Enforcement Network (GPEN). GPEN offers a framework for international cooperation and information sharing but no binding agreements to facilitate transfers of data.

Exam Essentials

Understand challenges related to international data transfers.   For U.S.-based multinational corporations, differing privacy laws may make it impossible to comply with conflicting privacy laws from two jurisdictions at the same time. Non-U.S. countries with strict privacy laws often require assurances that their citizens' personal data will be protected by their standards before allowing U.S. companies to handle their information.

Remember the key components of the GDPR.   The GDPR provides perhaps the most progressive example of comprehensive privacy regulation in the world. For the exam, it will be helpful to recall core concepts from the GDPR, such as jurisdiction, the definition of personal information, data controllers and processors, data subject rights, and the rules that permit data export beyond the EU.

Explain the various mechanisms for international data transfers.   In order to do business with some countries, such as EU member states, U.S. companies must adopt a mechanism for compliance with standards like the GDPR. These include SCCs, BCRs, and safe harbor programs. For the exam, it is helpful to be familiar with each of these mechanisms and how they work.

Be familiar with other international agreements that impact international data transfers.   The United States is a member of other international frameworks and agreements that assist with international data transfers. APEC provides a privacy framework, and it is a good idea to be familiar with its nine principles for the exam. APEC also provides a safe harbor program based on that framework, called the Cross Border Privacy Rules (CBPR) system. The United States is also a member of the OECD, which offers the GPEN program. Although GPEN is not a safe harbor program, it does support international cooperation for privacy enforcement issues, and it will be helpful to know GPEN's five part mission.

Understand the history of EU/U.S. data privacy decisions.   The EU has a history of regulating data transfers with the United States through mechanisms like adequacy decisions, safe harbor programs, and the Privacy Shield. Legal challenges, particularly the Schrems I and Schrems II cases, have repeatedly invalidated these frameworks due to concerns over U.S. surveillance practices. The latest attempt to address these issues is the EU–U.S. DPF, established in 2023, which aims to provide adequate protection for EU data subjects while allowing data transfers to the United States. U.S. companies can self-certify to the DPF, and compliance is enforceable under U.S. law by the Federal Trade Commission (FTC).

Review Questions

1. The EU's GDPR is most equivalent to which U.S. federal law?

    A. The Patriot Act

    B. The Privacy Act

    C. None

    D. The Civil Rights Act

2. Which of the following is *not* one of the nine principles of the APEC framework?

    A. Notice

    B. Integrity of Personal Information

    C. Security Safeguards

    D. Right to rectification

3. All of the following may qualify as circumstances that may allow international data transfers of personal information to take place under GDPR except:

    A. With the consent of the data subject

    B. To meet the terms of a contract with the data subject

    C. If the information is already public

    D. For research purposes

4. Grafton Street Coffee Co, based in Dublin, Ireland, has hired a neighboring business, AdCorp, to help it analyze customer preferences and send targeted marketing to drive repeat business. What legal roles are each of these businesses most likely playing when it comes to handling personal information?

    A. They are both data controllers.

    B. AdCorp is acting as a data controller, and Grafton Street Coffee is acting as a data processor.

    C. Grafton Street Coffee is acting as a data controller, and AdCorp is acting as a data processor.

    D. They are both acting as data processors.

5. Yuping is helping a small data analytics startup company based in the United States expand its business by offering analytics services for companies in the EU. Which of the following routes is Yuping most likely to recommend to facilitate data transfer from EU companies to the startup?

    A. DPF self-certification

    B. Standard Contractual Clauses

    C. Binding Corporate Rules

    D. APEC

6. Said's U.S.-based company holds personal information of EU data subjects. In the course of an eDiscovery request, Said is asked to turn over data sets that include this personal information. This disclosure is prohibited by the GDPR. What does this scenario illustrate?

    A. A failure of the EU/U.S. Privacy Shield program

    B. A multinational compliance conflict

    C. The weakness of U.S. privacy laws

    D. Jurisdictional overreach by the EU

7. A large, U.S.-based, multinational corporation wants to expand into the EU. The company wants to facilitate seamless international data transfers among its many subsidiaries operating in the United States and EU. What approach should this company take?

    A. Join the U.S.–EU Privacy Shield program.

    B. BCRs

    C. SCCs

    D. CBPR

8. Do U.S.-based companies have to comply with requests to exercise data subject rights under the GDPR even if the company is not operating an EU-facing business?

    A. Yes, if the company has assets in the EU.

    B. Unsure; this is an unsettled jurisdictional issue.

    C. Yes, if the personal information in question belongs to an EU data subject.

    D. No; the EU has no jurisdiction over companies in the United States.

9. What is the CBPR system?

    A. An EU-approved mechanism for international data transfer

    B. An APEC safe harbor program for international data transfer

    C. An international framework for privacy enforcement

    D. An APEC program to facilitate better understanding of member nations' privacy laws

10. What was the primary reason that the EU's Court of Justice struck down the U.S.–EU Privacy Shield program?

    A. Concerns that U.S. companies would not comply fully with the program

    B. Concerns that U.S. requirements for information security safeguards are inadequately enforced

    C. Concerns that the program couldn't protect personal data of EU subjects from U.S. government surveillance

    D. Concerns that U.S. companies lack the technical ability to fulfill all of the data subject rights conferred by the GDPR

11. Which of the following is not part of GPEN's mission?

   A. Encourage dialogue among enforcement agencies

   B. Share expertise and professional development

   C. Create a clearinghouse for sharing confidential information about ongoing investigations into privacy law violations

   D. Exchange information about relevant issues and trends

12. Pierre lives in Lyon, France, and notices a lot of Internet popup ads for his local boulangerie. He learns that the boulangerie uses a digital marketing service based in the United States. Pierre demands the boulangerie stop targeting him with these ads. On what provision is Pierre's demand most likely based?

   A. The right to erasure

   B. The CAN-SPAM Act

   C. The right to object

   D. The right to restriction of processing

13. After reviewing new progressive privacy laws enacted by another country, the EU decides to permit international data transfers with businesses based in that country. What is this international data transfer mechanism called?

   A. Adequacy decision

   B. Safe harbor

   C. BCR

   D. SCC

14. Carlos works for an international organization that helps member nations cooperate on issues of cross-border privacy enforcement. Which organization is most likely Carlos's employer?

   A. APEC

   B. GPEN

   C. NATO

   D. CJEU

15. Which of the following is not a data subject right conferred by the GDPR?

   A. Right to object

   B. Right to rectification

   C. Right of erasure

   D. Right of notice and choice

16. Nancy is a compliance manager at an import/export business that specializes in connecting U.S. cottage industries with buyers in Japan and Singapore. What could she do to make it easier for her company to legally transfer records between the United States, Japan, and Singapore?

    A. Join the CBPR program

    B. Use contracts with SCCs

    C. Join GPEN

    D. Follow the APEC Privacy Framework

17. A Swedish company named Digital Empire was found responsible for repeatedly and purposely violating multiple provisions of the GDPR. The resulting privacy violations caused some people in the EU to lose their jobs and exposed others to social stigmas and other harms. What is the largest penalty Digital Empire might face?

    A. €30,000,000

    B. €20,000,000 or 4% of annual revenue, whatever is greater

    C. 8% of annual revenue

    D. €10,000,000

18. A program that establishes a common regulatory framework to allow trade partners from multiple countries with differing data privacy laws to conduct international data transfers is called:

    A. Safe harbor program

    B. Binding corporate rules

    C. APEC privacy framework

    D. Bilateral trade agreement

19. Marco runs a creamery in Italy. He wants to send his customer data to a small company in the United States by employing SCCs. Based on the EU's requirements for using SCCs, what role in managing the international data transfers does Marco's company play?

    A. Data importer

    B. Data exporter

    C. Data manager

    D. Data owner

20. GDPR protects data privacy for which of the following populations?

    A. EU citizens

    B. EU data subjects

    C. EU citizens and foreign nationals

    D. UK citizens

Appendix

Answers to Review Questions

Chapter 1: Privacy in the Modern Era

1. A. All of these records are important to a business and may be considered sensitive. However, this does not mean that they would fall into the scope of a privacy program. Privacy programs are specifically intended to protect personal information and, of the information presented here, only customer records fall into that category. A cybersecurity program would be interested in protecting all these elements of information.

2. A. The three main goals of a cybersecurity program are confidentiality, integrity, and availability. Although privacy and security objectives are often linked and interdependent, privacy is not one of the three cybersecurity objectives.

3. C. Industry best practice calls for an annual privacy risk assessment designed to analyze the organization's current practices in light of the evolving privacy environment.

4. B. The special categories of information under GDPR include information about racial and ethnic origin, political opinions, religious or philosophical beliefs, trade union membership, genetic information, biometric information, health data, and data about a person's sex life or sexual orientation. Other categories of information may be sensitive but do not fit into this definition.

5. C. One of the provisions of the notice principle is that organizations should provide notice to data subjects before they use information for a purpose other than those that were previously disclosed.

6. C. Kara's organization is collecting and processing this information for its own business needs. Therefore, it is best described as the data controller.

7. C. ISO 27701 covers best practices for implementing privacy controls. ISO 27001 and ISO 27002 relate to an organization's information security program. ISO 27702 does not yet exist.

8. D. Unlike assessments, audits are always performed by an independent auditor who does not have a vested interest in the outcome. Audits may be performed at the request of internal management, a board of directors, or regulatory authorities.

9. A. The mission of a privacy program should be written at a high level as an enduring document. The goals, objectives, and procedures of a privacy program may change frequently as business needs and privacy requirements change.

10. D. The HHS guidelines for the de-identification of records specify that ZIP codes should be included only if the region represented by the ZIP code has 20,000 or more residents.

11. C. All of these statements are true, with the exception of the requirement to retain a third-party dispute resolution service. Although organizations should definitely maintain a dispute resolution process, there is no requirement that it be run by a third party.

12. B. The chief privacy officer is a senior executive who should be involved in strategic privacy tasks. It would be quite unusual for someone in this role to be involved in the actual encryption of personal information.

13. B. The gap analysis is the formal process of identifying deficiencies that prevent an organization from achieving its privacy objectives. The results of the gap analysis may be used to design new controls.

14. A. Active data collection techniques directly request data from the subject, such as in an online survey or other form. Passive data collection techniques gather and analyze data automatically, such as by analyzing a user's web browsing traffic.

15. C. The privacy notice may contain general descriptions of security controls, but it would not normally contain detailed descriptions of those controls.

16. D. There is a reasonable argument that each one of the three cybersecurity principles (confidentiality, integrity, and availability) was impacted by this incident. However, the most direct impact is that the records were irretrievably deleted, causing an availability breach.

17. A. This is an example of a layered privacy policy, where the simplified version appears first, followed by the full legal and technical detail.

18. D. Privacy should be embedded into design, rather than bolted on as an afterthought. Organizations should strive for a positive-sum approach to privacy that does not treat privacy as requiring trade-offs. Organizations should design privacy mechanisms with visibility and transparency in mind. Systems should be designed to prevent privacy risks from occurring in the first place, not to respond to privacy lapses that do occur.

19. A. Justice Louis Brandeis used the term "right to be let alone" in a dissenting opinion in *Olmstead v. United States*. This opinion was later cited in *Roe v. Wade*, *Katz v. United States*, and *Carpenter v. United States*.

20. C. This is an example of aggregation, a technique that only reports summary information about a population in a manner that avoids disclosing information that may be traced back to a single person.

Chapter 2: Legal Environment

1. A. The legislative branch holds two significant checks-and-balances on the executive branch. The first is the authority to allocate funds, known as the power of the purse. The second is the ability to remove executive branch officials from office through the impeachment process. Veto power and prosecutorial discretion are powers of the executive branch. Judicial review is a power of the judicial branch.

2. A. The legislative branch powers are defined in Article I of the U.S. Constitution. Executive branch powers are defined in Article II of the U.S. Constitution. Judicial branch powers are defined in Article III of the U.S. Constitution.

3. D. This is a tricky question. The Fourth Amendment has been interpreted to provide individuals with some privacy rights, but it does not explicitly establish a right to privacy. The word *privacy* appears nowhere in the text of the Constitution.

4. C. Administrative law is commonly documented in the Code of Federal Regulations (CFR). The U.S. Code contains legislative law. The U.S. Constitution and its amendments (including the Bill of Rights) contain constitutional law.

5. A. Although all of these statements are accurate, only one describes the principle of *stare decisis*: that courts should be guided by precedent. Translated from the Latin, *stare decisis* means "let the decision stand."

6. A. There are two elements to a court's jurisdiction. Personal jurisdiction refers to a court's authority over the parties being sued. The contract language establishes the New York courts' personal jurisdiction. The second jurisdictional element is subject matter jurisdiction, which refers to a court's authority to hear cases on a particular area of the law.

7. D. The legal definition of person may be a human being, a corporation, or another legal organization. U.S. citizens, legal residents, and corporations all fit within the legal definition of a person.

8. A. Most federal privacy laws, including FERPA, GLBA, and HIPAA, do not contain a private right of action. The California Consumer Privacy Act (CCPA) does contain a private right of action.

9. D. In order to prevail on a negligence claim, the plaintiff must establish that there were damages involved, meaning that they suffered some type of financial, physical, emotional, or reputational harm.

10. C. The tort of invasion of solitude involves actions that constitute a physical or electronic intrusion into the private affairs of a person, such as breaking into their home or accessing their email account.

11. B. The Senate consists of one hundred members, two from each state. The House of Representatives consists of 435 voting members, divided among the states in proportion to their population.

12. D. U.S. District Courts are the trial courts of the federal system and are the location where most disputes are first brought under federal law. Decisions of the district courts may be appealed to U.S. Circuit Courts of Appeal. Decisions of the circuit courts may be appealed to the U.S. Supreme Court.

13. D. The addition of an amendment to the U.S. Constitution under any process other than a constitutional convention requires ratification by three quarters of the states.

14. C. Many states do have laws requiring that some contracts be in written form, but there is no universal requirement that a contractual agreement take place in writing, although written contracts are clearly preferable. The conditions that must be met for a contract to be enforceable include that each party to the contract must have the capacity to agree to the contract, an offer must be made by one party and accepted by the other, consideration must be given, and there must be mutual intent to be bound.

15. B. The supremacy clause establishes preemption, a concept meaning that law stemming from a higher authority takes precedence over laws from a lower authority. In this case, the supremacy clause says that federal law preempts any conflicting state laws.

16. B. The base of common law began in the English court system and was exported to the British colonies. Many former colonies, including the United States, continue to rely on this base of common law today.

17. D. The Health Insurance Portability and Accountability Act (HIPAA) is legislation passed by Congress. However, the HIPAA Privacy Rule and HIPAA Security Rule did not go through the legislative process. They are examples of administrative law created by the Department of Health and Human Services to implement the requirements of HIPAA.

18. D. The Foreign Intelligence Surveillance Court is a specialized court established exclusively for the purpose of hearing cases related to government surveillance for intelligence gathering purposes. This court has a narrow subject matter jurisdiction tied to national security issues.

19. D. There is no indication in the question that the firm has any physical presence or place of business in the state, nor have they consented to the state's jurisdiction. However, state officials could make a claim of jurisdiction under the "minimum contacts" standard that includes conducting business within a state, regardless of physical presence.

20. D. False light is a legal term that applies when someone discloses information that causes another person to be falsely perceived by others.

Chapter 3: Regulatory Enforcement

1. C. The three prongs of the test used to determine whether a trade practice unfairly injures consumers are that the injury must be substantial; the injury must not be outweighed by countervailing benefits to consumers and to competition; and the injury must not be reasonably avoidable.

2. A. TRUSTe is a privacy certification firm that conducts privacy assessments of other firms seeking to participate in safe harbor agreements. The FTC charged them with failing to conduct required annual recertifications.

3. C. The U.S. Department of Health and Human Services (HHS) has responsibility for promulgating and enforcing the administrative law associated with HIPAA and the Health Information Technology for Economic and Clinical Health (HITECH) Act.

4. A. The FTC uses consent decrees to create formal agreements between companies and the government that dictate how the company will behave moving forward. If the company later violates the consent decree, the government can bring legal action against them.

5. B. There is no indication in the scenario that Acme Widgets made any false or misleading statements about their security. Therefore, this is not likely a deceptive practice. The FTC enforcement action was likely based on the practice being unfair.

6. B. In July 2019, the FTC charged Facebook with violating the terms of a 2012 court order and issued them a record fine of $5 billion, the largest fine ever imposed on a firm for privacy violations.

7. C. Educational institutions that receive certain types of federal funding are obligated under FERPA to protect the privacy of student educational records.

8. D. PCI DSS was created in 2004 by Visa, Mastercard, American Express, Discover, and JCB to regulate the credit card processing industry. The standard primarily focuses on security, rather than privacy, issues, but it does include data retention requirements that enhance consumer privacy.

9. B. The Better Business Bureau operates a self-regulatory framework for advertisers that target children. This is different from the broader digital advertising framework operated by the Network Advertising Initiative.

10. C. The Consumer Financial Protection Bureau (CFPB) has enforcement authority over consumer interactions with financial institutions.

11. B. The TRUSTe seal is an example of a trust mark issued to websites that meet certain privacy criteria.

12. A. The Children's Online Privacy Protection Act (COPPA) grants the FTC authority to regulate websites that are targeted at children under the age of 13.

13. A. Disputes related to FTC complaints are first heard by an administrative law judge (ALJ). They may then be appealed to the FTC commissioners before being brought into the U.S. federal court system.

14. B. Verizon inappropriately shared customer proprietary network information (CPNI) with its marketing division without customer consent. This practice violates the provisions of the Telecommunications Act of 1996.

15. D. State attorneys general are the chief law enforcement officers of their states and may bring legal action against firms for violations of the laws of their state.

16. A. The Department of Commerce was responsible for administering the U.S. side of the EU/U.S. Privacy Shield. In July 2020, the EU Court of Justice issued the Schrems II decision declaring the Privacy Shield illegal.

17. D. The National Credit Union Administration (NCUA) is responsible for the supervision of federal credit unions. The Consumer Financial Protection Bureau (CFPB) may regulate the trade practices of a credit union, but it does not have supervisory authority.

18. C. The three components of a deceptive trade practice are that there must be a representation, omission, or practice that is likely to mislead the consumer; the practice must be examined from the perspective of a consumer acting reasonably in the circumstances; and the representation, omission, or practice must be material. The criteria that an injury must not be outweighed by countervailing benefits to consumers and to competition is for judging an unfair practice, not a deceptive practice.

19. D. Nomi was a technology company that placed sensors in retail stores collecting information about cell phones visiting the stores. The FTC charged them with failing to obtain consent before collecting and storing this personal information.

20. A. The Federal Trade Commission (FTC) has the primary authority to bring enforcement actions against most U.S. firms who the agency believes are engaged in unfair and/or deceptive trade practices.

Chapter 4: Information Management

1. C. It is possible that a medical record could contain any type of personal information and medical records do generally contain personally identifiable information (PII). However, the most directly applicable category is protected health information (PHI), because it is a far more specific category than the general PII. When you take the CIPP/US exam, you may find yourself asked to choose from multiple answers that may seem correct. Be sure to read the question carefully and choose the *best* answer to the question.

2. A. Data flow diagrams do not necessarily need to include technical details of the environment. Although this is certainly an acceptable practice, it is not required, and some organizations choose to maintain high-level diagrams that are easier for laypeople to understand.

3. A. The Fair and Accurate Credit Transactions Act (FACTA) includes a Disposal Rule that requires that covered organizations take reasonable measures to protect against unauthorized access or use of consumer reports in connection with their disposal.

4. A. Employees should receive information during training that is appropriate to their role in the organization. This may mean that different employees receive different content. Privacy training should take place on a regular basis and include content on regulatory requirements. Individuals completing training should understand their role in protecting privacy.

5. D. Advanced persistent threats (APTs) are well-resourced organizations with access to sophisticated attack tools. Other types of attackers are unlikely to have access to tools with the same degree of sophistication.

6. C. The hallmark of a ransomware attack is that the malicious software encrypts the user's data and then demands payment of a ransom in exchange for the decryption key.

7. D. Security incidents occur when there is a violation or imminent threat of a violation of a security policy. The theft of the employee's password meets these criteria. Events and adverse events are elevated to the level of an incident when this type of violation occurs. There is no indication that social engineering techniques were used in this attack.

8. A, B, C, D. All of these systems are reasonable sources of security alerts that may indicate the need for a cybersecurity incident response effort.

9. D. The detection of security incidents occurs during the detection and analysis phase of incident response. The goals of the containment, eradication, and recovery phase are to select a containment strategy, implement that strategy to limit damage, gather additional evidence, identify the attackers, eradicate the effects of the incident, and recover normal operations.

10. A. The lessons learned review should be facilitated by an independent facilitator who was not involved in the incident response and who is perceived by everyone involved as an objective outsider. This allows the facilitator to guide the discussion in a productive manner without participants feeling that the facilitator is advancing a hidden agenda.

11. A. The European Union's General Data Protection Regulation (GDPR) contains a broad requirement for the notification of individuals affected by a breach of personal information. The other laws mentioned here apply to specific categories of information: HIPAA covers health records, GLBA covers financial records, and FERPA covers educational records.

12. D. Master service agreements (MSAs) provide an umbrella contract for the work that a vendor does with an organization over an extended period of time. The MSA typically includes detailed security and privacy requirements.

13. A. Each time the organization enters into a new project with the vendor, they may then create a statement of work (SOW) that contains project-specific details and that references the master service agreement (MSA).

14. B. This situation appears to directly violate the principle of purpose limitation. Information should only be used for the purpose that it was originally collected and that was consented to by the data subjects. In this case, it appears that the information was collected for healthcare purposes and that the proposed use is not consistent with providing healthcare.

15. C. Script kiddies, by definition, do not have access to advanced tools. They typically use only publicly available tools to conduct their attacks. Advanced persistent threat (APT) actors use sophisticated tools as one of their signature characteristics. Insiders and hacktivists may or may not have access to sophisticated tools, depending on their skill level.

16. C. The creation of incident response policies and procedures is one of the core tasks during the preparation phase of an incident response effort.

17. D. Playbooks describe the specific actions that an incident response team will take in the event of a specific type of cybersecurity incident. Therefore, this is the term that best describes Tonya's document.

18. A. Zero-day attacks exploit vulnerabilities that were recently discovered and may not yet be known to the cybersecurity community. There is no patch available to correct zero-day vulnerabilities, leaving organizations especially susceptible to these attacks.

19. C. Shredding and incineration are both appropriate mechanisms for the destruction of paper records, and the use of a qualified third-party disposal firm is also reasonable. Degaussing is a data destruction technique, but it works only for electronic media and is ineffective for paper records.

20. C. Although each of these practices represents an appropriate privacy practice, data classification is the one most directly aligned with the need to describe security controls for different categories of information. By assigning data elements classification levels, Rob can help other employees understand which types of information require protection.

Chapter 5: Private Sector Data Collection

1. B. The Red Flags rule was first created under FACTA in order to transfer some responsibility for identity protection to credit reporting agencies by requiring CRAs to watch for signs of apparent identity theft on consumer credit reports.

2. C. The Dodd–Frank Act created the Consumer Financial Protection Bureau (CFPB) to centralize authority for a variety of laws regulating the financial services industry. The CFPB has enforcement authority for the FCRA, FACTA, the Red Flags Rule, GLBA requirements regarding privacy, and many other financial regulations.

3. C. NetBank is likely violating the DNC rules in the TSR and TCPA. Although the FTC has enforcement authority for the DNC generally, the FTC does not have jurisdiction over banks. For this reason, the FCC would probably investigate this potential violation.

4. B. Although the FTC can pursue legal complaints that may even carry heavy fines, the FTC often opts to enter into consent decrees that bring businesses into compliance with the law without further legal action.

5. C. COPPA expands the definition of PII for children to include two or more pieces of information collected in combination, such as a location and photo, that may identify a child. COPPA requires prior parental consent before such information may be collected.

6. B. Under HIPAA, business associates are third-party firms that participate in the handling of PHI for a covered entity. Covered entities are required to have a business associate agreement (BAA) with such companies that confer responsibility for HIPAA compliance on the third party.

7. D. The FTC provides enforcement, education, and support to lawmakers. The FTC also collaborates with other federal agencies on enforcement and may even treat with non-U.S. authorities on arrangements such as safe harbor arrangements. However, the FTC does not have jurisdiction over state laws or legal proceedings.

8. B. GLBA distinguishes between customers and consumers. Customers are people like account holders who have ongoing relationships with the bank. Consumers may only conduct isolated transactions with the bank. This is important because the bank has fewer obligations to Dimitri under GLBA because he is not technically a customer.

9. D. The DNC rule allows an exception for existing business relationships. For the exception to apply, the caller also needs written permission to contact a customer listed on the DNC registry.

10. C. FACTA implements consumer protections against identity theft. Most famously, FACTA gives consumers the right to a free credit report each year from each of the major CRAs in order to check their reports for accuracy. FACTA also initiated the Red Flags Rule, which requires CRAs to monitor consumer credit reports for signs of identity theft.

11. D. HIPAA provides exceptions that allow covered entities to share PHI in limited ways for public health purposes; for the conduct of their business, including billing; and with the informal permission of the patient. However, PHI may never be shared for a preemployment background check without the consent of the patient.

12. D. Many regulations require information security practices that include a documented program, designated personnel, and appropriate workforce training. However, private sector privacy and security regulations generally allow organizations to determine the most appropriate strategies for safeguarding information. Though many companies may use forensics teams, they aren't required by legislation discussed in this chapter.

13. A. The Dodd–Frank Act builds on the practices identified in the FTC Act to include abusive acts. This is designed to keep financial institutions from harming consumers by exploiting people who don't understand the terms of a transaction. For example, obscuring the true interest rate of a loan may constitute an abusive act.

14. A, C, D. FERPA provides broad exceptions that allow colleges to share protected information, such as transcripts, with financial providers, graduate schools where a student is applying, and for educational research. Unless Bella is a minor, however, FERPA does not allow disclosure to her parents.

15. A. Although HIPAA does grant patients the right to see most elements of their medical records and to request corrections, there are a few exceptions. This includes information gathered to respond to legal proceedings, lab results restricted by CLIA, information that might lead to a patient harming themselves or others, and psychotherapy notes.

16. B, D. The FCRA defines credit reports more broadly than one may first assume. Credit reports naturally include information about a person's creditworthiness, standing, and capacity, but may also include information about a person's character, general reputations, and mode of living.

17. D. The HITECH Act includes requirements that, once a covered entity learns of a PHI breach, victims must be notified within 60 days. If the breach impacts over 500 individuals in a given state, then it is also required to notify prominent local media outlets. Any breach affecting over 500 people must also be reported to HHS within 60 days.

18. D. Although the VPAA appears to regulate an industry—videotape sales and rentals—that has largely vanished, the act is increasingly interpreted to apply to consumer privacy for streaming media services. This has huge implications for consumer data collected by online streaming companies for advertising and other purposes. This area of privacy law is being closely watched by privacy professionals.

19. C. CAN-SPAM regulates electronic messages generally, not only email, and courts have ruled that social media messages are in scope. Not every message that mentions a product is in scope of CAN-SPAM because the law considers the primary purpose of the message. In this case, the main reason for Mark's message was clearly selling tables at his new restaurant.

20. C. The 21st Century Cures Act was enacted to speed the development of medical treatments. One way this act improves efficiency in sharing medical information is by standardizing electronic health records (EHRs) and setting up rules for appropriate sharing of information.

Chapter 6: Government and Court Access to Private Sector Information

1. C. The Foreign Intelligence Surveillance Act (FISA) was established in 1978, soon after the Watergate scandal of the early 1970s. FISA regulates the government's ability to conduct surveillance and implements oversight and accountability processes for federal law enforcement.

2. D. When sharing cyber-threat information, CISA protects companies from liability, keeps company information confidential and proprietary, and requires that data be anonymized before sharing. Reprisal from cybercriminals has not been a legal concern when it comes to sharing cyber-threat intelligence confidentially with the government.

3. A. The Supreme Court set a landmark precedent in *Miller v. United States* when they ruled it was legal for law enforcement to obtain the defendant's banking records without a warrant. The Court reasoned that the records belonged to the bank, not to the customer, and therefore were not protected under the Fourth Amendment.

4. A. The Privacy Protection Act of 1980 allows "a person aggrieved by a search" they believe to be in violation of the act to pursue damages in civil court.

5. B. Since the Supreme Court ruled that financial records held by banks are not protected by the Fourth Amendment, Congress passed the RFPA in order to provide privacy protections for financial information.

6. D. The Patriot Act amended a large number of existing laws, including FISA, ECPA, BSA, RFPA, FCRA, and many more. Many of these modifications helped increase government intelligence gathering capabilities; others helped monitor immigration, track financial support for terrorism, and more. The USA Freedom Act, however, modified the Patriot Act—not the other way around.

7. A, B. There are several important exceptions to the customer notification requirements under the RFPA. The Bank Secrecy Act, for example, actually prohibits customer notification when a bank submits a suspicious activity report (SAR). Also, disclosures made to supervisory agencies engaged in regulating banks (such as the SEC) are permitted because these disclosures don't pose a legal risk to individual customers.

8. B. Pen registers track metadata about incoming calls and trap-and-trace devices track information about outgoing calls. Both of these functions may actually be performed by a single technology today, but they are still referred to separately in the law.

9. C. Under the Bank Secrecy Act (BSA), financial institutions are required to implement Anti-Money Laundering (AML) programs to monitor accounts for signs of criminal activity.

10. A. Edward Snowden revealed the NSA's programs for collecting bulk personal data on Americans just before the USA Patriot Act was scheduled for reauthorization in 2015. Via the USA Freedom Act, Congress reauthorized most provisions of the Patriot Act but added restrictions to end, among other things, the bulk collection of data on Americans.

11. D. In the *Zurcher* case, the Supreme Court ruled that the First and Fourth Amendments did not, in fact, protect journalists from authorized search warrants. In response, Congress enacted the Privacy Protection Act to better protect journalistic privacy.

12. B. Preservation occurs after relevant records have been identified. In the preservation step, the attorney orders the company to preserve and avoid destroying the identified records. This is known as a legal hold.

13. C. The minimization principle expressed in FISA requires the U.S. Attorney General to implement procedures to make sure that authorized surveillance does not inadvertently violate individual privacy except as authorized by the investigation.

14. D. Though all have important roles to play, the eDiscovery process is almost always led by the attorneys. eDiscovery occurs as a part of ongoing litigation or other legal disputes.

15. D. The RFPA grants customers the opportunity to challenge a request in court. The customer must file such a challenge within 10 days of receiving a request or within 14 days of a request being mailed. If the customer does not object, the disclosure may proceed. The RFPA does not require affirmative consent from the customer.

16. B. National Security Letters (NSLs) have been used broadly under the Patriot Act to demand the production of business records. NSLs are a form of administrative subpoena.

17. D. CALEA specifies that companies are not required to help the government break encryption unless the company itself provided the encryption and has the keys to decrypt it.

18. C. The USA Freedom Act did reform the practice of using National Security Letters (NSLs) by requiring selection terms and creating a process for recipients to challenge NSLs. However, NSLs were in use before the USA Freedom Act and the Patriot Act were implemented.

19. D. Several provisions included in the Patriot Act when it was passed in 2001 were set to sunset 2005 unless reauthorized by Congress. Congress has debated, revised, and reauthorized these provisions every few years since but has yet to make the provisions permanent.

20. C. The Fourth Amendment to the U.S. Constitution protects Americans' "persons, houses, papers, and effects against unreasonable searches and seizures." This has been interpreted to include protection from electronic searches as well as many forms of surveillance.

Chapter 7: Workplace Privacy

1. C. The Employee Polygraph Protection Act (EPPA) broadly bans polygraph testing in the private sector workplace. Law firms are not on the list of exceptions.

2. C. Protected classes under federal law include race, color, religion, national origin, LGBTQ identity, sex, pregnancy, marital status, disability, genetic information, and age (if over 40).

3. D. The Americans with Disabilities Act (ADA) prohibits discrimination based on disability for qualified applicants who can perform essential job functions with reasonable accommodations. Organizations may deny employment to people who cannot perform the essential functions of a job even with reasonable accommodations.

4. B. Human resources departments usually manage all stages of the employment relationship. HR also usually maintains personnel files and other records that contain private information collected from employees.

5. A. There is no federal law generally mandating drug testing. The Drug-Free Workplace Act did encourage employers to offer training and information discouraging drug use but stopped short of requiring drug testing programs.

6. B. The Age Discrimination in Employment Act (ADEA) prohibited employment discrimination against people over 40.

7. D. Regulations enforced by the National Labor Relations Board (NLRB) do not allow employers to engage in surveillance purely to spy on unionizing activities. Furthermore, employers may not even give the impression they are doing so.

8. D. When furnished by a third party, employee background screening meets the explicit Fair Credit Reporting Act (FCRA) definition of a consumer report, and FCRA compliance is enforced by the Federal Trade Commission (FTC) and the Consumer Financial Protection Bureau (CFPB).

9. D. When an employer uses an outside investigator for employee misconduct investigations, they are required to provide the employee with a summary of the report if the results of the report lead to the employer taking adverse action against the employee. The employer does not have an obligation to notify the employee in advance, obtain consent, or provide a complete copy of the report.

10. B. Transition management occurs as an employee is exiting a company and includes removing all access to private information for departing employees.

11. B. There is no comprehensive federal law governing workplace privacy in the United States. Some federal laws have provisions that create compliance requirements for workplace privacy, and many states have laws offering some privacy rights to employees. Contracts with labor unions may also contain additional privacy protections.

12. C. The National Labor Relations Board (NLRB) is charged with protecting workers' rights to organize into unions and engage in collective bargaining.

13. C. Good records retention policies usually mandate the destruction of records after a set period of time, depending on the type of record.

14. C. Employee misconduct investigations must balance the rights of employees bringing complaints as well as employees accused of misconduct at the same time.

15. A. The Occupational Safety and Health Administration (OSHA) enforces standards for workplace safety, and when a complaint is filed, OSHA inspects workplaces to ensure compliance. OSHA's enforcement strategy only works if employees feel comfortable filing complaints.

16. A. The risk of discrimination is reduced most effectively when hiring managers only ask interview questions in relation to a job seeker's qualifications for a position.

17. D No single federal agency is primarily responsible for regulating workplace privacy rules because there is no comprehensive federal law for workplace privacy.

18. B. The Electronic Communications and Privacy Act (ECPA) allows employers to intercept communications for business purposes or with the consent of employees.

19. D. The Genetic Information Nondiscrimination Act (GINA) prohibits employers from collecting most genetic information with only a few narrow exceptions. Medical information necessary for the Family and Medical Leave Act (FMLA) requests constitute one such exception.

20. D. Employers commonly monitor publicly available social media activity for job seekers and employees but must be careful not to collect information in violation of antidiscrimination laws or mistake the employee for someone else on social media.

Chapter 8: State Privacy Laws

1. C. California's CFIPA implements differential requirements for financial institutions to share personal data. When sharing with affiliated entities, consumers are entitled to notification and the chance to opt out. When sharing with unaffiliated third parties, such as outside marketing firms, financial institutions must obtain written consent.

2. C. Most states have data privacy laws that require companies to have written information security policies, a process for destroying personal information when it's no longer needed, and specific controls to safeguard personal information. Although cybersecurity insurance is a good idea, it is not usually legally mandated.

3. A. In most instances, Washington State's biometric privacy law requires that businesses obtain prior consent before "enrolling" personal biometric data in a database for commercial purposes.

4. A. The CCPA is enforced by the California Consumer Privacy Protection Agency. However, the CCPA also provides a limited private right of action, which increases potential civil penalties and litigation costs for violators.

5. B. The New York Department of Financial Services Cybersecurity Regulation requires financial institutions to implement data security controls in alignment with the U.S. Department of Commerce's NIST cybersecurity framework.

6. D. CAN-SPAM allows state attorneys general to sue violators. This greatly expands enforcement capabilities and provides an important role for states without the need for additional state-level regulation.

7. D. Although some federal statutes do include breach notification requirements, there is no comprehensive federal law that defines personal information and requires organizations to notify consumers when their personal information is compromised.

8. D. Although they vary by state, breach notification laws may require notification to consumers, state regulators, and credit reporting agencies.

9. A. Before SB 2005, breaches were only considered to have occurred if the data involved were not encrypted. Following SB 2005, however, disclosures of encrypted data could be considered breaches under certain circumstances.

10. C. Federal law preempts state law, but since there is no comprehensive federal privacy law, states are free to make their own laws so long as they don't conflict with existing federal statutes.

11. C. The Washington law specifically excludes photographs and audio/video records from its definition, making it potentially less useful in regulating facial recognition practices.

12. C. The main criticism of the use of credit reports in employment decisions is that it may disadvantage job seekers from nonaffluent backgrounds. For this reason, many states have restricted the use of credit reports for employment purposes.

13. D. Although not all states impose all these penalties, free credit monitoring, penalties sought by an attorney general, and civil suits arising from a private right of action are potential consequences for an organization. Unless some other criminal act has occurred, or employees caused the breach knowingly or were grossly negligent, criminal prosecution of employees is highly unlikely.

14. A. Indiana's breach notification law requires only that notifications be made without unreasonable delay.

15. B. Although state laws can add to requirements in federal legislation, federal laws preempt state laws. Even if state privacy requirements are less stringent, residents are still obligated to follow federal laws. Not only does federal law preempt state law, but states also do not have federal jurisdiction.

16. B. In 2018, Alabama became the last U.S. state to implement a breach notification law.

17. C. State laws usually require notifications when the personally identifiable information has been disclosed in a manner that constitutes a breach. Not all information is personally identifiable and not all disclosures are breaches, depending on each state's definition of these concepts.

18. B. This law specifically restricts the purposes for which a retailer may collect or scan information from a customer ID card and mandates the destruction of the information when it is no longer needed.

19. B. The Delaware Online Privacy and Protection Act (DOPPA) requires website operators to implement privacy policies, restricts certain forms of advertising to children, and prohibits "book service providers" from sharing information about consumer reading habits without a court order

20. C. CalECPA, or the California Electronic Communications and Privacy Act, builds on the privacy protections of the federal ECPA by protecting a broad swatch of electronic information from warrantless searches by state law enforcement.

Chapter 9: International Privacy Regulation

1. C. Unlike the EU, the United States does not have a single comprehensive law protecting individual data privacy rights.

2. D. The right to rectification is, in fact, a data subject right under the GDPR, not the APEC Privacy Framework.

3. D. The GDPR lists only very limited circumstances under which international data transfers of personal information may take place outside of adequacy decisions, BCRs, and SCCs. Research is not among these circumstances.

4. C. Under GDPR, a data controller decides how personal information should be processed and for what purpose. A data processor handles personal information for a controller.

5. B. Yuping is most likely to recommend DPF self-certification because it is a simpler and more straightforward process for U.S. companies to comply with EU data transfer requirements. The Data Privacy Framework allows U.S. companies to certify their compliance with EU privacy standards, making it an easier and faster option than other methods. Standard Contractual Clauses are more complex, requiring legal agreements to be signed for each data transfer. Binding Corporate Rules are typically used by large multinational corporations for internal data transfers, which wouldn't apply to a small startup. APEC is irrelevant here as it pertains to data transfers in the Asia-Pacific region, not the EU.

6. B. Multinational compliance conflicts occur when someone is asked to comply with two or more contradictory laws at the same time. It is not possible for Said to comply with both requirements. This type of situation is why legal mechanisms for international data transfers, like Binding Corporate Rules, are necessary.

7. B. Binding Corporate Rules (BCRs) are complex to set up, but allow corporate groups to transfer within the group inside and outside of the EU.

8. B. The Court of Justice of the European Union has ruled that GDPR does not grant the EU special extra-territorial jurisdiction for business that are neither established in the EU nor offering goods or services in the EU. However, the GDPR does apply to the personal information of all EU data subjects and the debate in the EU continues.

9. B. The Cross-Border Privacy Rules (CBPR) system is an APEC safe harbor program that allows members to safely transfer data internationally.

10. C. Following the revelations of Edward Snowden about the scope of the U.S. government's mass surveillance activities, the EU's highest Court decided that the privacy program could not guarantee protection consistent with GDPR requirements.

11. C. The Global Privacy Enforcement Network (GPEN) has five-point mission to facilitate better cooperation and dialogue among members. However, the mission stops short of creating a specific mechanism for sharing protected information.

12. D. Under GDPR, the U.S.-based digital marketing service is most likely operating as a data processor. The right to the restriction of processing allows Pierre to demand that the boulangerie, as the data controller, halt this processing activity.

13. A. When the EU makes an adequacy decision in the favor of another country, international data transfers are permitted to and from that country without the need for an additional legal mechanism.

14. B. The Global Privacy Enforcement Network (GPEN) has a five-point mission to help member nations cooperation around issues of cross-border privacy enforcement.

15. D. All of the above except the "right of notice and choice" are data subject rights under the EU's GDPR. Notice and choice is not a right, but is considered a traditional fair information practice in the United States.

16. A. CBPR is the APEC safe harbor program that will help Nancy's company facilitate international data transfers with member nations, such as Japan and Singapore.

17. B. Fines for egregious violations of GDPR provisions can be very steep. Data subjects may also seek additional damages for any harm they may have suffered from the violations.

18. A. Safe harbor programs are usually first joined by member nations, which each committed to enforcement and independent verification for participating companies. Once a country has joined a safe harbor program, private companies can seek third-party verification of compliance with the program in order to conduct data international data transfers.

19. B. The EU requires those using SCCs to designate parties as either data importers or data exporters and to use the appropriate set of SCCs, depending on the designation. Marco's company exports the data, the U.S. company imports the data.

20. B. The GDPR refers to the people to whom it provides privacy protection as data subjects in the EU. If a person is in the EU, then their data are protected by the GDPR, no matter their citizenship or immigration status.

Index

Get Certified!

 Security+

 CISSP

 CISM

 CISSP

 PenTest+

 SSCP

 Data +

 CCSP

 CC

 CIPP/US

 CIPM

 ITF+